Brand Thinking

Building Brands You Can Believe In

Allison J. Steinke
University of Minnesota, USA

Haseon Park
University of Minnesota, USA

Foreword by
Marty Brandt

BLOOMSBURY ACADEMIC
NEW YORK • LONDON • OXFORD • NEW DELHI • SYDNEY

BLOOMSBURY ACADEMIC

Bloomsbury Publishing Inc, 1359 Broadway, New York, NY 10018, USA
Bloomsbury Publishing Plc, 50 Bedford Square, London, WC1B 3DP, UK
Bloomsbury Publishing Ireland, 29 Earlsfort Terrace, Dublin 2, D02 AY28, Ireland

BLOOMSBURY, BLOOMSBURY ACADEMIC and the Diana logo are trademarks of Bloomsbury Publishing Plc

First published in the United States of America 2026

Copyright © Bloomsbury Publishing, Inc 2026

Cover design: Dustin Watson
Cover image © istock/Arnanzung

All rights reserved. No part of this publication may be: i) reproduced or transmitted in any form, electronic or mechanical, including photocopying, recording or by means of any information storage or retrieval system without prior permission in writing from the publishers; or ii) used or reproduced in any way for the training, development or operation of artificial intelligence (AI) technologies, including generative AI technologies. The rights holders expressly reserve this publication from the text and data mining exception as per Article 4(3) of the Digital Single Market Directive (EU) 2019/790.

Bloomsbury Publishing Inc does not have any control over, or responsibility for, any third-party websites referred to or in this book. All internet addresses given in this book were correct at the time of going to press. The author and publisher regret any inconvenience caused if addresses have changed or sites have ceased to exist, but can accept no responsibility for any such changes.

A catalog record for this book is available from the Library of Congress.

ISBN: HB: 978-1-5381-9519-2
PB: 978-1-5381-9520-8
ePDF: 979-8-7651-6083-1
eBook: 978-1-5381-9521-5

Typeset by Integra Software Services Pvt. Ltd.
Printed and bound in the United States of America

For product safety related questions contact productsafety@bloomsbury.com.

To find out more about our authors and books visit www.bloomsbury.com and sign up for our newsletters.

To Dr. Elisia Cohen and Dr. Valérie Bélair-Gagnon:
Thank you for your unwavering support and encouragement.
To Marty Brandt and Scott Meyer:
Your inspiration brought the concept of brand believability to life!

Brief Contents

Acknowledgments xi
Foreword, Marty Brandt xii

Introduction 1

Part I Brand Believability 9

1. **Brand Purpose** 37
2. **Brand Culture** 55
3. **Brand Design and Experience** 77

Part II Brand Growth 107

4. **Market Segmentation** 117
5. **Brand Channels and Outreach** 133
6. **Brand Communication** 153

Part III Brand Strategy 173

7. **Brand Research and Assessment** 181
8. **Brand Positioning** 201
9. **Brand Architecture** 221

Part IV Social Influence 235

10 Sustainability 249

11 Social Responsibility 269

12 Brand Resonance 291

Appendix A: Methods 310

Appendix B: Interviewees 312

Appendix C: Brand Believability Score Assessment Sample Survey 313

References 314
Index 333
About the Authors 338

Contents

Acknowledgments xi
Foreword, Marty Brandt xii

Introduction 1

Part I Brand Believability 9

I.1 Introduction: What Is Brand Believability? 10
I.2 The Problem: Brand Skepticism 14
I.3 The Solution: Brand Believability 14
I.4 Application: Brand Believability Score 28
I.5 Metrics: Engagement, Shareability, and Profitability 29

1 Brand Purpose 37

1.1 Introduction: What Is Brand Purpose? 38
1.2 The Problem: Post-Truth 39
1.3 The Solution: Believable Brand Purpose 39
1.4 Case: Seventh Generation 47
1.5 Application: Creating a Sticky and Spreadable Brand Story 50
1.6 Metrics: SMART Goals 51

2 Brand Culture 55

2.1 Introduction: What Is Brand Culture? 56
2.2 The Problem: Brand Drift 57
2.3 The Solution: Believable Brand Culture 57
2.4 Case: Trader Joe's 68
2.5 Application: Internal Branding 70
2.6 Metrics: Employee Engagement Pulse Surveys 72

3 Brand Design and Experience 77

3.1 Introduction: What Is Brand Design and Experience? 78
3.2 The Problem: No "It" Factor 79
3.3 The Solution: Believable Brand Design and Experience 80
3.4 Case: Chiro for Moms / Chiro for Kidz 91
3.5 Application: Journey Maps 95
3.6 Metrics: Customer Satisfaction Score (CSAT) 103

Part II Brand Growth 107

II.1 Introduction: What Is Brand Growth? 108
II.2 The Problem: Market Saturation 108
II.3 The Solution: Believable Brand Growth 109
II.4 Application: Responsibility Assignment Matrix (RACI) 111
II.5 Metrics: Market Share and Brand Penetration 112

4 Market Segmentation 117

4.1 Introduction: What Is Market Segmentation? 118
4.2 The Problem: Inauthentic and Impersonal Branding 118
4.3 The Solution: Believable Market Segmentation 119
4.4 Case: Halara Cannabis 126
4.5 Application: The Ansoff Matrix 130
4.6 Metrics: Types of Segmentation 131

5 Brand Channels and Outreach 133

5.1 Introduction: What Are Brand Channels and What Is Effective Outreach? 134
5.2 The Problem: Fragmented Media Landscape 136
5.3 The Solution: Believable Brand Channels and Outreach 137
5.4 Case: Chipotle 142
5.5 Application: Target Audiences and Personas 144
5.6 Metrics: Reach, Frequency, Gross Rating Points (GRPs), and Impressions 148

6 Brand Communication 153

6.1 Introduction: What Is Brand Communication? 154
6.2 The Problem: Echo Chambers and Filter Bubbles 155

6.3 The Solution: Believable Brand Communication 156
6.4 Case: Red Bull 165
6.5 Application: Linear Thinking 168
6.6 Metrics: Digital KPIs: Website and Social Media Analytics 170

Part III Brand Strategy 173

III.1 Introduction: What Is Brand Strategy? 174
III.2 The Problem: Brand Stagnancy 174
III.3 The Solution: Believable Brand Strategy 175
III.4 Application: Figure Storming 176
III.5 Metrics: Financial KPIs 176

7 Brand Research and Assessment 181

7.1 Introduction: What Is Brand Research and Assessment? 182
7.2 The Problem: Excessive Consumer Data 184
7.3 The Solution: Believable Brand Research and Assessment 186
7.4 Case: The College of Saint Benedict and Saint John's University 188
7.5 Application: SWOT Analysis 193
7.6 Metrics: Brand Monitoring, Social Listening, and Consumer Perception 196

8 Brand Positioning 201

8.1 Introduction: What Is Brand Positioning? 202
8.2 The Problem: Ad and Brand Bombardment 204
8.3 The Solution: Believable Brand Positioning 206
8.4 Case: Thrive Pet Healthcare 208
8.5 Application: Position Mapping 211
8.6 Metrics: Media Mix, Share of Voice, and Digital Presence Analysis 215

9 Brand Architecture 221

9.1 Introduction: What Is Brand Architecture? 222
9.2 The Problem: Misalignment 226
9.3 The Solution / Case: Believable Brand Architecture at CBS 226
9.4 Application: Building a Strategic Brand Architecture Model 230
9.5 Metrics: Brand Sentiment 231

Part IV Social Influence 235

IV.1 Introduction: What Is Social Influence? 236
IV.2 The Problem: Performative Activism and Exploitation 237
IV.3 The Solution: Believable Social Influence 239
IV.4 Application: B Corporations and Conscious Capitalism 242
IV.5 Metrics: Brand Awareness 245

10 Sustainability 249

10.1 Introduction: What Is Sustainability? 250
10.2 The Problem: Climate Crisis and Greenwashing 251
10.3 The Solution: Believable Sustainability 255
10.4 Application: Context, Strategy, and Goals 258
10.5 Metrics: Certifications and Credibility 260
10.6 Case: Patagonia 265

11 Social Responsibility 269

11.1 Introduction: What Is Social Responsibility? 270
11.2 The Problem: Miscommunication 272
11.3 The Solution: Believable Social Responsibility 274
11.4 Case: CONQUERing 277
11.5 Application: Conscious Consumers and Brand Value Co-creation 280
11.6 Metrics: Employee Experience (EX), Charitable Giving, and Philanthropy 283

12 Brand Resonance 291

12.1 Introduction: What Is Brand Resonance? 292
12.2 The Problem: Brand Indifference 292
12.3 The Solution: Believable Brand Resonance 294
12.4 Application: Artificial Intelligence (AI) 297
12.5 Case: Spotify 303
12.6 Metrics: Brand Affinity 306

Appendix A: Methods 310
Appendix B: Interviewees 312
Appendix C: Brand Believability Score Assessment Sample Survey 313

References 314
Index 333
About the Authors 338

Acknowledgments

This work is funded in part by Marty Brandt's Brandt Fund for Brand Thinking Studies at the University of Minnesota Hubbard School of Journalism and Mass Communication. The purpose of the Brandt Fund is to evolve, codify, and inspire adoption of the discipline of *Brand Thinking* for better business performance and societal impact through the University of Minnesota's Hubbard School programs and beyond.

Foreword
Marty Brandt

Dear Reader,

Before you dive into this book, I have a simple exercise for you. Over the years, I've found this helpful when starting a new discussion about branding and brands. Let's give it a try.

Take a moment to pause, have a deep breath, quiet your mind, and think of a brand. One that you know well and truly admire, a brand from any part of your life—could be a product or service, personal or business. Next, write down a few of the key reasons why you admire that brand. Then pause again, reflect on your answer, and observe what you believe is distinctive and appealing about your admired brand. Consider how it came to occupy that place in your life. Note that those beliefs result from various experiences you have with the brand directly or indirectly.

OK, now you're warmed up and ready to explore *Brand Thinking: Building Brands You Can Believe In.*

Brands and branding have long grappled with an identity dilemma. The word *brand* itself is burdened with some negative perceptions, no doubt the result of brand malpractice by a few brands over the years. Still, there is no denying that many businesses and organizations benefit greatly from the strong emotional attachment people have for their brand. Others, not so much. Why is that?

The difference is a brand-savvy leadership mindset and an organizational brand belief culture. An ethos, if you will. And leadership understands that brand thinking, which leads to a competitive advantage in the marketplace, is based on what customers believe is desirable, distinctive, and true about the brand—a brand they can believe in.

My career in branding has spanned multiple continents and industries, from the vibrant tech hubs of Silicon Valley to the dynamic markets of Asia and Europe. As founder of TrueBrand LLC, I have had the privilege of working with a diverse array of clients, including The Carlyle Group, Ampere Computing, and Dell, among many others. Each engagement has reinforced my conviction that the essence of a successful brand lies not just in its visual identity or marketing campaigns but in the values and beliefs it embodies.

Before TrueBrand, I founded and led proBRAND, a strategy consultancy specializing in building technology brands. This experience taught me the importance of aligning brand strategy with business objectives, ensuring that every brand element contributes to a cohesive narrative that resonates with both internal stakeholders and external audiences.

Building a brand people can believe in is a strategic imperative. When a brand is built on a foundation of authenticity, integrity, and purpose, it creates a meaningful bond with its audience that transcends mere customer loyalty. It fosters a community of believers who become champions for the brand, advocating for it with passion and conviction.

I have seen this phenomenon firsthand with clients like Intel and Logitech, where a well-crafted brand strategy not only enhanced their market presence but also inspired their employees to become brand believers. This internal alignment is crucial because when employees believe in the brand, they are more likely to embody its values in every interaction, reinforcing the brand's promise to customers.

I would like to commend the groundbreaking work of Drs. Allison Steinke and Haseon Park from the Hubbard School of Journalism and Mass Communication at the University of Minnesota. Their research has been instrumental in shaping our understanding of branding and its impact on both businesses and society. Their findings, which delve into the intricacies of brand communication and strategic thinking, will undoubtedly influence the direction of branding for years to come. By exploring how brands can effectively express their values and build meaningful connections with their audiences, their work provides valuable insights for anyone seeking to create brands that resonate deeply with people.

Brand Thinking is more than a methodology; it is a mindset. It involves understanding that branding is not just about creating a logo or a tagline but about crafting a narrative that resonates with people's aspirations, values, and emotions. It requires leaders to think holistically about their brand, considering how every decision, from product development to customer service, contributes to its overall meaning.

In my work with clients like HP and Deloitte Consulting, I have seen how this holistic approach can transform a brand's impact. By integrating brand strategy into every aspect of the business, these companies have been able to communicate their value proposition more effectively, differentiate themselves in crowded markets, and build lasting relationships with their stakeholders.

My experience working across different regions has taught me that while cultural nuances vary, the fundamental desire for authenticity and connection remains constant. Whether in Europe, Asia, or Africa, people want to engage with brands that stand for something meaningful. This universal desire presents both opportunities and challenges. On one hand, it allows brands to connect with a global audience on a deeper level. On the other hand, it demands that brands be sensitive to local contexts while remaining true to their core values. I recall the challenges and successes of developing brand strategies for clients like Acer and MTN Telephone Network in diverse markets, where understanding local preferences was crucial to building a loyal customer base.

Over the years, the landscape of branding has evolved significantly. Digital technologies have democratized access to information, making it easier for brands to reach their audiences while increasing the noise and competition. In this environment, the need for brands to stand out through authenticity and relevance has never been more pressing. Brands like Apple, Trader Joe's, Patagonia, and Costco have successfully adapted to these changes by leveraging storytelling, community engagement, and a deep understanding of their customers' values. Apple's commitment to innovation and design, Trader Joe's unique shopping experience, Patagonia's environmental activism, and Costco's customer-centric approach have all contributed to their ability to build strong connections with their audiences. By focusing on these elements, these brands have managed to stand out in crowded markets and foster a loyal following.

As I look back on my journey and reflect on the principles outlined in *Brand Thinking*, I am reminded that the most enduring brands are those that inspire belief. They are built on a foundation of purpose, integrity, and authenticity—and they resonate with people on a deep level.

In the following pages, you will discover insights and strategies for building brands that people can believe in. Whether you are a seasoned brand leader or just starting your journey, I hope that the principles of *Brand Thinking* will inspire you to create brands that make a lasting impact on the world.

—Marty Brandt

Introduction

What is brand thinking? How can you build a believable brand? Why does brand believability matter? *Brand Thinking: Building Brands You Can Believe In* provides an innovative and comprehensive framework that answers these questions and provides brand leaders, students, and innovators alike with an actionable plan. The concepts, applications, and metrics in this book can be leveraged to build, evaluate, and measure the believability of various brands. Effective brand building can provide organizations of all kinds with the competitive advantage needed for success. From helping drive stakeholder engagement to building overall brand value, brand thinking plays a central role in the way today's most dynamic organizations build brands people can believe in.

Based on perspectives from chief marketing officers (CMOs) and consumers and grounded in industry-leading research, this book is designed to help students, educators, and brand leaders:

- understand the various dimensions of brand thinking, including believability, growth, strategy, and social influence;
- define the building blocks of brand believability, including emotional attachment, credibility, authenticity, consistency, innovation, and quality;
- become familiar with priorities in contemporary brand building, including artificial intelligence, social and digital media marketing, sustainability, social influence, and social responsibility;
- apply the key elements of brand thinking to build believable brands;
- evaluate the believability and value of various brands in the competitive landscape;

- employ digital and financial metrics to build and evaluate brands across sectors;
- create comprehensive brands and purpose-driven value propositions;
- comprehend problems facing brands in today's contemporary media and marketing environments to see how brand thinking can provide believable solutions;
- use concrete applications to execute the brand thinking framework;
- increase understanding of concepts ranging from brand purpose and culture to market segmentation and brand communication;
- learn best practices from chief marketing officers and see how leading brands in health care, entertainment, foodservice, and more uphold the brand thinking framework in practice.

Each chapter includes key terms, discussion questions, and an activity to facilitate conversation and develop concrete application of each chapter's concepts for students and brand leaders to gain competitive advantage in the marketplace.

Brand Thinking: The Core Concepts

Brand thinking comprises four "Core Concepts:" Belief System, Growth, Strategy, and Social Influence. These concepts all build into a central focus point: Believability.

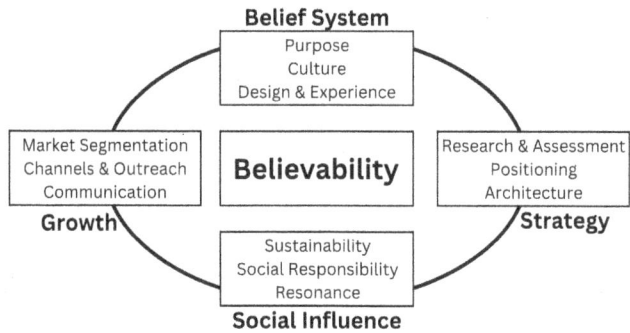

Brand Thinking Framework   © Allison J. Steinke and Haseon Park, University of Minnesota

Figure 0.1 Brand Thinking Framework.

Brand thinking is a tool educators, students, and industry professionals can use to better understand the believability of brands and the value of brand creation and brand meaning in a post-truth era. The principles presented in this book are informed by industry experience, thought leadership, and academic research—including interviews with chief marketing officers and executives at various organizations and focus groups with Generation Z consumers. See Appendix A and Appendix B for more information on our methods and research interviewees. Brand thinking is supported by our mixed-method research completed at and affiliated with the University of Minnesota's Hubbard School of Journalism and Mass Communication. Brand thinking research findings inform interdisciplinary fields including, but not limited to: Branding, strategic communication, marketing, advertising, and public relations. Brand thinking comprises metrics and original research as tools that brands and organizations can use to qualify and quantify believability in the competitive landscape.

Goals and Objectives

Brand Thinking fills an important blind spot in brand management by providing a road map to integrate, operationalize, and execute functional and emotional elements into brand planning and brand experience. Identifying and implementing how the softer side of brand management impacts the bottom line is often a struggle for C-suite executives in the face of pressure to deliver more immediate sales results and promotional campaign results.

Brand Thinking builds a bridge between commercially driven brand managers and their colleagues advocating for important brand thinking elements including purpose, growth, strategy, and social influence.

Marketing today does not sufficiently take into account what constitutes the actionable ingredients for a brand strategy that really connects with customers across generations. *Brand Thinking* highlights how and why brand thinking elements—for example, emotional attachment to purpose-based attributes—in fact lead to more resilient and lasting brands where sales revenue is noticeably better both during the growth phase as well as during brand maturity.

In addition to robust theoretical framing, *Brand Thinking* provides concrete case studies of companies across industry sectors that exemplify the cornerstones of the brand thinking framework including but not limited to: CBS, Chipotle, Mayo Clinic, Trader Joe's, and Patagonia.

Generally, believability and emotional attachment to a brand exerts a continuous attractive force even in spite of other marketplace pressures including price, competition, emerging social trends, and cultural revolutions. In other words, the bigger the brand believability magnet, the greater the attractive force.

Believable brands create deep and meaningful customer attachment and are more profitable, valuable, and better equipped to withstand adversity. Brand thinking is a critical tool and framework for current and future digital marketing strategists, content creators, advertising managers, CMOs, and more to use to fulfill their goals across generations.

With theory, applications, metrics, and case studies from industry, this book will walk you through the key components of brand thinking and how to build a brand you can believe in, from cultivating purpose to creating a unique design and experience.

Building Brand Believability

The fundamental brand concept of value exchange between brand owners and consumers and stakeholders is under stress. We are at an inflection point that provides us with an opportunity to make fundamental changes in branding practices. The Covid-19 pandemic, the calls for increased social activism for companies, the mistrust of business, and the rise of corporate purpose make developing and implementing our *Brand Thinking* framework imperative.

Brands and branding have long grappled with an identity dilemma. Most people agree on the origins of branding. Still, over the years, no widely accepted definition or consistent practices have emerged. Yet there is no denying that some businesses, organizations, and products benefit greatly from the emotional attachment people and loyal customers have to specific brands. Other businesses? Not so much. It's time to assert that the brand and branding ideals should come forward and into focus, in a more enlightened way, for the benefit of every organization—and for society, as well.

That's where brand thinking comes in—by helping build believability. Believability is an outcome aligning an organization's values, culture, and initiatives, and integrates elements of a brand's belief system, strategies, growth, and social influence. We present the key components of brand thinking and brand believability throughout this book as follows:

- Brand Believability: A combination of emotional attachment and credibility, bolstered by values including authenticity, consistency, innovation, and quality;
- Brand Purpose: An organization's "why"—its reason for being and the things it stands for;
- Brand Culture: How a company lives out its values and mission by instilling the knowledge and support of brand behaviors into brand learning;
- Brand Design and Experience: How a brand represents its identity to the public visually and experientially;
- Brand Growth: How a brand gains and maintains competitive advantage in the market;
- Market Segmentation: Dividing target markets into approachable groups;
- Brand Channels and Outreach: Matching brand values with appropriate channels to plan effective outreach to target audiences;
- Brand Communication: Connecting a brand with the market through paid, earned, and owned media;
- Brand Strategy: Consistent analysis and evaluation of multiple aspects of a brand to identify where the brand is situated in the market;
- Brand Research and Assessment: Timely, insightful analysis that identifies a brand's competitive positioning while creating solutions that elevate the brand experience;
- Brand Positioning: The space a brand owns in the mind of a customer and how a brand differentiates itself from competitors;
- Brand Architecture: The relationship between brands within an organization and how they interact;
- Social Influence: How brands contribute to the public good by implementing and supporting prosocial efforts and initiatives;
- Sustainability: How brands act in environmentally responsible ways;

- Social Responsibility: Brands' commitments to promote well-being among employees, stakeholders, clients, customers, and communities around the world;
- Brand Resonance: A combination of emotional attachment and credibility brands develop and sustain with employees, stakeholders, clients, and customers.

The goal of these principles is to help brand leaders create brands people can believe in. Believability incorporates elements of liking, relating to, identifying with, loving, trusting, desiring over time, and preferring over all competition.

What does it mean to be a believable brand, and why does brand believability matter? This book answers these questions by introducing brand thinking as an actionable framework that can be leveraged to build, evaluate, and measure the believability of various brands. Effective brand building can provide organizations of all kinds with the competitive advantage needed for success. From helping drive stakeholder engagement to building overall brand value, brand thinking plays a central role in the way today's most dynamic organizations build brands people can believe in.

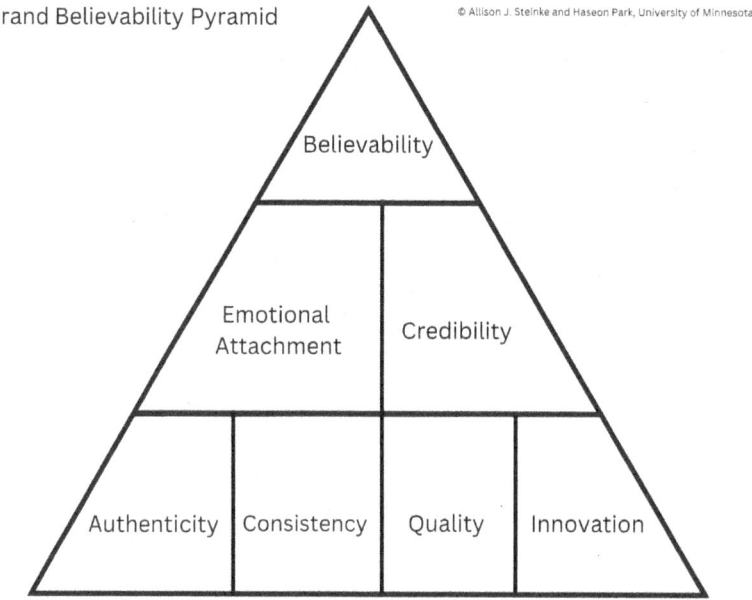

Figure 0.2 Brand Believability Pyramid.

Our research with chief marketing officers and consumers shows that brand believability—what executives leverage in their branding and marketing practices and what employees and customers believe to be true about a particular brand—is the central component of brand thinking. We argue that brand believability is the ultimate goal for all brands. Its building blocks include the following values co-created by brands and consumers: Emotional attachment, credibility, authenticity, consistency, innovation, and quality (Figure 0.2). This book will equip and empower you to communicate your brand's story with authenticity and passion to forge deeper connections with your audience and leave a meaningful and lasting impact on the world.

Part I

Brand Believability

What is brand believability and why does it matter? How can brands build believability? We define brand believability as a combination of emotional attachment and credibility, bolstered by values including authenticity, consistency, innovation, and quality. Brands and consumers co-create the norms and values that build brand believability. Our brand thinking framework provides the rules and values that believable brands abide by and uphold. Over time, brands' believability is quantified by metrics including engagement, shareability, and profitability. We also present a basic application of brand believability—the Brand Believability Score—that can help brands begin to quantify their believability with various audiences and stakeholders. Part I introduces the concept of brand believability, leveraging insights and perspectives from our research with chief marketing officers (CMOs) and consumers.

Outline

I.1 Introduction: What Is Brand Believability?	10
I.2 The Problem: Brand Skepticism	14
I.3 The Solution: Brand Believability	14
I.4 Application: Brand Believability Score	28
I.5 Metrics: Engagement, Shareability, and Profitability	29
Key Terms	35
Discussion Questions	35
Activity	36

I.1 Introduction: What Is Brand Believability?

Brand Believability: A combination of emotional attachment and credibility, bolstered by values including authenticity, consistency, innovation, and quality.

Branding is changing at a breakneck pace in a hyperconnected world. With the evolution of the digital and social media landscape dominated by activism, advocacy, social commerce, and influencers, foundational branding concepts and principles are being upended and revolutionized by the increasingly collaborative role of consumers. Consumers' desires for purpose-driven and conscientious branding are driving innovation among brands worldwide (Aaker, 2022; Iglesias & Ind, 2020).

Consumers are playing a more active role than ever in shaping the conversation around the success of brands and organizations worldwide. Brands are making renewed commitments to authenticity and transparency in communications in the interest of engaging clients and consumers. Shareholders are committing to sustainability as seen in the rise of B Corporations. There is constant innovation in digital content marketing practices, and social commerce—or selling goods, products, and services directly on and within social media platforms, including the utilization of non-fungible tokens and digital currency—is revolutionizing economies worldwide. From ratings and reviews to social media content and shareholder reports, there is more information available to consumers about brands than ever before. Brands have shifted from single ownership to shared ownership as heightened access to information allows more stakeholders—including customers and clients—to co-create brand meanings and experiences alongside traditional brand owners and managers (Swaminathan et al., 2020).

The rise of artificial intelligence (AI) has enhanced and also impeded brands' efforts to connect with consumers in a meaningful way, especially in the customer service realm. Some scholars argue AI threatens what it means to put the customer first. Other scholars argue AI has and can help facilitate meaningful connections and boost efficiency generated by technology including web and social media analytics, chat bots, algorithmic recommendations and advertisements

(Varsha et al., 2021). Research shows that personalized advertising boosts brand engagement and reduces privacy concerns on social media (Loureiro et al., 2023).

Social media's role in the consumer purchase journey has expanded as consumers search and make purchases directly through social media platforms themselves, a phenomenon known as social commerce. Social commerce is an affordance of social media apps including Facebook, Instagram, and TikTok, enabling consumers to buy and sell goods or services directly without leaving the app—consumers can make purchases almost instantly, with the swipe of a finger. Social commerce was an $89.4 billion market in 2020, and is projected to grow to $604.5 billion by 2027 (Charello, 2024). For these reasons, brand thinking is a more important framework than ever to help brands adapt and change with the rise and influence of digital and social marketing tools and platforms.

What Is a Brand?

The definition of *brand* varies widely. We define a brand as a collective set of perceptions, associations, and attributes attached to a product, service, or company by people inside and outside of the organization.

A brand is also formed by the direct and indirect experiences people have with product/service performance, communications, and employees, as well as, increasingly, with governance, citizenship, and workplace behaviors.

Brands are social processes that involve multiple stakeholders (Iglesias et al., 2017). Executives, consumers, and employees play key roles in co-creating, developing, and sustaining brand values in physical and digital realms (Ramaswamy & Ozcan, 2016). Storytelling on social media plays a crucial role in shaping perceptions and influencing decision-making processes inside and outside of a brand as social media empowers consumers to actively participate in brands and how they are developing (Lund et al., 2020). Ratings, reviews, and other forms of user-generated content can be used to co-create brands, and can also co-destruct them. Negative information and stories shared between stakeholders on social media in particular can harm brand value significantly as content generated on social media can have many different impacts on a brand ranging from creation to destruction—also known as a brand value continuum (Lund et al., 2020).

Brand can be defined as "a stand-in, a euphemism, a shortcut for a whole bunch of expectations, experiences and promises" (Millman, 2013). A brand can also be "a person's gut feeling about a product, service or company" (Neumeier, 2005). After significant social and economic changes caused by the global Covid-19 pandemic, brands have faced increased expectations from consumers for social activism, corporate purpose, and the greater social good. Consumers care about what brands contribute to society as a whole. It is therefore critical for brands to communicate these priorities to consumers.

David Aaker is Professor Emeritus at the University of California Berkeley's Haas School of Business and vice chairman of the San Francisco–based growth consulting company Prophet. A widely published brand strategist often called the father of modern branding, Aaker defines *brand* as "an organization's promise to a customer to deliver… not only… functional benefits but also emotional, self-expressive and social benefits." Aaker also argues that brand is "more than delivering on a promise. It's also an evolving relationship based on the perceptions and experiences a customer has every time they connect with the brand" (2014).

What Is Brand Thinking?

Brand thinking is a flexible and adaptable framework that executives, entrepreneurs, scholars, and students can use to evaluate, study, understand, form, and shape the marketing, communication, and mission/purpose/vision of any given brand. Brand thinking is also an actionable framework that can be applied among professionals to give their brands an edge in the competitive landscape.

Brand Thinking comprises five core concepts: Believability, Belief System(s), Growth, Strategy, and Social Influence (Figure I.1). This structure is described in detail throughout this book, and comprises values and meanings that inform branding in a consistent, clear, and meaningful way.

We argue that the central component of brand thinking is brand believability—also known as the creation of brand meaning in a post-truth era.

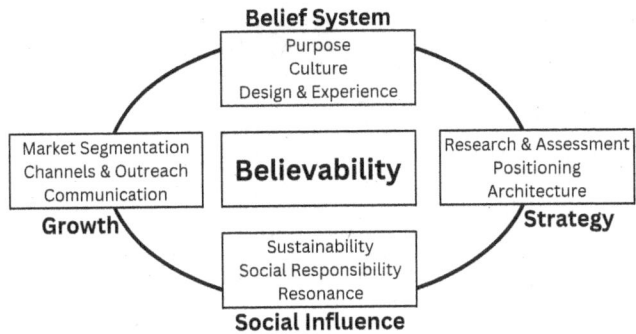

Figure I.1 Brand Thinking Framework.

In today's post-truth era, executives, employees, and consumers are co-creating values that build believable brands. Oxford Languages named *post-truth* the 2016 word of the year, being "an adjective defined as 'relating to or denoting circumstances in which objective facts are less influential in shaping public opinion than appeals to emotion and personal belief.'" *Cambridge Dictionary* (2024) defines *post-truth* as "relating to a situation in which people are more likely to accept an argument based on their emotions and beliefs, rather than one based on facts." Following these definitions, post-truth has impacted branding in significant ways. Most significantly, post-truth provides some opportunities for building believable brands: Appealing to consumers' emotion and beliefs. Emotional attachment is a key way brands cultivate believability. This book defines brand believability as a combination of emotional attachment and credibility, bolstered by values including authenticity, consistency, innovation, and quality. Believability is co-created by clients, consumers, employees, and stakeholders, and is validated by our research presented throughout this book.

Brand Thinking provides an organizing framework that integrates the emotional and functional benefits of branding. Before presenting believability as the central component of the brand thinking framework, we'll unpack one of branding's major obstacles: Brand skepticism.

I.2 The Problem: Brand Skepticism

There are some serious, influential brand skeptics around, including Roy Disney, who once said: "If you'll forgive me, I can't use that word—brand. I find the word repugnant. It means all the things that we're not. We're Snow White, Mickey Mouse, Donald, Goofy, and all those guys and gals. We're in people's hearts and people's souls. Calling Disney a brand demeans it" (Gunther, 2004).

Similarly, Sir James Dyson—founder of Dyson Ltd.—banned the word *brand* in his company. As Dyson stated at *Wired* magazine's "Disruptive by Design" conference in 2012: "There's only one word banned in our company: brand. We're only as good as our latest product. I don't believe in brand at all" (Creamer, 2012).

Author and thought leader Malcolm Gladwell wonders if we wouldn't be better off setting the word *brand* aside altogether: "I have the same feeling toward the word 'brand' as I do toward the word 'Africa.' It's a word used with great frequency to describe an intricately complex area.... The word gets thrown around so recklessly that I wonder whether we wouldn't be better off setting it aside" (Millman, 2013).

Consumers are sometimes skeptical of brands. At the same time, brands are the biggest wealth drivers for corporations. This skepticism is a catalyst as to why it's important to prove the value of brand thinking as an effective organizing framework for corporations and organizations everywhere. Beyond persuading skeptics to adopt a framework to understand and appreciate the potential impacts of branding, brand thinking builds the foundation for believability—the most powerful way for brands to engage consumers, clients, employees, and stakeholders across the board.

I.3 The Solution: Brand Believability

Believability is the central component of the brand thinking framework (Figure I.1). Believability is a combination of emotional attachment and credibility, and is bolstered by co-created values including authenticity, consistency, innovation, and quality. In other words: The building blocks of brand believability, presented throughout this book, are:

- emotional attachment
- credibility

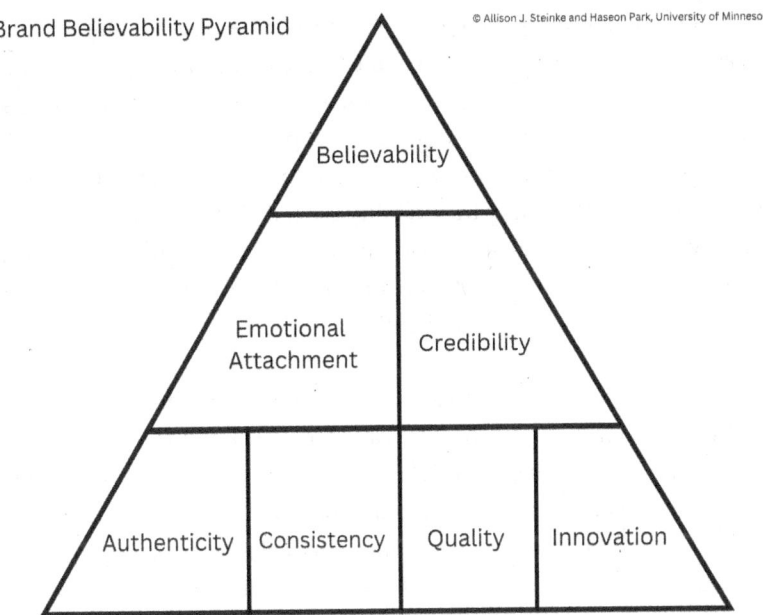

Figure I.2 Brand Believability Pyramid.

- authenticity
- consistency
- innovation
- quality

Believability is built through authentic branding practices including vulnerability and transparency in brand communications. Believability is also built with consistent and innovative branding practices. One way brands build believability is by consistently focusing and aligning an organization's values, culture, and initiatives. Another way brands build believability is with innovative brand behaviors and marketing practices. All products and services must be high quality and perceived as such by stakeholders, employees, clients, and consumers. Brand thinking asserts that believability is the highest order of brand meaning and serves the needs and expectations of all stakeholders, clients, employees, and consumers.

Believability, as a co-created and co-constructed paradigm, comprises what executives leverage in their branding and marketing practices and what employees and customers believe to be true about a particular brand. Brand believability is codified in brands' mission, vision, and purpose statements; value propositions; and brand promises. Believability is also co-created through user-generated content, social media content, reviews, and recommendations of brands' products and experiences by clients, consumers, employees, and stakeholders in physical and digital realms. Our research supports existing research that brand communications play a significant role in building believability especially in and through social media (Mulcahy et al., 2024). Based on our findings, brand believability comprises norms of emotional attachment and credibility, supported by co-created values including authenticity, consistency, innovation, and quality.

In addition to defining what believability is, it's important to differentiate believability from related concepts. Brand believability is not the same thing as brand loyalty or brand trust—but, as our research shows, loyalty and trust are byproducts of a believable brand. Trust is a byproduct of believability, and believability is a foundational element of trust.

Brand thinking thus asserts that believability—in the context of brand value creation, purpose delivery and brand strength—is the highest order of brand meaning and will serve the needs and expectations of all stakeholders.

The Co-Creation of Brand Values

Structuration theory is a sociological framework that helps to show how brand believability is built (Gibbs, 2024). All brands exist within economic, sociological, and organizational structures. Social actors—in this case, chief marketing officers (CMOs) and consumers—co-create rules, norms, and values within these social structures including governance and regulatory agencies and authorities, communities, and economic markets.

Value co-creation builds, defines, and shapes brand believability. At the same time, according to new institutionalism, rules, norms, and values comprise the legitimacy of brands and organizations (Steinke, 2022). The co-creation of brand values thus builds, defines, and shapes brand credibility and believability.

When social actors—including CMOs and consumers—act in a compliant manner with socially constructed rules, existing structures are reinforced. Recognizing that these structures are socially constructed and co-created with various rules, norms, and values, social actors—including chief marketing officers (CMOs) and consumers—can innovate in an attempt to act outside the constraints the structures place on them. Innovation can, in turn, improve the structures for the good of both consumers and the brand but can also destroy brands when not supported or sustained by social actors. Brand value co-creation is the result of a process in which executives, consumers, and employees engage with a brand and each other in digital and physical realms to build believability (Cheung et al., 2020).

Our research utilizes a qualitative triangulated approach to further develop the brand value co-creation model originally developed by Merz et al. (2009). Our research identifies authenticity, consistency, innovation, and quality as the co-created values that build brand believability—the core concept of brand thinking. These values—along with norms of emotional attachment and credibility—exist within the structure of brand thinking as an actionable framework (Figure I.2). We discovered the rules, norms, and values of brand believability inductively through in-depth qualitative data collection and analysis comprising in-depth interviews with chief marketing officers (CMOs), focus groups with consumers, and analysis of industry reports and data (Appendix A). From this point forward, we will refer to these norms and values as the building blocks of brand believability. They are introduced below and described throughout each chapter of this book.

The Building Blocks of Brand Believability

All brands abide by various economic, sociological, and organizational rules. One example of a brand believability rule is that all brands must be rooted in a deeply embedded purpose. In addition to this rule, there are many rules that challenge brand growth and innovation. Rules that constrain and challenge brand believability include structural constraints from federal regulations and agencies. For example: While many brands and organizations aspire to be prosocial, environmentally friendly, and to advocate for social causes, it's expensive to do so. It costs to become a B Corporation, to attain sustainability certifications, to produce sustainable products, and to source organic and fair-trade materials. Thus, structural constraints that keep brands from thriving might include a lack of monetary resources to attain the prosocial status that clients, consumers, stakeholders, and employees desire. A tension that comes with these constraints is that investors find socially responsible companies and organizations committed to sustainability incredibly lucrative, but these prosocial commitments are sometimes only possible for wealthy brands and organizations—a tension that will be unpacked throughout this book's narrative.

Brand Believability Norms: Emotional Attachment and Credibility

Normative outlooks are developed and established in line with the organizational and sociological rules that brands abide by. Two norms that all believable brands uphold are emotional attachment and credibility. Emotional attachment is defined as a positive affect with clients, consumers, employees, and stakeholders.

We define credibility as whether or not a brand delivers on their promises to provide high-quality products and/or services. Part of credibility is education. Education helps to build credibility, which is key to cultivating buy-in and believability among consumers, especially in the introduction of a new product or service. Consumers and brand leaders find value in brands that educate and provide thought leadership, which helps the consumer feel respected and empowered intellectually.

CMOs see themselves as educators within their brands and with consumers. In the introduction of new and innovative products and services, education helps brands cultivate consumer buy-in. Lizzie Spier, CMO of Halara Cannabis, notes that educating and teaching consumers about the industry at large helps open up conversations about why their product might be the best fit for them.

"For a lot of consumers, our product is a different consumption method than they've done before," Spier says. "We're creating buy-in by explaining how our technology is better than what they've known about cannabis before."

Education is a key part of Mayo Clinic's culture—both for staff and for clients/patients. Mayo's CMO Sherri Gilligan recognizes Mayo's commitment to vetted, accurate, and rigorous research is what gives Mayo their believability. The education that their doctors participate in and create is then shared broadly with the world.

Part of educating consumers is informing them of the quality the product or service is and can provide to them as well.

Building Believability with Brand Values: Authenticity, Consistency, Innovation, and Quality

Brand values are co-created between brands and consumers in a reflexive and iterative fashion (Lund et al., 2020). Brands' normative outlooks align with brand values including authenticity, consistency, innovation, and quality. These values build reflexively into brands' rules and norms to establish believability across the board.

Consistent and persistent brand behaviors, grounded in brand values and equity, can contribute to winning competitive advantage over other competitors in the market, ultimately leading to business success. Over time, brands' believability can be quantified by metrics including engagement, shareability, and profitability. These metrics are discussed at the end of this chapter. Authenticity, consistency, innovation, and quality are values that create and cultivate brand believability as described below.

Authenticity

Building believability involves elements of authenticity with consumers and business partners alike. Authenticity is defined as vulnerability, accepting feedback, being willing to make mistakes, and being persistent and authentic in pursuing fixes.

Chipotle's chief brand officer and CMO Chris Brandt says that Chipotle's success to date lies in their ability to be authentic, believable, and transparent: "just telling the truth, showing people what we do, and not getting lost with too many bells and whistles and everything else."

Mike Benson, president and CMO of CBS, says that authenticity leads to believability and trust that creates opportunities for innovation.

"Creating an emotional connection between your brand and the audience builds a bond that allows you to experiment, as long as you remain authentic," Benson says. "If you make a mistake, you can own it and explain your intentions: 'We tried, we're sorry, but we want to keep working to serve you as best we can.' Authenticity and honesty are essential when building and managing a brand, and especially critical when evolving a brand that's almost a hundred years old, like CBS."

Being a hundred years old—or young—presents its share of opportunities and challenges.

Consistency

Consistency is a predictability or rhythm marked by regular communication and engagement between brands' stakeholders and consumers. Consistency is also a commitment to quality and stability between brand promise and deliverables. Delivering consistent results, products, services, and experiences are foundational values and elements of building a believable brand. Consistency also plays into authenticity, especially as it relates to recovering from and working through failure. For innovative brands entering new markets, consistency is key to wooing new partners and customers. Consistent, authentic brand communication optimally leads to endemicity—a value that speaks to the power of connection.

Clare Scott, the CMO of Ryan Companies US, Inc., a real estate and construction company based out of Minneapolis, Minnesota, articulated consistency as following through with what you say you're going to do, year over year, which cultivates and helps to gain trust.

"It's about saying you're going to do something and then actually doing it, and then people start to buy in and believe it," Scott says.

Creating consistency—quality experiences that are meaningful day in and day out—helps build believability. Consistency can be either positive or negative. For example: If a consumer or company has consistently positive interactions with a brand, they are more likely to continue engaging with that brand. Repeated negative experiences also create consistency, just not as a desirable outcome. Consistency is also internal and external. Consistent branding is bolstered by employee behavior, employee and brand performance, and brand communication (Henkel et al., 2007). Brand consistency shifts across international boundaries as well. Consumers who are sometimes critical of U.S.-based brands including McDonalds and Starbucks have been found to be more favorable to them in international contexts as they evoke feelings in U.S. consumers of comfort, predictability, safety, and national pride while abroad (Bengtsson et al., 2010).

Jon Althoff is president and chief marketing/mission officer of the Dakota County Regional Chamber of Commerce. A chamber of commerce is a membership-based organization that brings together local businesses and professionals to act together to promote and protect the interests of its members by advocating for policies that benefit the local economy and improve the quality of life in the area. In addition to acting as a collective voice for businesses, brands, and organizations within a region to influence local government and community initiatives, chambers of commerce are networking organizations that help to mutually support and encourage fellow members' missions and purpose. "Truth may be another word for believability, and I was once told by a former mentor, Mark Bendix, that trust is truth over time. I like that definition," Althoff says. "A consumer of a service or of a good has to trust your brand. That means they're getting truthful experiences that are meaningful to them day in, day out. That's what builds long-term brand growth, brand strength."

Authenticity and consistency are two sides of the believability coin.

"First, you have to be authentic to who you actually are and what you're going to market with, especially with Generation Z and Generation Alpha coming up behind them, because they'll see right through inauthentic brand messaging. I could put forth all the beautiful advertising in the whole world, but it has to be authentic and believable," Katie Alvino, CMO of College of Saint Benedict and Saint John's University, says.

> Second, it's believable if your brand's able to deliver on that brand promise that you're promising in your marketing. So if what I'm selling isn't coming through in the product experience—in this case it's higher ed—it just falls flat. And then your reputation starts to unravel over a period of time because you are not delivering on what you are selling—your brand promise.

In these ways, delivering consistent results, products, services, and experiences are foundational values and elements of building a believable brand. Consistency also plays into authenticity, especially as it relates to recovering from and working through failure. For innovative brands entering new markets, consistency is key. Lizzie Spier, CMO of Halara Cannabis, knows this journey firsthand.

"When we were first getting started, there was so much that we had to do to really create buy-in and convince a lot of the dispensary owners that we were a product worth bringing on," Spier says.

Even with consumers in some of these more established areas like Northern California in the Emerald Triangle, a very historical area for just—that's where a lot of cannabis has been grown since the 1960s. A lot of people there are skeptical. So, for us, it took a lot of being vulnerable and being willing to be making mistakes and being willing for them to be like, "Oh, this sucks. Come back and try again." And just being persistent and being authentic to say, "Hey, we are trying, we're learning, we're discovering, but we want to be better. So we want that feedback. We want you to tell us more." And so a long relationship of really just being receptive to feedback and taking it in stride and actually improving our product really helped us create trust and buy-in.

Clare Scott, CMO of Ryan Companies, knows from experience that consistency in pursuing face-to-face communication with clients and partners enables educational opportunities that sell.

Again and again, I hear people come back from our presentations to clients saying, "Once we met with them, we had them." Just yesterday, I was in Chicago talking to one of our guys who has been cultivating this relationship with the health care system down there for years… he just said, "It took us so long to get this client in the door. But once we met with them, we had them." To me, that's believability: "Gosh, if we can just get in front of you, you are going to buy into what we bring, what we offer, why we're different."

Longevity—a cousin of consistency—plays a part in establishing the credibility of a brand, but it can both help and hurt brands looking to evolve and change. Glenn Bottomly, CMO of Taylor Corporation, says Taylor has "a really good grasp" on its belief system in part due to the fact they've been in existence for fifty years. On the other hand, CBS president and CMO Mike Benson wrestles with the value in one hundred years.

"Will it help us to tell people we're one hundred years old, or will it hurt us?" Benson says. "How do we articulate such a milestone, so it ultimately adds value for everyone? I want people to feel like we're one hundred years new, not one hundred years old."

Innovation can be difficult to attain or pursue depending on the context of the brand or organization. As a brand that's been around for nearly one hundred years, longevity can sometimes be the enemy of innovation.

For decades, we've been engaging our audience in much the same way, but as audience behaviors have evolved and changed, we've had to evolve our style of marketing. Creating new ways to engage audiences to provide a more relevant relationship with our brand and IP is at the heart of that evolution. We need to meet audiences where they are, and that might not be on the CBS Television Network. A lot of what I do on a daily basis is push our team to innovate around building, growing and developing audiences in ways that are more meaningful and authentic for us, and the audience we want to reach. For teams that had been wired to do the same type of work for decades, that innovation has been both challenging and exciting,

At the same time, Glenn Bottomly, CMO of Taylor Corporation, says Taylor has "a really good grasp" on its belief system in part due to the fact they've been in existence for forty-eight years.

While consistency helps bolster brand value, if a brand maintains a high quality of their products and services, the introduction of some inconsistency in product design in particular can help consumers to take a more active role in brand value co-creation (Charters, 2009). This inconsistency can be introduced through innovation, which is crucial to a brand's believability.

Innovation

We define innovation as the ability to ideate, develop, deliver, and scale new products, services, processes, and experiences efficiently and effectively. Ideally, innovation has a positive influence on the brand and its clients, customers, employees, and stakeholders. Digital and social media—and the increasingly collaborative role of consumers with desires for purpose-driven and conscientious branding—are driving innovation among brands worldwide (Aaker, 2022; Iglesias & Ind, 2020; Iglesias et al., 2017).

The rise of artificial intelligence (AI) has enhanced and also impeded brands' efforts to connect with consumers in a meaningful way, especially in the customer service realm. Some scholars argue AI threatens what it means to put the customer first. Other scholars argue there are meaningful connections to be made and brand equity to be built thanks to the efficiency provided by AI-generated technology including web and social media analytics, chat bots, algorithmic recommendations, and advertisements (Varsha et al., 2021). Studies show that personalized advertising boosts brand engagement and reduces privacy concerns on social media (Loureiro et al., 2023).

Innovation solves problems. For example, at BlueGrace Logistics—a B2B company that provides supply chain management and logistics technology to customers throughout North America—innovation leads to efficiency. "We are a culture of providing frictionless experiences to the vendors and suppliers we work with because their jobs are equally chaotic and have an equal number of problems in doing this transportation and logistics piece," Mark Derks, BlueGrace CMO, says. "We're a culture of innovation and technology, and also a people-first culture, high on recognition and reward."

CMOs relate innovation to technology, and note that quantifying their commitment is important. "I think we have about eight different categories that we're evaluating to see that we're moving over time to a marketing operation that is innovative, creative, and data-driven," Jaime Hunt, CMO of Old Dominion University, says. "One of our measurements is our use of technology. How are we using marketing technologies that either automate or help us be more efficient or better at what we do?"

Innovation is a value that informs believability by engaging customers and employees in the product or service. "There's no such thing as a brand lifecycle, there is only ineffective brand marketing," Althoff says. "The brand may not have life anymore, but it's only because you haven't figured out how to shift, pivot, or morph your brand into something that's more usable in the current environment. A lot of our planning process is how we can do things differently based on the way people need access to data, information, and help."

Innovation is engrained into many brands' and organizations' mission, vision, and purpose statements. Leah Larson is CMO of Madison Air, an indoor air quality company. She describes her brand as "disruptive innovators who believe in the transformative power of air." Larson went on to say that the brand is built on a "shared belief in the transformative power of air, meaning that we and our customers all are united under this belief that air can quantifiably improve business and human lives."

Innovation can be difficult to attain or pursue depending on the context of the brand or organization. Benson spends much of his time encouraging his team to innovate because they aren't used to it. As a brand that's been around for nearly one hundred years, longevity can sometimes be the enemy of innovation.

Darren Wennen, CCO of Caerus Corp., a medical startup, has spent years in senior leadership roles at medical companies and organizations.

Wennen has seen firsthand one major reason brands fail to innovate: they fear cannibalizing their existing products or services. "You don't get much real innovation out of companies like Medtronic, Boston Scientific, or Abbott now because it's much easier to focus effort on existing products than it is to innovate to new ones," Wennen says. "One of the best examples of this is Kodak, I'll say. They invented digital photo technology in the 1970s. They didn't commercialize it because it cannibalized their existing film business."

For Lizzie Spier, CMO of Halara Cannabis, innovation is a part of their daily routine as a marketer in an emerging market with recent regulations.

> We determine a new sleep product, research that line, source the product, test the product, bring it to market, and down to the consumer level. We're constantly working to just improve that experience. This is a relatively new industry, and in ten years' time, I know the technology that we'll be using is going to be drastically different than we are today. We are constantly in this cycle of innovation and change because on a monthly basis there are new things that people are learning about this plant, as well as the methods of consumption. It's a lot of iteration and change, but I do feel like with where we've come, it's been a very rewarding experience with a lot of lessons along the way.

Spier continues,

> Innovation is really about debunking people's myths. A lot of people are coming in with information that's either what they've heard or what they've known. But once again, like I said, this industry is in such a fast cycle of innovation. There are so many new things coming out that on the business side, we're constantly aware of these changes, but the consumers already know so little about the plant and the product that when there are these new things that come out that are scientific and technology and all this stuff, it's coming to them at a spot that they didn't expect cannabis to be.

Innovation is key to thriving corporate cultures, too, and often encourages brands to find a fresh way of doing things, including through hackathons and internal mock Shark Tank competitions. Glenn Bottomly, CMO of Taylor Corporation, says,

> A couple years ago, we introduced Shark Tank to our organization as an internal competition. Shark Tank was an opportunity for us to leverage the expertise of our employees, create strategic new opportunities that we can bring into the market, ensure that those are going to be reliable when we scale them, and ensure that innovation gets propagated across

the organization that we can then drive to our customers. Innovation helps brands find a better way.

Bottomly continues,

> One of the things I think that we talk about a lot internally is, "We want to be the expert in the room." The people that we bring into our organization are extremely bright. They bring with them years and years of experience, and that expertise and creativity is really key for us. So that would be one key aspect of the positioning. Another key is being strategic in our thinking and in our deployment. So, as I mentioned a little bit earlier, we have a phrase, "There's always a better way," and so we say that a lot. We challenge each other. Something's not working right, and sometimes we'll say in meetings, "There's got to be a better way." And so, whatever that is, if it's bringing in new employees, if it is improving the process that a customer has, if they've been using and having a horrible experience maybe with another company, we can bring in some innovative thinking and show how there's a better way to do that.

For Chris Brandt, CMO and chief brand officer of Chipotle, innovation leads to excellence in product, experience, and operations. Through its mission to Cultivate a Better World, the brand is working toward more sustainable restaurant designs featuring solar panels, energy-efficient lighting, all-electric equipment, and more as well as continuing to commit to locally and ethically sourced food and products. These commitments are all codified in this brand's annual sustainability report released to shareholders and the public. "We believe that no one else is doing anything like what we do. At its core, Chipotle is craveable food you feel good about eating and that itself is pretty special," Brandt says.

Quality

Quality is proof that partnership or investment in a brand is worthwhile. Consumers desire quality products and experiences, so consistently delivering that quality builds a reciprocal believability with consumers.

Mike Benson, president and CMO of CBS, says: "I've always believed that a brand must offer a clear quality and value proposition that resonates with consumers, making them feel the brand holds specific emotional value for them." He emphasizes that believability stems from trust and the assurance that the brand consistently delivers something reliable and trustworthy.

Brands must offer products and services that deeply connect with consumers. In health care, this connection takes the form of life-changing diagnoses and treatments. For Mayo Clinic, the world's top-ranked hospital, innovation and quality have been inseparable for more than a century.

"We diagnose conditions that others can't, and our outcomes far exceed those of other institutions, which makes us a trusted brand," says Sherri Gilligan, chief marketing officer, Mayo Clinic. "When Mayo Clinic speaks, people listen."

For third party logistics companies like BlueGrace, quality comes in the form of efficiency and process. CMO Mark Derks notes that efficiency improves bottom-line ROI.

> It's one thing to call somebody and say, "Hey, can I move your freight from point A to point B?" It's another thing to call somebody and say, "Hey, can we reduce your order-to-order management to service customer time by 7 percent? That will save you X number of millions of dollars." It's a completely different conversation. So, process and supply chain engineering become a differentiator.

Believability in product-oriented brands comes from connection with consumers. With an established emotional connection and quality products, brands can innovate more freely to create even more engaging shareable quality products.

"Believability translates into authenticity and the quality of our products, trust that the consumers have in the quality of our product, connection with the consumers as well, just by the nature of what cannabis is for so many people that have that legacy relationship," Lizzie Spier, CMO of Halara Cannabis, says.

> So, I would say that's a big part and for us, that believability translates to justifying the price of our product, the way that we fit into the market. But then it also allows us to try to push the envelope with new products and new ideas. That believability and that trust allows us to come into an established industry, in an established market and say, "Okay, we're going to try some new things that are maybe a little bit out of norm or maybe not what a lot of people have come to know," but through this believability and trust and quality, we're able to have them on board as we explore these new things.

Innovation has pros and cons and plenty of risks and benefits. A brand can innovate with boundaries of quality but can't push so far that the quality of the brand gets shaken. A motto common among tech startups in Silicon Valley is to "fail fast, fail often" (Carroll, 2014). Evaluated experience is the best kind, and when it comes to innovation, three ways to ensure lessons are learned from failure are to (1) pick your battles wisely; (2) don't ask who or why, but what; and to (3) make sure the people around you feel comfortable speaking up (Yildirim, 2023).

As an example of interfacing with donors at a higher education institution, Old Dominion University CMO Jaime Hunt says:

> Believability is about making sure that you have sort of the proof that's in the pudding, that shows you donated these dollars, and this was the outcome we told you that we would get for those dollars, and this is what you got. It's critical to have that sort of two-way communication with donors in particular and lots of touch points with them to be able to see how their dollars are supporting the institution.

Consistent, authentic brand communication in support of quality products and/or services allows brands to educate consumers—a quality that contributes to credibility, one norm that upholds believable brands.

I.4 Application: Brand Believability Score

Brand thinking is a framework that outlines the components necessary to build a believable brand: A belief system, strategy, growth, and social influence. Within these components, as our research shows, brand believability is a combination of emotional attachment, credibility, authenticity, consistency, innovation, and quality. It's important for every brand to consistently assess their believability within all areas of the brand thinking framework. Our intention is to provide a clear road map for this assessment to help brands navigate and evaluate their success and opportunities within the brand thinking framework.

You can begin by bringing your team together to assess the status of your brand's success in each area of the brand thinking framework with informal discussion about your brand's belief system, strategy, growth, and social influence. Then, you can calculate your brand's Brand Believability Score with an assessment survey you can personalize and tailor for your team, internal stakeholders, and/or external clients or consumers.

The Brand Believability Score is calculated with an assessment survey that tallies the points in each category of the brand thinking framework to present a Brand Believability Score. The score is out of 6 total points, which can also be quantified as a percentage. The goal is 100 percent both for internal and external stakeholders. If your brand scores below 100 percent in any category of the brand thinking framework, you can clearly see areas of opportunity to develop believability by utilizing and interpreting findings of the Brand Believability Score assessment survey. The Brand Believability Score is meant to answer the question: "Is your brand believable?" A sample of a Brand Believability Score assessment survey is shown below and also in Appendix C.

- Is your brand believable?: Total /6 = %
  - Emotional Attachment /1
    - Are you emotionally attached to this brand? (Yes/No)
  - Credibility /1
    - Is this brand credible? (Yes/No)
  - Authenticity /1
    - Is this brand authentic? (Yes/No)
  - Consistency /1
    - Is this brand consistent? (Yes/No)
  - Innovation /1
    - Is this brand innovative? (Yes/No)
  - Quality /1
    - Does this brand provide high-quality products/services? (Yes/No)

I.5 Metrics: Engagement, Shareability, and Profitability

One of the popular industry metrics to quantify brand performance is the *Net Promoter Score (NPS)*, a trademark of Satmetrix Systems, Bain & Company, and Fred Reichheld. NPS quantifies how likely consumers are to recommend their brand experience to others (Reichheld, 2006).

Another metric is *Brand Intimacy*, which measures customers' emotional connections to and satisfaction with various brands (Natarelli & Plapler, 2017).

This book will explore various metrics that show how to quantify believability, including the Brand Believability Score assessment survey, a sample of which is included in Appendix C. Overarching concepts that build believability include engagement, shareability, and profitability. These metrics are introduced below.

Engagement

From an internal and organizational perspective, chief marketing officers (CMOs) track and attempt to quantify believability—engagement being a key performance indicator (KPI)—using various metrics and dashboards.

According to Mike Benson, president and CMO at CBS, the key values of CBS are unification, accessibility, and optimism. As the former head of marketing at Amazon Studios, responsible for the promotion of original series on Amazon Prime Video, Benson values arguments grounded in data, but also in creativity and innovation. He values data-driven decision-making but recognizes the difficulty of implementing data-driven decision-making at an organization that traditionally hadn't leveraged it.

> I went from Amazon, a company where we had an overwhelming abundance of our own proprietary customer data, to CBS that had relatively little data outside of what we'd get from third-party vendors. At Amazon, we had access to a wide range of data and insights to help us build campaigns with greater efficacy, but at CBS we've had to develop new ways to collect and interpret data to help us build better marketing strategies, as well as help us to innovate.

CMOs see engagement with audiences and authenticity as key to brand growth. At the same time, CMOs are attempting to figure out ways to follow consumers and their behavior in ways that are meaningful and relevant.

CMOs note that Google and YouTube analytics and the value of building social media communities are underrated and underutilized in marketing strategy. Analytics and social media communities are two areas CMOs are attempting to lean into effectively. A desire to increase the size of their staff(s) and to hire data analytics professionals are ways CMOs seek to further develop their expertise and engagement in this area.

CMOs value data-driven decisions and insist they are paramount to marketing success. At the same time, CMOs admit their organizations are lagging in their use, understanding, and appreciation of data and analytics in making marketing decisions.

CMOs argue that one of the best ways to build awareness, grow, and gather consumers is to gather competitors, become a category, and create a "brand block" with key retailers.

Our research shows that social listening is key in this process as it's important to gather communities on social media to give consumers and followers more of what they love—and one concrete way to measure engagement is within digital and social media realms.

Engagement rate is defined as the percentage of a brand's audience that has engaged with their content. Engagement rate can be measured as a formula. To calculate engagement rate, divide the number of engagements by the total reach: (Engagements / Reach) × 100. Engagements are defined as how many times a person interacted with your content, and includes likes, comments, shares, and in some cases, clicks. Reach is the total number of unique people who have seen a brand's content. To calculate engagement rate on a website, you can look at your website's analytics dashboard or integrate for free with Google Analytics to track real-time analytics data including engagements and reach.

Engagement helps believable brands create deeper fans, followers, brand ambassadors, and advocates. As brand ambassadors and advocates multiply, brands can leverage that advocacy to create and scale new audiences. In these ways, shareability is another key metric for measuring brand believability.

Shareability

Leah Larson, CMO of Madison Air, notes that referrals and word of mouth create brand believability, especially in the B2B space.

Glenn Bottomly, CMO of Taylor Corporation, notes that word-of-mouth referrals matter, and that when a customer has a good experience, they have the potential to become brand ambassadors.

"We have just found that when a customer has a really good experience working with Taylor, they will share that," Bottomly says.

They will be a great source of marketing testimonials that we can use on our website and in marketing materials. We can invite them to be speakers at trade shows that we're working at, and that just continues to build that relationship over time. It's a partnership, and so driving growth ultimately equates to trust and, ultimately, believability that gets earned over time.

Jeehye Jung is CMO of Amuse Agency and has consulted for brands for over a decade. She's found that the amount of shares brands receive is the best metric you can get to prove a brand's believability among followers and stakeholders.

"It's one thing to like something or look at overall impressions, but it's another thing to be like, 'Ooh, I really believe in this so much that I'm going to risk my own personal brand and also share it for you,'" Jung says. "So for me, shares show believability and the peak embodiment of whatever message your company is saying at that given point."

Once you get buy-in and support from a couple of key people or influencers, the doors start opening for the brand to create a brand community. Word-of-mouth referrals are typically more effective than advertising of any kind, and this includes referrals from influencers on social media. Call-to-Action (CTA) messages on all marketing materials are important and often persuade people to share content or perform a desired action. An example of a CTA would be "Register Today!" with a link to a registration form. Shareability can be quantified in digital and social media realms with shares—how many times people share a brand's content on the web or social media—and mentions, or the number of times a person or organization tags a brand in social media post(s) or on websites, including blog posts, ratings, and reviews.

Profitability

The bottom line matters for brands everywhere in for-profit and nonprofit sectors. As Jeehye Jung, CMO of Amuse Agency, says,

As a CMO, my ultimate goal is to drive product sales, and for me, believability is defined by the number of returning customers for a specific product. That metric encapsulates several key aspects: it suggests we're effectively building a long-term brand connection, even at the basic level of dependability. It also reflects credibility, as a product that consistently meets expectations will naturally bring customers back. This return rate serves as a measure of both emotional attachment and the product's performance.

In digital and social media realms, one way to quantify profitability is to keep track of return on investment (ROI) on each campaign or effort as a measurement of the value gained from digital and social media marketing and advertising. Profitability of digital and social media marketing campaigns can be a wonderful representation of net profit and the cost of investment: (Profit / Total Investment) × 100. Tracking profitability and ROI is key in all areas of the brand thinking framework.

Conclusion

Brand thinking requires a strong leadership team committed to a deeply embedded purpose, meaningful values that inspire persistent brand behaviors, and a mindset that recognizes the importance of believability as a competitive advantage and vital contributor to business success. Behavior is an important factor related to the execution and establishment of belief systems in branding.

In Debbie Millman's 2013 book titled *Brand Thinking and Other Noble Pursuits*, Canadian anthropologist and author Grant McCracken argues that branding is a process of "meaning manufacture that begins with the biggest, boldest gestures of the corporation and works its way down to the tiniest gestures."

Endemic is a term that originated in the medical world to signify the constant prevalence of a disease in a given population. Adopted into the branding world, endemicity—or, becoming endemic—is a value attained when a brand becomes "regularly found and very common among a particular group or in a particular area" (*Cambridge Dictionary*, 2024).

Endemicity is synonym for believability as it represents a combination of credibility and emotional attachment with clients and customers, and it speaks to the embeddedness of a brand within consumer lifestyles. Chris Brandt, CMO and chief brand officer of Chipotle and former CMO of Taco Bell, spent time at General Mills where he was first exposed to the term as part of advertising Nature Valley products to the skiing community.

Here at Chipotle, we talk about being endemic. The first time I heard that word, I was at General Mills working on the Nature Valley brand. I was talking to the guys at *Ski* Magazine. And I said, "How's your business?" And they said, "Well, it's pretty good with the endemic advertisers, but not so good with the other ones." And I didn't really know what it meant, but then I got it from the context, oh, the endemic advertisers for *Ski* Magazine are skis and poles and jackets and ski equipment, right? And I said, "I want Nature Valley to be endemic to skiing. I want skiers to feel like their equipment isn't complete until they tuck a Nature Valley bar into their jacket pocket as they head out to the mountain." And so, here at Chipotle, we've really tried to be endemic to anything that we do, whether it's gaming, whether it's with athletes. Because if we get athletes who eat at Chipotle all the time saying "This is what my order is," "I think my order's better than yours," "I'm willing to share it," all of those things… we want to feel like we're just a natural part of it—because we are!

One example Brandt gave was of Chipotle's effort to join digital gaming platform Roblox. Chipotle's marketing team invested in a Roblox initiative to provide users with free burritos, and while it was a risk, the campaign was wildly successful.

"We're part of Roblox because we did it in the right way," Brandt says. "We did it in a way that users of Roblox would really like. And they reward you with their time, they reward you with their interest, they reward you with all those things."

Community embeddedness plays into endemicity, too. Cultivating relationships with and being connected and authentic in communities with established markets is a priority, and education plays a key part in building believability especially for new and emerging brands, or for brands introducing new products and services. Dr. Jesse Lillejord, founder and CMO of Chiro for Moms / Chiro for Kidz, says that listening—both in person and on social media—is key to cultivating emotional attachment and building credibility.

"Believability is everything for us," Dr. Jesse says.

With us being so niche and so specialty, everything that we do is based around the believability of what we are. Our patient base needs to understand—they need to believe—that we will listen to them because that's the very thing that creates the conversation that keeps them paying attention. So, they have to constantly believe in not just the way that we treat and the fact that they'll get relief, but the fact that we'll listen because the second that they don't, it's over. They stop showing up on social media, they stop looking at our emails, they stop sending emails to ask questions, and it's over. Believability is of the utmost importance for us.

Part I of this book discusses brand believability and brand belief systems. Belief Systems are defined as how brand purpose, culture, design and experience build believability. Here are the three elements of brands' belief systems that we'll explore in Part I of this book:

- *Brand Purpose:* An organization's "why"—its reason for being and the things it stands for.
- *Brand Culture:* How a company lives out its values and mission by instilling the knowledge and support of brand behaviors into brand learning.
- *Brand Design and Experience:* How a brand represents its identity to the public visually and experientially.

Key Terms

Authenticity
Consistency
Credibility
Emotional attachment
Endemic

Engagement
Innovation
Profitability
Quality
Shareability

Discussion Questions

1 Which area of the brand thinking framework—belief system, strategy, growth, or social influence—is most important for brands to build? Why?
2 Which element of believability—emotional attachment, credibility, authenticity, consistency, innovation, or quality—is most important for brands to pursue? Why?
3 What concepts should brands consider in their pursuits that aren't included here?

Activity

The Most Believable Brand Ever: Choose your favorite brand of all time. Rank each element of the brand thinking framework in order of effectiveness. Why did you rank these elements like you did? Is your favorite brand of all time believable? Why or why not?

1

Brand Purpose

What is brand purpose and what does it have to do with believability? To build a believable brand, it must be rooted in a deeply embedded purpose—an organization must have a "why," or its reason for being and things it stands for. In a post-truth era where truth is secondary to belief, building and telling a compelling brand story is a powerful way to create and sustain brand purpose. Brand stories are bolstered by brand values including authenticity, consistency, innovation, and quality. This chapter introduces the concept of brand purpose, discusses post-truth, provides a case of the purpose-driven brand *Seventh Generation*, shows how to create a sticky and spreadable brand story, and gives an example of how to quantify purpose with SMART Goals.

Chapter Outline

1.1 Introduction: What Is Brand Purpose?	38
1.2 The Problem: Post-Truth	39
1.3 The Solution: Believable Brand Purpose	39
1.4 Case: Seventh Generation	47
1.5 Application: Creating a Sticky and Spreadable Brand Story	50
1.6 Metrics: SMART Goals	51
Key Terms	53
Discussion Questions	53
Activity	53

1.1 Introduction: What Is Brand Purpose?

Brand Purpose: An organization's "why." Its reason for being and the things it stands for.

A majority of working professionals prefer to work for a purpose-led organization where they can do work that reflects their passions and personal values (Mitchell, 2021). A majority of consumers prefer to invest in purpose-driven brands (BLVR, 2023; Peters, 2021).

Brands' belief systems and values are core to understanding branding and brand thinking. Scott Bedbury supports this argument in his book, *A New Brand World* (Bedbury & Fenichell, 2003). A brand game-changer at Nike and Starbucks, Bedbury argues that "brands are complicated concepts. Their power comes from many different people and how well they understand and respect the brand and its values." With regard to brand purpose, or an organization's "why," Bedbury argues that "a brand gives employees a common understanding of what they do for a living and how they must do it." He also says that brands provide companies with a "conscience" and they give it a "heart."

Hatch and Schultz (2008) assert that a "successful" corporate brand is "coherence between what leadership wants to accomplish (vision, purpose), what is known or believed by employees, and what external stakeholders expect from the company (their images of it)." This commitment to purpose is part of belief systems, and also overlaps into the core concept of believability.

The Purpose of Purpose

Brand purpose is not about what you do, it's about who you are (Mainwaring, 2023). Purpose can be codified in a company's charter, personified in their shareholders and stakeholders, and owned by conscious consumers.

Stanley Hainsworth is principal and creative director of Tether, a multidisciplinary design firm in Seattle, and former vice president creative director of Starbucks. He asserts that "genuinely good branding involves examining every single way the brand, the product and the experience is viewed. Everything that you do, everything that you say, is the cumulative expression of the brand" (Millman, 2011).

1.2 The Problem: Post-Truth

Post-truth is defined as the prioritization of personal beliefs over factual accuracy, disregarding the importance of truth and instead focusing on appealing to emotion (O'Callaghan, 2020). Oxford Languages named *post-truth* the 2016 word of the year, crediting the EU referendum in the United Kingdom and the presidential election in the United States with its surge in popularity. *Post-truth* is also "an adjective defined as 'relating to or denoting circumstances in which objective facts are less influential in shaping public opinion than appeals to emotion and personal belief'" (Oxford Languages, 2016). *Cambridge Dictionary* defines *post-truth* as "relating to a situation in which people are more likely to accept an argument based on their emotions and beliefs, rather than one based on facts" (2024).

Post-truth has impacted branding in significant ways. Four main problems that have come from post-truth include not knowing how to know, fallible ways of knowing, not caring about truth, and disagreeing about how to know (Barzilai & Chinn, 2020).

At the same time, post-truth provides some opportunities for building believable brands: Appealing to consumers' emotion and beliefs.

As described in the previous chapter, emotional attachment is a key way brands cultivate believability, and is one element that informs the creation of brand purpose. Other elements of building a believable, purpose-driven brand include purpose statements / pillars, partnerships, and a compelling brand story.

1.3 The Solution: Believable Brand Purpose

Brand purpose is defined as an organization's "why"—its reason for being and the things it stands for.

Purpose is developed and codified in brands and organizations in and through employees, purpose statements, brand story, and the establishment of various partnerships. One way to build brand purpose is by prioritizing people. Chief Purpose Officers (CPOs) are a C-suite position characterized by commitments to mission, vision, corporate and social partnerships, collaborations, and goals (Kohler, 2022). Regardless of whether a brand or organization has a CPO or not, Chief Marketing Officers (CMOs), especially those who identified as founders or who had knowledge of their organization's founding principles, note that founders of their organizations often had purpose-driven personal and emotional pain points that inspired them to start their companies/organizations—purpose is most compelling when carried from the top down. Thomas Kolster of Do Goodvertising argues that one way to prioritize people is by adhering to functional, emotional, social, and transformational statements that work together to build a brand promise while providing value for the customer (Kolster, 2020). For example: If you're marketing a car, a functional statement about the product could be that it is "a faster car"; an emotional statement could be to describe it as "a masculine car"; a social statement could be "an environmentally friendly car"; and the penultimate transformational statement would be "a conscious traveler." Hiring chief purpose officers is one strategy to consistently implement purpose-driven marketing and messaging.

Brands pursue purpose to better their company and better the world. Consumers are more likely to remember a brand with a strong purpose, and consumers feel a stronger emotional connection to purpose-driven companies (BLVR, 2023). The following guiding principles are key to establishing a purpose-driven and believable brand.

Purpose Statements

Purpose statements represent brands' and organizations' aspirations, send signals to employees about what the company stands for, and are the starting points for embedding and activating authentic purpose (Bailey et al., 2023). Purpose statements and mission statements are similar and often overlap, but are occasionally distinct. Here are the definitions of each:

- Purpose statement: Represent brands' and organizations' aspirations, send signals to employees about what the company stands for, and is the starting point for embedding and activating authentic purpose (Bailey et al., 2023).
- Mission statement: What a company or an organization is trying to achieve with all its activities (*Cambridge Dictionary*, 2025).

Vision statements are another kind of statement that provide purpose for brands, and brand promise is a concept that can be purposeful, but is distinct from purpose statements, mission statements, and vision statements. Vision statements and brand promise can be defined as follows:

- **Vision statement:** A clear, specific, compelling picture of what the organization will look like at a specific time in the future (one, two, or five years), including a few key metrics that define success (Raman, 2017).
- **Brand promise:** A commitment made by a brand to its clients and customers that presents the value and experience they can expect when using its products or services.

Purpose statements often align with advocacy and activism. As brands evolve over time, purpose can become elusive. Gaining buy-in from employees is key to delivering on and distilling brand purpose—to clarify purpose over time, it's important to check in with employees to ensure they are bought into the brand's story and purpose statements or if it needs to evolve.

A vast majority of Fortune 500 companies have mission statements, but not many have distinct purpose statements. Here are some examples of Fortune 500 brands with distinct purpose statements:

- **AT&T:** Connecting people to greater possibility—with expertise, simplicity, and inspiration.
- **General Mills:** Making food the world loves.
- **Southwest Airlines:** Connect people to what's important in their lives through friendly, reliable, and low-cost air travel.

At the same time, for brands without purpose statements, mission statements can be purposeful—as is the case with many of the brands we showcase in this book. Three buckets of brands we present include those that promote consumer-oriented products; client-facing services; and/or prosocial organizations. Prosocial purposes proliferate many product- and service-oriented brands today, and those that don't have a distinct purpose statement and often implement purpose to their mission statements. Product-oriented brands, including jewelry brand CONQUERing, connect their purpose to consumers. For example, CONQUERing's purpose is to make people feel empowered (CONQUERing, 2024).

Service-oriented brands and organizations often have relational mission statements, like Thrive Pet Healthcare. CMO Amy Halford notes: "We aim to create the future of pet well-being through medical excellence, innovative technology, and a connected community of teams and partners. We exist to nurture both pets and people through meaningful relationships and exceptional veterinary care." Halford's personal draw to work in veterinary health care was because of how important pets are in the lives of their owners.

"As a marketer, the ability to work in a space that has so much emotional relevance and impact in people's lives feels good," Halford says. "It's a good mix of purpose and relevance."

"Our purpose, our brand promise, is to make businesses better," Mark Derks, CMO of BlueGrace Logistics, says. "It's a three word promise that we will make your business better. In addition to purpose, I also shift and talk about brand understanding, brand reach, and brand awareness. I want to make sure people understand what our brand is, what the purpose is, and how it can help their organization and add value to the goals they have."

Other brands pursue a prosocial mission, tied to a cultural movement, like remedying the climate crisis. Leah Larson, CMO of Madison Air, says that their purpose is tied to creating a better world by providing better air.

"About 90 percent of your time is spent indoors and most indoor air has got all sorts of things in it that aren't good for people," Larson says. "We think about air as a force for good, similar to the Carlson School of Management's belief that business is a force for good. This is the mission that we're on. Our internal culture and values also support our mission and where we're going."

Brand story is how a brand infuses their purpose statements throughout their marketing and communications.

Brand Story

Brand story is a narrative that communicates a brand's identity, purpose, and values in an authentic and memorable way that builds credibility and emotional connections with stakeholders, employees, clients, and consumers. To create a compelling brand story, it's important to create a series of plot points that summarize a brand's history, mission, purpose, and values, then to bring it to life in a narrative way. Tactically, a helpful starting point is to identify various pain points clients, customers, and stakeholders face, and to illustrate how the brand presents solutions to those pain points in authentic, consistent, innovative, and quality ways.

Jeehye Jung, CMO of Amuse Agency, recognizes that consumers are smart and picky, and often want to know your origin story, where you come from, and what you have to back it up. Brands led by thought and opinion leaders who embody and have lived experiences relevant to consumers are key to brands' success.

"There's really no other better way to express a company's visions to the world than by really lifting up the people who just embody it in their everyday lives," Jung says. "It's just so much easier when there's that human-to-human connection rather than just a company speaking to you."

Jung mentioned Oatly as a brand that effectively humanized their marketing by printing statements about employees on their packaging—for example: "Hey, John bottled this Oatly. He likes cats."

Glossier is another brand Jung mentioned that effectively leverages their salespeople to be the spokespeople for the product.

"Humanized marketing is what sells," Jung says. "I think brands and companies still have an important role to play, but the days where companies can just build emotional attachment on their own is over."

Integrating brand story in and throughout organizational culture(s) is important for brands and organizations in hiring practices and performance management.

"When assimilating new employees, we spend a lot of time on our brand story to ensure they have a comprehensive understanding of every element of our brand platform—including our values," Andrew Farrant, CMO of Global Jet Capital, says.

> A clearly defined culture allows us to sit down with an employee and say, "Last month, when we were trying to get X, Y, Z out the door, you weren't exactly the most collaborative person to deal with, and we value collaboration." This clarity and organization-based alignment also helps when considering candidates or dealing with performance issues, we're able to have very specific discussions about whether or not they are exhibiting behavior that is aligned with our values and culture.

Brand Profile: Ryan Companies US, Inc.

Ryan Companies US, Inc., a U.S.-based commercial real estate company that specializes in construction, architecture, engineering, development, real estate management, and capital markets, works with clients across the United States. Their purpose is exemplified through seven values: Safety, Integrity, Respect, Stewardship, Family, Excellence, and Fun. Ryan Companies describes their purpose in part as: "From commercial real estate project conception to completion and beyond, we put our hearts into creating spaces that bring your story to life" (Ryan Companies, 2016).

One example of Ryan Company's purpose exemplified is through how they leveraged their brand story to carry out a contract to help build the Krause Gateway Center, Kum & Go's international headquarters located in Des Moines, Iowa. This contract was an unconventional and creative partnership with internationally renowned Italian architecture firm Renzo Piano Building Workshop and OPN Architects of Des Moines. The project came with contention at the executive level at times, but was ultimately executed through telling an authentic brand story and bringing in Renzo as a unique partner.

"Mr. Krause hired internationally renowned Italian architect Renzo Piano to build the space, which would be the company headquarters in addition to a home for his internationally recognized, personal art collection," Clare Scott, Ryan Company's CMO, says. "His collection is phenomenal, and houses valuable and important and beautiful pieces. He wanted it to be a legacy to what his company had built for the community. The design for the HQ was so precise that it required someone with top-notch execution capabilities on the construction site."

At this point in time, Ryan Companies had never worked with an international architect with a global pedigree, and had never built a building with such precise specifications.

"And yet, they hired us," Clare says. "They hired us on the basis of us telling the story of the way we approach things and the way we honor commitments and the way we solve problems that others don't even think of."

Clare notes the project proposal was a controversial pursuit because she made the decision to bring in an outside agency to custom design the proposal in the style of Kum & Go instead of in the typical / traditional Ryan brand—something Ryan's CEO disagreed with. But Clare, as CMO, wanted to ensure she communicated Ryan's brand story while valuing and appreciating Kum & Go's brand story at the same time—so she went with her gut and against her CEO's wishes.

"I did it because I wanted to show Mr. Krause that we understood his vision and what he was trying to build, not only for his family legacy, but for the Des Moines community," Clare says. "And against all odds, against competitors who had much better, more specific, greater experience than we did, we won that work."

In the end, Ryan Company's CEO came back to Clare and said, "You read this guy, you read what he needed to hear."

"So it wasn't as much about the proposal as it was the way our people showed up and brought earnest authenticity to the table," Clare Scott says.

> We said, "We're really good at hard things, and we can do this hard thing for you." And it was really, really hard. But it's a beautiful building, and the guy loved it so much that he hired us to build his custom home on Lake Okoboji, even though we don't build homes. It was just a really positive outcome from something that seemed like a long shot for us.

Brand Profile: Chipotle

Chris Brandt worked for Fortune 500 brands including General Mills and Taco Bell before landing at Chipotle as CMO and chief brand officer. Brandt notes that he has "never been at a brand that had such a rich brand purpose." Chipotle's brand purpose was inspired by its founder, Chef Steve Ells, whose aspirations led him to create Chipotle, a restaurant committed to quality ingredients and sourcing from local, organic, sustainable farms. Ells's commitment to quality ingredients continues to shine through the brand's story today.

> Quality ingredients were just what he wanted as a chef, and the stories are legend of some of the suppliers that have grown up with us, from a handful of stores to 3,700 restaurants today. Steve would tell suppliers to keep the food very clean and natural the way it should be. There are some things that the industry does to add more weight to cows or to meat, and Steve just said, "Promise me you'll never do those things to anything we have at Chipotle." That kind commitment and founder-inspired purpose helps to cultivate a better world.

Brandt says, "We believe food has the power to change the world. And that purpose and our commitment to real food really is a big motivator for people." Brandt notes that Chipotle's purpose is tangibly felt inside of their restaurants as part of employee culture in addition to providing food that creates an emotional bond with consumers. "You feel our purpose in our restaurants—our employees are proud to serve this food to their families and their communities and their friends, and this isn't the case at most QSRs or even other fast casuals."

> At its core, Chipotle is craveable food you feel good about eating. Think about how rare that is in your life. Because most things that taste really good, you don't feel that good about eating. Chipotle has that unique combination. The more we get people to understand the respect and thoughtfulness with which we treat our food, in addition to being great tasting, that's the emotional bond that Chipotle builds. That's what drives a lot of emotional connection to Chipotle that has really helped the brand take off, for sure.

On the other hand, not all brands come with an embedded purpose.

Brandt also spent time at Taco Bell, where he worked to create the slogan "Live Màs." "Chipotle is lucky to have a founder-inspired brand, but not every brand is that lucky," Brandt says.

> Sometimes you have to invent a purpose, and you have to find the right thing. That's hard. It's hard to create a purpose, and it's hard for the purpose to manifest itself in the creative and the company's actions. When we created "Live Màs," which became our tagline, we were asking: "How do you get a little bit more out of life?" Most people's lives are boring. They drive to work. They do the same thing every day. So, if you can give them a little fun and something that's a little different in their life, they like you. And that was Live Màs—just get a little bit more out of life, live more, right? So, living màs and a little bit more became a brand purpose for Taco Bell that just made sense for the brand.

> Branded businesses that have a positive, prosocial influence in the world are grounded in convictions that must come from the top down.

The key to building and maintaining a solid sense of purpose is to develop and tell a consistent brand story. Beyond purpose statements and brand story, brands also pursue purposeful partnerships. All of these support a consistent brand story and belief system.

Partnerships

Cause marketing and corporate social responsibility or corporate social advocacy campaigns help bolster purpose for brands and organizations. These marketing and advocacy campaigns often manifest in partnerships. As one example: Aveda partners with charity: water, an organization that helps provide clean water to millions around the world. In addition to external partnerships, partnering with clients is another way brands cultivate purpose.

Another form of partnership is through philanthropic giving. CONQUERing's purpose statement—to help people feel empowered—emanates through everything they do from product development to marketing strategy and philanthropic efforts. CONQUERing donates a portion of their profits to organizations that share their passion for empowering others, which is one form of partnership.

Andrew Farrant, CMO of Global Jet Capital, notes that when an employee group came together to work on the company's purpose, they rebuilt the brand's story, complete with a new purpose statement that integrates partnership as a cornerstone. "We partner with our customers to surpass their expectations by proudly leveraging our dedication and expertise in business jet financing," Farrant says.

Brands' executives in particular can partner with community organizations as board members. Mark Derks, CMO of BlueGrace Logistics, notes that BlueGrace's executive team members serve on boards of various organizations ranging from higher education institutions to nonprofits. External service on boards is something all executives benefit from.

1.4 Case: Seventh Generation

One of the first B Corps was Seventh Generation, a household cleaning brand. In the mid-1990s, chemical engineers were just beginning to refine the science around green cleaning. At the same time, investors were looking to capitalize on a market opportunity among new parents—a turning point in consumer purchasing decisions. Seventh Generation was born, the science evolved, and sales scaled upward through distribution at Whole Foods Market, Target, and eventually e-commerce via Amazon.

Seventh Generation's success was due in large part to the creation of a green cleaning brand block. As competitors gathered in stores and online, Seventh Generation was able to become a category captain. It built its brand while bringing competitors along for the ride to increase options for consumers and overall interest in the brand block. For Seventh

Generation, that meant flocking together with "frenemies" including Target's brand Method, and attempting to give consumers more options in the green cleaning realm.

Seventh Generation, a household cleaning brand with over one hundred products distributed globally, has been ranked as one of the most purpose-driven brands in the world year-over-year (StrawberryFrog & Dynata, 2024). This is due in part to the brand's compelling brand story and commitment to purpose-driven branding and production.

Brand Story

Seventh Generation's cofounder Jeffrey Hollender founded the brand in 1988 as a result of a pain point in his life story. Jeffrey's son developed asthma, which he traced back to toxins in their home environment. As a result, Jeffrey wanted a solution that would help his son—and other individuals with chronic health issues catalyzed by toxins—thrive (Mccuan, 2004).

When Seventh Generation was founded in 1988 in Burlington, Vermont, it began as a niche mail-order catalog business that curated energy-, water-, and resource-saving products. At the same time, chemical engineers were just beginning to refine the science around green cleaning, and investors were looking to capitalize on a market opportunity that would become endemic among parents starting families—a huge market segment and major turning point in consumer purchasing decisions.

By 1990, Jeffrey sold the catalog and began to focus on product innovation and gaining momentum in retail markets. Jeffrey aggregated a small cohort of consumers and advocates that cared about health, wellness, and the environment. At the same time, the brand's early stakeholders began to recruit shareholders that caught and supported the brand's purpose-driven mission.

The Seventh Generation team became the first homecare company to market unbleached, 100 percent recycled paper products—bathroom and facial tissue—while setting new industry standards for the chlorine processing of fibers (Seventh Generation, 2024). This effort wasn't without trials and failures—early iterations of Seventh Generation paper products were likened to sandpaper—but Jeffrey's persistence and investment in green chemistry that didn't pollute water or cut down virgin forests paid off.

Seventh Generation's early shareholders were aligned with Jeffrey's vision and mission, set long-term goals, and paid close attention to financial metrics including profit margins, marketing and advertising spend, and product quality. As a result of a small but committed consumer base and shareholders who bought into their long-term value proposition—that green chemistry would keep getting better and that the product would continue to improve over time through innovation—Seventh Generation found success with their entry into the retail space in thirty-three Boston-area markets with their liquid laundry detergent, chlorine-free bleach, and dishwasher detergent.

Seventh Generation's rise to success was due to their commitment to innovation, authenticity, and radical transparency. Their commitment to innovation and quality sustained the brand's evolution. As green cleaning science evolved, Seventh Generation's product quality improved. Their growth also resulted from the creation of a green cleaning brand block, comprising a number of major competitors. Seventh Generation's success shows that, when it comes to brand building, it's important to bring your competitors with you to build a brand block.

Seventh Generation was sold to Unilever in 2016 for over $600 million. The brand has maintained its commitment to purpose-driven products and branding in part through adherence to a clear mission statement, value propositions, and partnerships.

Purpose Statement, Value Propositions, and Partnerships

Seventh Generation's name was inspired by an ancient Iroquois philosophy: "In our every deliberation, we must consider the impact of our decisions on the next seven generations."

This commitment to making sustainable choices in the interest of providing for seven generations beyond informs Seventh Generation's mission statement: "To transform the world into a healthy, sustainable, and equitable place for the next seven generations—and beyond."

To solidify their commitments to purpose-driven production, Seventh Generation became a founding B Corporation in 2008. To support their commitment to authenticity and radical transparency, they began to publish annual corporate consciousness reports in 2004. To educate consumers, Seventh Generation regularly lobbies for the removal of toxic phosphates from household cleaning products and clearly prints all ingredients on their product packaging. They also pursue certifications including USDA Certified Biobased and EPA Safer Choice. They continually support innovation in reducing their products' carbon footprints and partner with climate justice organizations to call for an end to the era of fossil fuels and a just transition to renewable energy. They have a Social Mission Board and Foundation that gives 100 percent of their funds to Indigenous-led organizations and communities, which supports their mission statement inspired by Iroquois ideology.

Seventh Generation is one example of a purpose-driven brand that seeks to innovate in the interest of bettering the planet and creating quality products.

1.5 Application: Creating a Sticky and Spreadable Brand Story

Integrating elements of spreadability and stickiness is key to any branding and storytelling initiative. Sticky and spreadable brand stories ultimately cultivate and uphold the six building blocks of brand believability—emotional attachment, credibility, authenticity, consistency, innovation, and quality—and can be inspired by Jenkins et al.'s (2013) spreadable and sticky storytelling principles:

- Spreadable stories involve technical features of platforms and affordances, carry economic incentives and textual characteristics, and are created to be sent across social networks. Spreadable stories are made to circulate and be shared among brand communities. They give rise to networked culture; can be remade; and can have cultural, personal, political, and economic motivations. To be spreadable, stories must be accessible.
- Sticky stories are created to draw readers and consumers in for an in-depth experience with the brand. Sticky stories are created for deep audience engagement and have the potential to pique interest and drive user action.

Similarly, sticky and spreadable stories can be created with application of the following storytelling principles (Heath & Heath, 2007):

- Simple: What's the core of your message? Prioritize the main concept of your brand.
- Unexpected: Get attention by asking questions, violating schemas, and using curiosity gaps.
- Concrete: Use sensory language to paint a mental picture.
- Credible: Gain credibility by drawing from authorities outside and inside the brand. Also use statistics and details.
- Emotional: Tell stories about people, not numbers—what's in it for the customer? Use identity appeals.
- Stories: Drive action through simulation and inspiration—how can an existing problem change? Encourage readers to take action and be inspired to do so.

1.6 Metrics: SMART Goals

CMOs and executives strive to quantify purpose in various ways. Experts including Net Promoter Score founder Fred Reichheld asserts that it's important to identify purpose as early as possible and benchmark it "so you can gauge progress, learn from both successes and mistakes, and set the stage for further improvements down the road" (Reichheld et al., 2021). For Chick-fil-A, Reichheld found that the thing that most energized founder Dan Truett was "turning a person's frown into a smile." Frowns and smiles may be difficult to measure in a concrete way, but the Net Promoter Score (NPS) has a framework for this in application.

Purpose is also manifest through customer and consumer feedback, which can be quantified through customer ratings and reviews. Thrive Pet Healthcare CMO Amy Halford says,

> Our purpose talks about building relationships, and our veterinarians and the staff that look to connect with the client as much as they love the pet are the ones who do this really well. Then, we'll see higher ratings and reviews for those hospitals. What they'll say in the ratings and reviews is, "I felt cared for. They clearly cared about my fur baby as much as I do." That's the feedback that we get. It's all around care and listening.

Brand purpose can be quantified through metrics including bottom line ROI.

Mark Derks, CMO of BlueGrace Logistics, says,

> The ultimate measure of brand success is growth in our business, and I believe any business, including a nonprofit, reflected through revenue, or financials. Are your financials advancing to meet the expectations of your goals as a business, organization, or nonprofit? Nonprofits only operate because they generate income that goes back into programs and administration. Without income, revenue, and financials, their impact becomes nothing.

To measure your brand's purpose, you can set SMART Goals that align with your selected brand story and purpose statement. Here are examples from our research and Romanchuk (2024) of how you can apply the SMART Goals framework in a way that can measure the effectiveness of your brand story and purpose:

- Specific: State exactly what needs to be accomplished.
  - What tasks will help accomplish these goals?
  - What personnel will accomplish these goals?
  - What responsibilities will team members carry out to accomplish these goals?
  - Can this be accomplished in house or does it need to be outsourced?
- Measurable: Make sure the specific goal has a target metric or key performance indicator (KPI).
  - How will we ensure and quantify success throughout?
  - What are our key metrics or key performance indicators (KPIs)?
  - Is this goal clear and actionable?
  - Is there anything subjective about this goal?
- Attainable: Challenging yet still achievable.
  - How will this goal stretch us?
  - How is this goal innovative?
  - How is this goal different from anything we've done before?
  - How does this goal fall in line with our team's strengths?
- Relevant: Goals are consistent with the other goals that have been established, and the overall goals of the company or marketing department.
  - How does this goal support our organization's broader vision, mission, and purpose?

- Time-Based: Including a time limit for achieving the goal.
  - When will our goal be accomplished?
  - How often will we check in on the progress of our work toward achieving our goal?
  - What contingencies do we have to accommodate changes in schedule or timeline?

Key Terms

Brand promise
Brand story
Chief purpose officer
Mission statement
Purpose statement

Shareholders
SMART Goals
Stakeholders
Value proposition
Vision statement

Discussion Questions

1. How can you create an effective brand story?
2. Is your brand's purpose tied to a product, service, or prosocial mission?
3. How does humanized marketing help brands' authenticity?

Activity

Create a Believable Purpose Statement: Create a sticky and spreadable purpose statement for a brand. Draw from the five values of brand believability—emotional attachment, credibility, authenticity, consistency, innovation, and quality—by answering the following questions: How is this purpose statement authentic? How are you going to communicate this purpose statement to this brand's various stakeholders/audiences? What are your value propositions and how do they uphold your purpose statement?

2

Brand Culture

What is brand culture? We argue that by instilling the knowledge and support of brand behaviors into brand learning, a company can effectively live out its values and mission in a believable way. This chapter introduces the concept of believable brand culture and discusses the problem of brand drift. Trader Joe's is presented as an example of an authentic and believable brand culture. This chapter also provides an internal branding application exercise and employee engagement pulse surveys as a metric that can help to quantify the quality of a brand's culture.

Chapter Outline

2.1 Introduction: What Is Brand Culture?	56
2.2 The Problem: Brand Drift	57
2.3 The Solution: Believable Brand Culture	57
2.4 Case: Trader Joe's	68
2.5 Application: Internal Branding	70
2.6 Metrics: Employee Engagement Pulse Surveys	72
Key Terms	75
Discussion Questions	75
Activity	75

2.1 Introduction: What Is Brand Culture?

Brand Culture: How a company lives out its values and mission by instilling the knowledge and support of brand behaviors into brand learning.

A believable brand culture is built both internally and externally. Internally, employee experience (EX) is a key way that believable brand cultures are built. Believable brand culture involves employees who feel empowered to be authentic; clear communication and education about brand values; consistent feedback, affirmation, and reward; creating credibility by encouraging and empowering employees to grow in knowledge and skill; and using innovation to produce high-quality products and services. A believable brand culture is authentic: a culture where every employee is aligned with the brand values and understands their personal role in delivering on them. A believable brand culture is innovative, where employees have consistent access to real-time data and feedback about their performance in addition to clients'/customers' product and service experiences. A believable brand culture is consistent: A culture where the day-to-day behaviors of every employee are inspired by the brand vision and values. A believable brand culture is credible: Employees feel empowered by the culture and believe leadership will make decisions to do what's right for the employees, clients, and stakeholders.

Externally, believability is linked to the willingness of consumers to participate, validate, and believe in brand promises. Employees are a brand's most important ambassadors, and brand culture is reflected back by consumers who engage with the education, empowerment, and experimentation that a brand presents. Brands that prioritize people and cater to the needs and objectives of each team are important elements to activate employees toward a purposeful brand culture (Mitchell, 2023).

Researchers and industry consultants insist that innovation is key to gaining and maintaining competitive advantage. According to Dr. Nadya Zhexembayeva of Reinvention Academy, companies must reinvent every ten years minimum to survive, and 20.6 percent of companies reinvent themselves every twelve months or less (Zhexembayeva, 2023). At the same time, reinvention must be consistent with a brand's cultural values and promises.

This chapter presents an internal branding application exercise and employee engagement pulse surveys as a way to measure the quality of brand culture. Before we discuss how to measure the believability of a brand's culture, it's important to understand one of the major roadblocks to building a believable brand culture—brand drift—and the solutions that can help brands get past this problem.

2.2 The Problem: Brand Drift

Brand drift is the gradual deviation or divergence of a brand from its original identity, values, or positioning. It occurs when a brand's messaging, image, or actions start to stray from the core principles or promises it was built upon. This shift can happen due to various factors such as changes in leadership, market trends, consumer preferences, or internal, organizational changes. Brand drift can undermine customer trust and loyalty, as it can lead to confusion, inconsistency, and disconnects between brands and audiences. Inconsistency in branding practices leads to a lack of commitment among key stakeholders. Therefore, managing and maintaining brand consistency is crucial to avoid brand drift and sustain a strong brand reputation (Grimes et al., 2019).

Changes in leadership, market conditions, technological advancements, and shifts in the competitive landscape are all factors that contribute to brand drift. To prevent brand drift, a brand must be committed to consistent evaluation of the key elements that comprise believable brand culture: employee experience, emotional attachment, and credibility.

What combats or prevents brand drift? Our research shows that a believable brand culture is characterized by authenticity, consistency, innovation, and quality. A believable brand culture helps to combat and prevent brand drift.

2.3 The Solution: Believable Brand Culture

To build a believable brand culture, a brand's key stakeholders must be authentic and transparent with employees and consumers in their communication about the brand's innovations, trajectory, mission, and vision; must proactively educate and gain buy-in from employees about and for major organizational changes; and must maintain consistency with the brand's original purpose, mission, and vision. Consistent and high-quality feedback and assessment of the brand's mission, values, and goals are important and can be gathered to ensure that strategies and actions remain aligned with these foundational elements.

Our research shows that a believable brand culture starts with employee experience. A believable brand culture comprises employees who are emotionally attached to the brand and support the brand's credibility. A believable brand culture is characterized by:

1 employees who feel empowered to be authentic;
2 clear communication and education about brand values;
3 consistent feedback, affirmation, and reward;
4 creating credibility by encouraging and empowering employees to grow in knowledge and skill;
5 using innovation to produce high-quality products and services.

These five key points help to ensure the strength and vitality of a brand's culture by ensuring employees are engaged emotionally and invested in the brand's credibility. Evaluating employee and key stakeholders' emotional attachment to the brand and perceptions and beliefs about the brand's credibility can help quantify employee engagement.

Cultural fit is an important part of building a believable brand culture. Emotional attachment draws talent—but it's important to recognize what sort of talent is best.

"I've been intentional about hiring more people that are more T-shaped—they have some broad expertise, but some really deep expertise in needed areas," Jaime Hunt, CMO of Old Dominion University, says. "This has enabled us to collaborate and work together across silos, and then work across silos across the institution."

Brands are more believable if employees live in a way that is congruent with the brand promise (Henkel et al., 2007). At the same time, diverse identities, approaches, and thoughts also lead to richer employee experience and need to be cultivated accordingly (Corritore et al., 2020). Brands and organizations with the healthiest cultures encourage cognitive diversity—but need a shared core belief system (Corritore et al., 2020).

"There are billions of cultures in the world and every one that exists is held together by some shared belief," Leah Larson, CMO of Madison Air, says. "Being anchored in a belief system is potentially the space that may be overlooked or missed today and is a really interesting area to further explore."

Educating and Empowering Employees Toward Authentic, Genuine Collaboration

Employees are brand ambassadors. Even when they aren't on the clock, they are representing their employer in various ways—from how they talk about the brand to the way they design and order their schedule and activities relative to their work responsibilities and obligations. Authenticity helps to empower employees to bring their whole selves to work. Encouraging employees to be authentic empowers them to engage with brand initiatives and culture in a more voluntary and enthusiastic way. Encouraging and enabling a collaborative culture where employees can be authentic leads to an increased amount of emotional attachment, too (Quaratino & Mazzei, 2018).

To feel emotionally engaged and to cultivate authenticity, employees must have the freedom to share feedback and ideas with leadership and to be affirmed that their ideas are valid and worthy of being shared.

Building a collaborative culture can be difficult, but it is worthwhile. Brand cultures that are characterized by cold and direct communication can be changed, but executives and employees alike need to educate their peers and direct reports about the benefits of authentic and collaborative correspondence.

CMOs expressed how education can be used as a tool to enable employees to innovate and collaborate with authenticity, innovation, and creativity. Jaime Hunt, CMO of Old Dominion University, developed a marketing maturity framework (Hunt, 2023) that she leverages in her work on a daily basis.

"I use a marketing maturity framework to both evaluate where we are today in terms of the maturity of our marketing and set a path for where we need to go and to evaluate how we've been getting there," Hunt says. "We're tracking over time how we're moving into a more mature organization."

Authenticity enables cultures to transform and grow well. Hunt goes on,

> We're moving from not even telling each other what we're working on, or we're not even telling the campus community what we're working on, to a culture of openness, transparency, and approachability—we measure our success with the marketing maturity matrix that allows us to say, okay, this is where we are today. This is where we want to be in a year.

Mike Benson, president and CMO of CBS, has spent decades in the entertainment industry. At one point in his career, he went to work at Amazon Studios to build a marketing team to support new, original content offerings from Amazon Prime Video. This "startup" environment within the larger Amazon corporation enabled him to draw from his experience in the entertainment industry, but also showed him how to effectively use data to help sell-through new ideas and build better marketing campaigns.

> The marketing culture at CBS was built primarily around gut instinct, experience and opinion, not necessarily data-driven insights, so I started to use data to help our team at CBS better understand why we needed to innovate. I would bring new ideas to the team, backed with data and insights, that helped to provide more context for the idea. Then, I would press the team to bring data and insights to support their own ideas. Teaching the team how to use data to innovate has been an important part of the evolution of our culture, and our brand.

Using data to have debates about decisions is one way to create an authentic and innovative brand culture. Benson continues,

> Amazon hired me to build an entertainment marketing team within a tech company. Amazon Studios had just started producing original content, and they lacked both a brand for this new venture and experience in marketing original IP. I had a background in building entertainment brands and attracting large audiences to various entertainment types, but I had never worked in a tech company. From me, Amazon learned how to effectively market their new original content, and I learned how to innovate and operate within Amazon's tech-focused environment. Together, we built a brand and culture for Amazon Studios and Prime Video, grounded in Amazon's existing brand and culture.

Benson brought his expertise on how to best generate awareness and interest in the new Amazon-produced content, and manage relationships with showrunners, filmmakers, producers, talent, and agents, while learning from his colleagues at Amazon about how to use data to have a healthy, spirited debate about decisions that needed to be made to build a business around this new product offering.

Culture change isn't always easy and always takes time. "Debates haven't been part of the culture at CBS Marketing, so I'm working on flipping the script," Benson says. "For me, it's important that diverse points-of-view and opinions are welcomed and discussed, so we can mold ideas in ways that get to an outcome that will best meet our objectives. A culture of healthy, spirited debate helps us get there."

Clear, Consistent Communication About Brand Values

Brands' and organizations' core belief systems comprise various values that are instilled by leadership and reflected by the employee base. Some brands' core values are internal—for example, to create opportunities for employees. "Our core value is our key message, and that is, 'We exist to create opportunity and security for our employees,'" Glenn Bottomly, CMO of Taylor Corporation, says.

> We have a passion for our customers and for our work. It's why we are here. We believe that there is always a better way. We are always about solutioning and continuous improvement. We respect the potential and significance of every individual. So, every single employee that we have plays a vital role in advancing both our mission and also supporting our customers. And then we embrace personal as well as shared responsibility and accountability. So, at the end of the day, it's the results that matter, and we look at it as, "A marketing team is one thing, but if we're not helping sales grow revenue, then it doesn't matter because the revenue drives it all."

At Taylor Corporation—a brand that began as a wedding invitation brand that grew into an industry-leading provider of print, marketing, labeling, packaging, warehousing, and fulfillment solutions—the values of opportunity and security for employees are showcased in various employee resource groups and growth opportunities that come with being the sixth-largest graphics arts company in North America. According to Bottomly, in their fifty years of existence, Taylor has acquired more than two hundred companies. One way to maintain consistent culture but also some autonomy and independence is by providing centers of excellence to support and educate elements of the organization about everything from marketing to legal to supply chain management.

The Marketing Center of Excellence is one of several centers of excellence across Taylor Corporation that provides support to our entire Taylor enterprise. We have multiple centers of excellence that provide centralized support to all of the businesses so that they themselves don't have to have redundancy and everybody having all of their own functional resources. You can have a centralized team to do that, and so from a marketing perspective, I lead the Marketing Center of Excellence. Some of our businesses have their own marketing teams, others have none, and so we provide, in some cases, 100 percent of a business unit's marketing and other times, we provide 10 or 15 percent of their marketing.

Education also helps create a believable brand culture by helping stakeholders and employees assess their strengths and weaknesses in the interest of sharing out with others. At Old Dominion University, the marketing team assesses their strengths and weaknesses with application of the Marketing Maturity Model and then hosts workshops for teams across the institution to help educate campus teams about ODU's brand.

CMO Jaime Hunt says, "We do a lot of workshops and trainings for the campus community and are seeing a lot of growth in how communicators across campus talk about ODU. While we're doing this, we're also developing a brand," she explains, "so we need to be on somewhat of the same page while we wait for that. And so, getting more communicators and marketers on that page over the past ten months has been really important."

Some brands are built around customer-centric values. For Mayo Clinic, an academic medical center, everything they do demonstrates and exemplifies that the needs of the patient come first.

"This core value extends to the needs of people everywhere," says Sherri Gilligan, chief marketing officer, Mayo Clinic.

Mayo Clinic shares its discoveries with the world through a commitment to openness and collaboration. It openly publishes its research, clinical trials, and medical innovations in peer-reviewed journals, ensuring that advancements in medical science are accessible to health care professionals globally. By prioritizing transparency and knowledge-sharing, Mayo Clinic aims to improve patient care and health outcomes worldwide.

"We take an integrated approach to medicine, where our physicians work together across specialties to ensure the best possible care for each patient," says Gilligan. "The focus is always on doing what's best for the patient, coordinating efforts to provide comprehensive, personalized care."

A believable brand culture is co-created between key stakeholders and the employee base. Fred Reichheld, creator of the Net Promoter Score, asserts that brand culture starts with influence from the top down.

> The job of a leader is to ensure that the team is on the right mission, that they understand it and have the resources required to succeed, and, most important, that they know their leader will do everything possible to take care of their safety and well-being. Great leaders wake up in the morning worrying about that, and they go to bed worrying about it (Reichheld et al., 2021).

At the same time, it can be beneficial to encourage employees to engage with the creation of brand values. Internal research and assessment through discussion with employee groups led Global Jet Capital to reverse-engineer their corporate values: We Care, We Collaborate, We Never Settle, and We Get Up and Go.

"Each of our values was reverse-engineered—it started with employee groups agreeing, 'These are the behaviors we want to see and the behavior we believe will make us successful.' And then as a group we said, 'Well, let's segment those behaviors into clusters that seem to fit well together,'" CMO Andrew Farrant says. "Having an employee-based brand team to help develop brand components—like purpose and values—is critical. Starting with employee perspectives supports authenticity and will ultimately deliver believability for the brand through their delivery of products and services."

Within higher education—or any brand or organization that involves multiple stakeholders—believability is often built collaboratively, or is co-created across teams. James Plesser is CMO of the Carlson School of Management at the University of Minnesota. The Carlson School is a top-ranked business school that enrolls thousands of students each year at undergraduate and graduate levels, with stakeholders ranging from faculty to staff to administration.

"Faculty are responsible for research, teaching, and service—this includes devising our degree programs. The brand organically originates there for our students, and is then delivered through curriculum, co-curriculum, programming, student services, and more. The brand experience and its believability and credibility are delivered far outside the scope of my department," Plesser says.

> Brand is an accumulation of all the touch points and experiences that a customer has with that brand. Here that means it is about the classroom experience, the career placement services, and other elements a student encounters—all of those add up to the believability of the brand. A core aspect of my role is to tap into which of those resonate and are drivers for different audiences. Our group spends a lot of time focusing on prospective students: how do we identify their needs, what gaps exist when it comes to their student journey, and what can we tap into from a marketing and communication standpoint to meet those needs?

Believability is a combination of authenticity, consistency, and credibility, and leadership helps to create a believable culture. The employee base is the most important stakeholder in enacting culture through behavior and commitment to the brand. Employees' commitments to the brand are evident in whether or not the products and services delivered are quality.

"Brand believability is linked to relevance, authenticity, credibility, and endurability," Andrew Farrant, CMO of Global Jet Capital, says.

> Our main offering is an operating lease, which is not a product per se that you can touch and feel—it's more of an approach to financing an asset—in our case a business jet. Our brand lives in the interaction we have with clients and the way the lease is shaped and negotiated. It takes time and education to get that across to the marketplace and more specifically—prospects. If key elements of the brand platform have not come from the employee base—who ultimately need to deliver the value proposition—the likelihood of achieving believability is diminished.

Creating Emotional Attachment with Employee Affirmation, Recognition, Reward

Part of creating a believable brand culture is creating emotional attachment. Mary Jo Hatch and Majken Schultz, coauthors of *Taking Brand Initiative*, published results of a controlled, three-year Corporate Branding Initiative (CBI) study with LEGO, Nissan, Johnson & Johnson, Intel, and others. Hatch and Schultz noted that believability comprises two things: "a mix of functional and emotional content and the whole company has to believe in what it is doing" (Hatch & Schultz, 2008). Our research shows clearly that emotional attachment is a major component of building a believable brand culture.

"Culture is something that you can't say—you have to feel," Thrive Pet Healthcare CMO Amy Halford says.

Clare Scott, CMO of Ryan Companies, says that before she applied to work at Ryan, she "fell in love with the culture," a feeling that eventually brought her to work for them full-time.

Feelings matter, and employee recognition is a way to ensure an employee base is engaged emotionally. Leah Larson, CMO of Madison Air, says that ensuring employees feel affirmed in their work is an emotional thing: "We want to ensure that our employees walk away with that emotional feeling of, 'I'm good at my job and I am making the world better.'"

Mark Derks, CMO of BlueGrace Logistics, says that cultivating a "people-first culture, high on recognition and reward brings good feelings—along with elements of teamwork and inclusivity."

Companies that have a strong belief-based brand attract talent more easily and are also able to attract customers. Inclusivity and belonging are important to employees, customers, and stakeholders; it's difficult to market a product, service, or experience if employees don't feel like they belong and can't see themselves reflected among the employee base. Creating emotional attachment and credibility are ways to establish inclusivity and belonging.

Certifications, Innovation, and Credibility

In highly institutionalized fields including law and medicine, practitioners are required to pursue continuing education credits annually. Doctors are also required to take board exams regularly throughout their careers. In branding, certifications have come into play in recent years; advanced degrees play a role in solidifying the credibility of executives and employees as well.

Mayo Clinic physicians are dedicated lifelong learners who build credibility through rigorous research and ongoing education. This commitment to excellence drives the discovery of new cures, the development of innovative therapies, and the advancement of medical practices. The result is a continuous cycle of expertise and quality, leading to proven, positive outcomes for patients.

"As an academic and research institution, our physicians not only practice medicine but also engage in rigorous research and contribute to our educational programs by teaching," says Sherri Gilligan, chief marketing officer, Mayo Clinic.

Innovation happens through research, mergers, acquisitions, points of inflection, and more. Maintaining consistency through innovation is a challenge but through consistent communication and evaluation of a brand's culture through consistent check-ins with employee groups, it's possible to execute on new ideas and approaches effectively.

"Our purpose, our brand promise, is to make businesses better," Mark Derks, CMO of BlueGrace Logistics, says. "It's a three-word promise that we will make your business better. We deploy a culture of teamwork and inclusivity that supports this purpose. We have operators and employees that work together to solve shipper problems. In supply chain logistics specifically, there are many problems. Every day our clients come to their desk and they have issues to solve."

Education as a value informs brand culture both through internal learning and collaboration and from gleaning intellectual capital from outside sources. Certification courses, collaboration, and partnerships all lend themselves toward education that bolsters a believable brand culture.

When it comes to solidifying the credibility of a brand itself, the more a brand can be authentic—especially in the face of failures—the better.

Brand Profile: Chipotle

Chipotle Mexican Grill, Inc., is consistently ranked on the Fortune 500, is recognized on *Fortune*'s Most Admired Companies list, and has been named one of *Time* magazine's most influential companies. Accepting limitations, being authentic about them, and pursuing fixes are important elements to building strong brand culture. After a series of food safety scandals in 2015, consumers' trust in Chipotle plummeted. In response, the company doubled down on concerted efforts to prioritize the health of their employees and customers above anything else, build a reliable and diversified supply chain, and institute new policies to ensure employees do not work when they are sick. Chipotle also pursued innovative digital ordering processes through their mobile app. Digital ordering enabled Chipotle to withstand the Coronavirus pandemic—at one point, digital ordering accounted for a majority of Chipotle's revenue during the pandemic. To further lean into their digital ordering processes, Chipotle invested heavily in Chipotlanes—a drive-up window where customers can place mobile orders ahead of time then drive to the window to pick up their order at a specific time without leaving their cars. These efforts, in addition to authentic and consistent communication about the quality of their products, have helped Chipotle's revenue more than double and its stock price to increase by more than ten times in the past decade, reestablishing their leadership position in the restaurant industry. Beyond emotional attachment, credibility comes into play.

Chipotle CMO Chris Brandt helped introduce Chipotle's first Super Bowl advertisement ever in 2021. Chipotle's 2021 Super Bowl activation was an opportunity to create an advertisement that tied emotion to credibility. "If we made an ad that the employees were proud of, I felt like the consumers would really embrace it too—and that's what happened," Brandt says.

> So, we made an ad about our brand values. Most companies don't do it. Most companies don't have the courage or that strength of purpose that they can back up. But when you see our ingredients, how our restaurant experience is open and has nothing to hide, and you see the fresh ingredients and you see the grill and you can smell the chicken cooking and see employees hand mashing guacamole, and the food tastes clean and is clean, that backs up what we're trying to do in advertising.

"If we stopped buying organic cilantro, nobody would know, but our employees would know," Brandt says. "When we were making our Super Bowl spot, it was called 'Can a Burrito Change the World?' And the answer is no for a single burrito, but the way we make it just might." Brandt's team's strategy was to make an advertisement that he knew Chipotle employees would love. This type of approach—in addition to Roblox games, social media videos showcasing recipes, and collaborations and challenges with influencers—has led Chipotle to maintain its position as a leading innovator in the foodservice industry.

2.4 Case: Trader Joe's

Trader Joe's is a privately held direct-to-consumer (D2C) company founded in 1967 by Joe Coulombe. In 1958, Joe Coulombe took over a small chain of corner markets or convenience stores called Pronto Markets in Los Angeles. Pronto Markets were a one-stop-shop for all kinds of inventory ranging from gum to pantyhose to ammunition.

In 1967, Joe moved away from convenience stores toward grocery and opened the first Trader Joe's in Pasadena, California. Business was slow at first, but picked up in 1972 with the introduction of a Trader Joe's private-label granola.

Culture is cultivated at Trader Joe's by and through the people: It's the quality of the people which sets Trader Joe's apart. "Forget the merchandise, forget all the other stuff, it's the quality of the people in the stores," Joe says (Trader Joe's, 2018).

Trader Joe's has only had three CEOs in its more than fifty years of existence, including Joe, who was CEO for the first twenty-one years. During this time, Joe cast the vision of a nautical theme in all Trader Joe's stores, a theme that has carried through into the twenty-first century. Inspired by Joe's reading of *White Shadows in the South Seas* followed by a visit to the Disneyland jungle cruise, all Trader Joe's stores have nautical-themed elements, including store managers being called store captains who wear Hawaiian shirts, store employees being called traders on the high seas—all things Joe said "kind of sorta worked" (Trader Joe's, 2018).

By 1988, Joe had grown Trader Joe's to 19 stores around Pasadena, California. At this point, John Shields took over as CEO and created a growth strategy that enabled Trader Joe's to grow from 19 to 150 stores. In 2001, Dan Bane took over as chairman and CEO. As of 2024, Trader Joe's had 574 stores with a focused strategy to make Trader Joe's the "best grocery store in the world" (Trader Joe's, 2018). According to Bane, Trader Joe's has seven brand values that support its strategy:

1) Integrity: Treat others the way you want to be treated.
2) Product-driven company: Trader Joe's calls their buyers product innovators who travel around the world looking for innovative products to introduce on Trader Joe's shelves. Trader Joe's also has a Tasting Panel, comprising employees who taste every product before it hits the shelves.

3) Wow customer service.
4) No bureaucracy.
5) Kaizen: *Kaizen* is a Japanese term meaning change for the better or continuous improvement. It is a Japanese business philosophy that concerns the processes that continuously improve operations and involve all employees.
6) The store is our brand.
7) We're a national chain of neighborhood grocery stores.

In 1979, Coulombe sold the chain to Aldi founder Theo Albrecht, who owned it until his death in 2010. Today, Trader Joe's is owned by families that also own part of Aldi Nord, but the two companies operate independently. Trader Joe's has no business or ownership relationship with Aldi Süd (including Aldi U.S.) (Trader Joe's, 2024).

Part of Trader Joe's brand culture is a local outreach program called Neighborhood Shares (Trader Joe's, 2023). Every day of every year, Trader Joe's donates products that go unsold but are fit to be enjoyed to nonprofit partners including local food banks and other nonprofit food recovery partners. In 2023 alone, Trader Joe's donated more than 469 million dollars' worth of quality products to their network of nonprofit partners across the United States "to avoid unnecessary waste, support people in need, and deepen our neighborhood connections" (Trader Joe's, 2023; 2024).

Emotional attachment at Trader Joe's is endemic to the store's operations. Brand love is key to this brand's culture and is exemplified through employee engagement.

Trader Joe's hires people who really like people. According to Parker, Colorado store captain Ty Poe, "We can teach the crew to run register and stock shelves. That kind of stuff is not what's important. What's important is if you really like people."

Ty also mentions how it's hard to talk about Trader Joe's without talking about love—"because if you talk to anybody about Trader Joe's, they're eventually gonna mention it. They love a product, or they love shopping at our stores, but a lot of it is, they love working here, you know, and that in and of itself is sort of our culture, right?" (Trader Joe's, 2022).

Brand love at Trader Joe's starts with the employment application.

"The people who express their love for Trader Joe's in the application are the ones that really catch our eye," Ty says. "They put a couple sentences about why they wanna work here. They've shopped with us for years or they grew up on Trader Joe's. That's a big one" (Trader Joe's, 2022).

President of Trader Joe's stores Jon Basalone says, "The goal is to hire nice, kind, empathetic individuals, and then just turn them loose. And so the customer service training is pretty simple. It's, you know, be yourself. We hired you for a reason. We hired you for you. You don't have to become something else or transform yourself into something to work at Trader Joe's" (Trader Joe's, 2022).

Our research shows that the emotional attachment and engagement of employees throughout each Trader Joe's store creates a culture of fandom that pours out into customers who love Trader Joe's for their nutritious ingredients, clean eating options, and because the culture is "fun, exciting, and cheap." Our research also shows that consumers think "every Trader Joe's employee is hot and nice."

2.5 Application: Internal Branding

Internal branding is an organizational behavior management exercise developed by Marty Brandt, founder of global brand consulting firm TrueBrand. Internal branding creates the conditions for employees to respect the brand goals and work together to deliver consistent brand experiences across all customer touchpoints (Brandt, 2010). This process involves teaching and learning through administration of employee communications campaigns, workshops, guidelines about conformance to the brand identity, employee branding for HR and recruitment purposes, and more. Executing an internal branding exercise can help build a believable brand culture through implementation of three main concepts—Knowing, Caring, and Doing—as follows:

- Knowing: The first stage of internal branding is to ensure that all employees understand brand goals and strategies, use the same vocabulary, and have common views of the brand and their clients/consumers. Key questions to evaluate knowing include:
  - Do employees know and understand the brand's mission, purpose, vision, and values?
  - Do employees know the brand goals and promise?

- Do employees know who the key target clients, customers, or consumers are, along with their needs and motivations?
- Do they know what their role is to drive brand growth and deliver the brand promise?
- Caring: The second stage of internal branding is that employees need to find inspiration and motivation in the meaning of the brand. This inspiration and motivation should be found at both collective—team and departmental—and individual/personal levels. Key questions to evaluate about caring include:
  - Do employees personally believe in the brand's mission, purpose, vision, and values?
  - Do employees believe others in the company believe in them, especially the leadership team?
  - Does the brand feel authentic to employees?
  - Do employees believe clients/customers recognize and appreciate the brand's values?
  - Do employees believe the brand's mission, purpose, vision, and values create important distinction for the company?
- Doing: The payoff is when employees are actually delivering—consistently and with quality—on brand promises through their everyday behavior. It's only in the doing that clients/customers can experience the distinction and real value of the brand. Questions to pose about doing include:
  - Are employees living up to the brand mission, vision, purpose, and values in their actions and deliverables?
  - Is management committed to the brand mission, vision, purpose, and values as demonstrated by their actions?
  - Does the brand have the right resources and processes in place to deliver the brand promises?
  - Is there a consistent, high-quality reward and recognition system for employees?
  - Is there a collective drive toward continuous improvement and innovation among employees and management?

Moving employees through the three stages of internal branding—Knowing, Caring, and Doing—is a challenge, and every brand has different realities whether it be differences in business models, stages of growth, core competencies, and more. Internal branding is best done through experiential learning, which allows people to discover what's required for success and how they can contribute to achieving the brand's desired goals. Two specific experiential learning approaches Brandt (2010) emphasizes are "Moments of Truth" and "Living the Brand." Employees that experience moments of truth through internal branding exercises and live the brand accordingly are more productive, more willing to stay with the company, and become the key asset of a branded business.

One metric that can help to measure the believability of a brand's culture is employee engagement. Pulse surveys are one way to quantify employee engagement.

2.6 Metrics: Employee Engagement Pulse Surveys

Employee engagement is defined as the involvement and enthusiasm of employees in their work and workplace (Gallup, 2025). Research continually shows that employee engagement is an uphill battle, as less than half of employees are consistently engaged at work. Engaged employees build a believable brand culture, and the amount of employee engagement can help quantify the believability of a brand's culture. Employees desire purpose and meaning in and through their work. Employees want to be recognized and known for their achievements, skills, and talents. Industry research shows that the key drivers of employee engagement are purpose, development, a caring manager, ongoing conversations, and a focus on strengths (Gallup, 2025). To lean into these drivers and build brand believability, it's necessary for brand leaders to commit to practices of humble inquiry, an approach defined as "the art of drawing someone out by asking questions to which you do not already know the answer, thereby building a relationship based on curiosity and interest in the other person" (Somers, 2024). Along these lines, it's important for leaders to ask rather than tell: "For people to work better in teams, build relationships founded on trust, and find better solutions to problems… the culture of the United States needs to become better at asking and do less telling" (Schein & Schein, 2021).

One way to be better at asking and to do less telling is to conduct surveys. Employee engagement surveys are typically issued annually and measure how employees think, feel, and act—or, in light of internal branding principles, how employees know, care, and do. Pulse surveys garner feedback on specific topics in a brief, frequent, and consistent way. Pulse surveys are similar to employee engagement surveys but are dynamic and agile, issued more frequently, and narrower in scope. Pulse surveys are often sent weekly, monthly, or quarterly, and focus on one concept consistently over time—as with this application and example: Employee engagement. Frequent inputs allow brand leaders to react and implement solutions more often than one time a year, which is crucial as employees who feel validated and heard are more likely to be engaged and recommend their employer to others.

To construct a pulse survey that measures employee engagement effectively, we recommend that brands utilize the concepts presented in the Brand Believability Pyramid to focus on one element of internal branding at a time. Here's a sample set of pulse survey questions drawn from the Brand Believability Pyramid concepts—emotional attachment, credibility, authenticity, consistency, quality, and innovation—in line with the Knowing, Caring, and Doing framework. Brands can select whichever topic they'd like to evaluate over time—the brand's mission, vision, purpose, values, or other criteria:

- Knowing
    - Are you emotionally attached to the brand's <insert mission, vision purpose, values, and/or other criteria here>? (Yes/No)
    - Are the brand's <insert mission, vision purpose, values, and/or other criteria here> credible? (Yes/No)
    - Are the brand's <insert mission, vision purpose, values, and/or other criteria here> authentic? (Yes/No)
    - Are the brand's <insert mission, vision purpose, values, and/or other criteria here> consistent? (Yes/No)
    - Are the brand's <insert mission, vision purpose, values, and/or other criteria here> innovative? (Yes/No)
    - Are the brand's <insert mission, vision purpose, values, and/or other criteria here> high quality? (Yes/No)
- Caring
    - Are you emotionally attached to your teammates? (Yes/No)

- Do you feel like the work your teammates do is credible? (Yes/No)
- Do you feel like your teammates are authentic? (Yes/No)
- Do you feel like your teammates are consistent? (Yes/No)
- Is there an innovative drive among your teammates and management? (Yes/No)
- Do you feel like the work your teammates produce is high quality? (Yes/No)
- Doing
  - Are you emotionally attached to the work that you do? (Yes/No)
  - Are you living up to the brand's <insert mission, vision purpose, values, and/or other criteria here> in your actions and deliverables? (Yes/No)
  - Do you bring your authentic self to work every day? (Yes/No)
  - Is your work consistent day to day? (Yes/No)
  - Are you innovative at work? (Yes/No)
  - Do you have the right resources and processes in place to deliver the best quality work you possibly can? (Yes/No)

Ultimately, the metric of this survey—in simplest terms—is the percentage of respondents who answered "yes" to the survey questions, providing a measurement of whether or not your brand culture is believable:

- Is your brand culture believable? Total /18 = X%
  - Knowing: Total /6 = X%
  - Caring: Total /6 = X%
  - Doing: Total /6 = X%

To investigate pain points revealed through pulse survey results, brand leaders can conduct focus groups and interviews with employees to explore and develop solutions accordingly. Additional metrics to help quantify the believability of a brand's culture include amount of employee retention/turnover, levels of training and development participation, and cultural alignment assessments—evaluations to determine how well employees' values align with the brand's values.

Key Terms

Brand ambassador
Brand mission
Brand promise
Brand values
Brand vision

Cultural fit
Customer experience (CX)
Employee experience (EX)
Employee resource groups
Internal branding

Discussion Questions

1 What is the most important part of internal branding: Knowing, caring, or doing? Why?
2 What value do you think is most important in building a believable brand culture: Emotional attachment, credibility, authenticity, consistency, innovation, or quality? Why?
3 How can negative employee experiences be redeemed to enhance brand culture?

Activity

Pulse Survey: Build an employee engagement pulse survey for your brand. Draw from concepts presented within the Brand Believability Pyramid in line with the Knowing, Caring, Doing framework.

3

Brand Design and Experience

All brands represent themselves visually through logos, color palettes, design, and aesthetic. In addition to visual design, brands' product and service designs facilitate emotional and sensory experiences that build believability. This chapter introduces the concept of brand design and experience as a key element of brand believability. Many brands have problems with a lack of charisma and fail to find an "it" factor. We argue that building a believable brand design and experience with authenticity, consistency, innovation, and quality can create charisma and help brands find their "it" factor. Creating journey maps and calculating brands' Customer Satisfaction Score (CSAT) over time can help to quantify the believability of a brand's design and experience.

Chapter Outline

3.1 Introduction: What Is Brand Design and Experience?	78
3.2 The Problem: No "It" Factor	79
3.3 The Solution: Believable Brand Design and Experience	80
3.4 Case: Chiro for Moms / Chiro for Kidz	91
3.5 Application: Journey Maps	95
3.6 Metrics: Customer Satisfaction Score (CSAT)	103
Key Terms	104
Discussion Questions	105
Activity	105

3.1 Introduction: What Is Brand Design and Experience?

Brand Design and Experience: How a brand represents its identity to the public visually and experientially.

Brand design and experience refers to the overall perception and interaction that customers have with a brand across all digital and physical touchpoints—spatially, in and through products and services, and via communication channels. Brand design and experience encompasses every aspect of the customer journey, from initial awareness to interest to desire to action and, ultimately, loyalty—also known as the AIDA funnel. Brand design and experience includes elements of customer service; user experience (UX) online and in-person; physical spaces including retail stores and offices; communication including advertising, social media, emails, and customer support; and emotional connections.

But what makes a brand admirable? Memorable? Believable?

Brand design and experience is sensory. It's also experiential. A brand is a marketing tool used to create a meaningful, distinct image of a company and its offerings in people's minds and hearts. By doing so, brands create value for customers and influence their market behavior, thus creating value for the company. Everything a company does when creating and managing its brands is driven by its ultimate purpose: "to create value for the company, its customers and collaborators" (Chernev, 2020).

Brand design and experience form an essential component of a brand's identity and how it interacts with its audience. How does a brand ensure it stands apart from its competitors visually and experientially? How can a brand ensure it's recalled by consumers more frequently than other competitors? Brand design and experience is how a brand represents its identity to the public visually and experientially. A brand's aesthetic directly influences how a brand is experienced by stakeholders and consumers.

Brand design and experience includes elements of spatial design, product design, service design, and communication design (Montaña et al., 2007). Spatial design encompasses the different ways and possibilities in which information and material are organized and presented in three-dimensional digital and physical environments. These environments can include physical spaces like office buildings and even digital environments like virtual reality (VR), augmented reality (AR), or mixed reality: a combination of VR and AR (Estudio, 2024).

Brand design comprises all the visual aspects that convey the brand's identity, including logos; color palettes; typography; imagery; illustrations; and visual elements used by the brand such as photographs and graphics.

Product design relates primarily to the design and experience of products that D2C brands deliver to consumers, but it can also relate to services that D2C or B2B brands deliver to clients (service design). For consumer-oriented products, product packaging is part of a brand's product design—a direct touchpoint with consumers. For D2C and B2B brands, service design is the process by which a service is delivered to a client.

Communication design is how a brand's design and experience is delivered across digital and physical mediums, including websites, mobile apps, and print and digital ads.

Authentic, consistent, innovative, and high-quality brand design and experience builds brand believability. Brand design and experience reinforces the visual and aesthetic representation of a brand in addition to the overall perception and interaction that customers have with the brand across mediums. Consistency across all touchpoints is crucial. When a brand lacks a consistent and innovative design and experience, they lack an "it" factor. The solution to the lack of an "it" factor is an authentic, consistent, and innovative design and experience across platforms.

3.2 The Problem: No "It" Factor

An "it" factor is what sets a brand apart from its competitors. According to leadership expert Craig Groeschel, the definition of "it" is elusive, but "it" is characterized by a consistent and compelling vision that is unique, powerful, and life-changing. An "it" factor carries an exquisite intensity that attracts fans and also critics (Groeschel, 2008). Some brands struggle to find and develop an "it" factor, but brand charisma and brand allure are two concrete concepts that can help brands identify an "it" factor which, in turn, builds brand believability.

Research shows that consumers desire brands to be visionary, articulate, ethical, unconventional, trusted, admired, attractive, powerful/dominant, sophisticated, iconic, and magical (Semaan et al., 2019). Similar to brand believability, brand charisma is co-created in the marketplace by brands, their leaders and key stakeholders, and consumers (Wieser et al., 2021). A part of brand charisma is the composition of a brand's leadership. If brand leaders are authentic, consistent, and innovative, the brand is more likely to reflect that persona.

Brand allure is another concept related to brand charisma. Brand allure is the way consumers affectively and cognitively connect to brands. What draws consumers into connection with a brand? On social media in particular, aesthetic appreciation and entertainment are key ways consumers can emotionally connect with brands. Information sharing is another way that consumers connect with brands in a cognitive way that helps to build the credibility of a brand (Athwal et al., 2018).

One example of brands that have lost their "it" factor include Blockbuster Video, a brand that filed for bankruptcy in 2011 (Antioco, 2011). This brand in particular lost their "it" factor due to a lack of consistency in leadership and a lack of innovation—two things that are key to building and sustaining believable brands (Davis & Higgins, 2013).

If a brand lacks charisma and allure, it won't be believable. Beyond these concepts, the values of brand believability—authenticity, consistency, innovation, and quality—are ways that brands can build and establish allure and charisma to find their "it" factor.

3.3 The Solution: Believable Brand Design and Experience

Brands are a strategic platform for interacting with customers. Brands are psychological concepts that offer value and embody experiences; and must be designed with the needs of its target segments in mind (Montaña et al., 2007). Innovative brand design can help to build consistent brand experiences all around the world, and must be consistent to build believability (Liu et al., 2017).

How can a brand create and deliver a believable brand design and experience? Montaña et al.'s (2007) brand design management model is a strong starting point: Their model argues that innovation is the most important part of developing a brand design and experience. Within the innovation process, brands must commit to concept generation, or coming up with concepts and ideas inspired by internal and external information from consumers and stakeholders; pursue a design strategy, which includes coming up with the teams necessary to carry out the design and experience effectively; commit to resource procurement, or recruiting all resources and funding necessary to carry out an innovative brand design and experience; and implement the design strategy consistently across elements of spatial design, product design, brand design, and communication design.

Keeping these elements in mind, the rest of this chapter will walk through the importance of authenticity, consistency, innovation, and quality in building a believable brand design and experience.

Creating Authentic Experiences

Authentic brand design and experience begins with key stakeholders and leadership. If key stakeholders and leaders are authentic and innovative, brand believability will follow. At Chipotle Mexican Grill, an authentic brand design and experience began with its founder, chef Steve Ells. Ells founded Chipotle with an intentional and innovative commitment to being as open and authentic as possible. All 3,700 Chipotle restaurants today have an open kitchen. "The open kitchen in the 1990s was an innovation because back then, food was fuel—our founder made food an experience," Chipotle's CMO and chief brand officer, Chris Brandt, said. "When you have food this great, we want to show it to everybody. We don't have anything to hide."

How can authentic brand design and experience help to build a believable brand?

"Believability is always going to come down to people's actual experience with the brand," Amy Halford, CMO of Thrive Pet Healthcare, says. "Believability is nothing without authentic experience."

For a D2C consumer product brand, the brand experience must be consistent with the brand promise.

"Believability is another way of saying authenticity," Tammy Nelson, CMO of CONQUERing, says.

> And so for us, we really believe in the idea of show versus tell. I can market all day long and I can say, "Our products are great, our service is awesome,

our shipping is fast, it's high quality, it's unique," but unless the experience consumers have with our product and the experience that they have with our service match what we're saying, that ruins believability and takes away from the authenticity of our brand and what we stand for.

Inclusivity and belonging are key parts of brand experience.

"Our designs are very universal, and we try not to label things as men's versus women's and/or kids versus adults," Nelson says. "It's all tied back to how we can have the most people to feel empowered."

Consistency Across Touchpoints

Every consumer, client, and employee will experience various touchpoints with a brand over time. The AIDA funnel is a helpful framework to illustrate the journey of how stakeholders move through various stages of

Figure 3.1 The AIDA Funnel.

relationship with brands. For a D2C brand, the highlight of a consumer journey is purchase intention. For a B2B brand, the highlight of a client's journey is partnership.

It is crucial for a brand design and experience to be consistent across digital and physical touchpoints. Customer service is one experience that can tie together design and experience from initial encounters with websites, social media handles, and employees through the end point of purchasing a product or service. One element of consistency is personalization. Consumers appreciate personalization of products and experiences. For example, our research shows that believable brands have a personality, engage with customers proactively on social media, and prioritize engagement with clients, customers, and employees by seeking out and commenting on customers' social media posts to offer returns, refunds, exchanges—and to simply comment on customers' experiences. Brands with believable design and experience include, but are not limited to Chick-fil-A, for their commitment to positive customer service digitally with a rewards program on their app and physically, in stores; Trader Joe's, for their consistent, cohesive, and creative social media marketing campaigns that match the excitement and community they cultivate in their stores with friendly employees; and Tesla, a brand which, according to our research with Generation Z consumers, is headed up by an authentic leader. As a consumer said in one of our focus groups: "Elon Musk might not be the best person in the world, but he's real and unapologetically himself, and he believes in his brand, so I do, too."

For example, at higher education institutions, believability is built through touchpoints with recruiters, the admissions office, and professors, to name a few.

James Plesser, CMO of the University of Minnesota's Carlson School of Management, says, "Brand is an accumulation of all the touch points and all the experiences of the customer with the brand. It's not just the communication pieces. What is it like as a student when they're submitting their admissions application? What is it like when they are watching a marketing video? What is their experience when sitting in class?"

Consistency in communicating across silos in organizational structures means interdepartmental communication and connections. The way an organization is structured internally speaks to the consistency of a brand's design and experience. The more an organization's departments can collaborate, the better. If there's not enough cohesion in leadership across touchpoints—for example, a CMO committed to effective marketing who works closely with a COO committed to effective service delivery—brands lose consistency and authenticity, which leads to the collapse of believability.

"As CMO of an insurance company, the customer experience team reports to me—so I have a lot of influence over not only the branding and what we say, but also the experience and what we do, which is critical," Tammy Nelson, CMO of CONQUERing, says. "I'm also the CEO and CMO of my jewelry brand, which means I'm involved in product development, service delivery, and marketing, everything. And so I can make sure that they all work together."

Consumers note that messy websites that are hard to navigate deter them from converting and making purchases, especially on retail sites. If a consumer can expect consistent delivery of a brand across platforms and mediums—from logo to social media platforms to website design—they can believe in a brand.

Entertaining and trendy content leads to positive referrals on social media platforms, which is a key way consumers co-create brand value and loyalty (Cheung et al., 2020).

Innovative Brand Design and Experience

All brands present a visual identity which includes a logo, photography, illustrations, graphics, social media posts, and website elements.

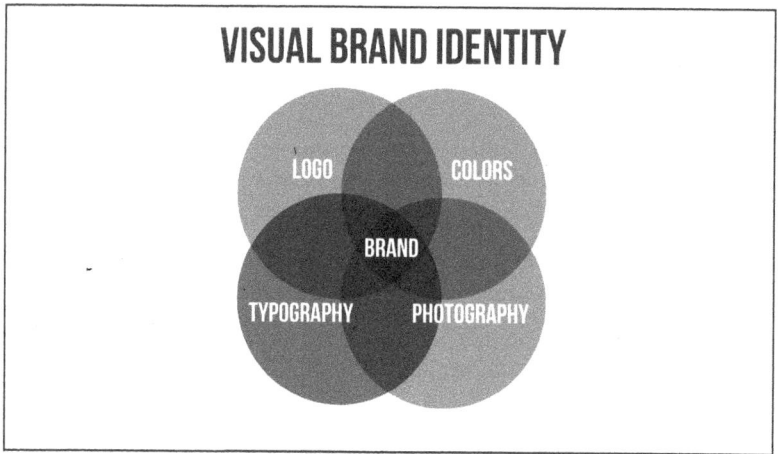

Figure 3.2 Visual Brand Identity.

Consumers encounter these elements intentionally through paid marketing or advertising; owned media including website and social media content; and through earned media when clients and consumers provide user-generated content (UGC) about their experiences with brands across the board.

Visual design is one of the most immediate and direct ways of influencing how someone feels about your business by leaving an emotional impression on potential clients, customers, and employees (Mailchimp, 2023). A brand identity starts with what you see, but it is also the feelings that arise as customers, clients, and employees interact with the brand. If a brand is able to build a relatable experience that resonates with customers, they will want to continue coming back for more (Zerkalenkov, 2024).

An innovative visual design can help a brand be more engaging by establishing a unique brand personality that influences all digital and physical content the brand creates. Education plays an important role in innovation, too, as brands can educate consumers through photography, which can provide an inside look at a brand or company's experience. Is a brand upscale and polished? Studio shoots or stock photographs showcasing refined and neat subjects and artifacts can present this brand personality. At the same time, candid and unfiltered photographs may capture a more informal vibe. For D2C companies with handmade goods, a hand-drawn logo may capture the essence of the handmade product. For a long-standing brand, a classic typeface can illustrate a historic essence.

In addition to creating a logo, selecting typefaces, color palettes, graphics, and more, a brand must ensure consistency of visual design across touchpoints. A consistent presentation of a brand's visual design across the company website, social media, advertising, packaging, and communication ensures a strong and cohesive brand identity that reinforces brand recall and fosters consumer confidence (Sabrina, 2023). These elements build brand believability.

Consumer-oriented packaging is an opportunity to educate and inspire consumers to invest in a certain product. For example, in addition to open kitchens, Chipotle educates consumers by printing all of their ingredients on their website and product packaging. Halara Cannabis prints their ingredients on their packaging, too, in an attempt to be as authentic as possible for consumers.

Brand Profile: Halara Cannabis

Halara Cannabis is based in California and has many regulations they are required to place on their packaging, including warnings, regulations, and restrictions. They also provide product information and survey cards inside of every box to educate consumers and break down pieces of the product in a tangible way.

"Because of the chemical engineering background of our founders, we want people to see our clean look, clean image, and simple design, and perceive our product as higher quality than our competitors," Lizzie Spier, CMO of Halara Cannabis, says. "At the same time, we have a lot of information to present to consumers, and we also want to present our brand's take-it-easy mood and image through openness, cleanliness, and quality."

Another piece of the design strategy is to set Halara apart from competitors. Lizzie Spier leads the brand's design strategy. She explains, "In the cannabis space, there are many hype brands that appeal to young male consumers with dark colors and graphic fonts. We're trying to generally appeal to a larger audience with our packaging and design as well."

Community Engagement

In addition to product packaging, a brand's design comes through on physical and digital signage through logos.

"Physical signage—the signs on the building and how that shows up—is the biggest driver of awareness and piquing interest in our brand," Amy Halford, CMO of Thrive Pet Healthcare, says.

Beyond physical signage, design and experience of a brand is carried out in digital and physical communities. D2C brands can create apps to provide users with a seamless experience that enables them to engage with the brand digitally; they may also have physical storefronts that reflect visual identities presented on digital platforms.

"Digital is one channel, but I think the other channel that is incredibly important is local community outreach and guerilla marketing within the community," Halford says.

> We're really encouraging our hospitals to get out there in their communities so people can see them, so that they can experience them and that they can

say, "Oh yeah, this isn't just some brand that's advertising to me, these are real people that are in my community that I know." The notion of local marketing is very, very important for our service and it's building that trust and that credibility. "There are real people that have been here [in my community] that care about my pet."

Guerilla marketing is another way to tap into the groundswell, or people using online social technologies—including blogs, social networking platforms, YouTube, and podcasts—to discuss products and companies, write their own news, and find their own deals (Li & Bernoff, 2008).

Spatial design speaks to the physical experience of a brand. At residential higher education institutions, the campus in particular is a key part of their design and experience.

"We have a residential leadership curriculum that develops the whole student and creates that true college experience with 3,500 acres of lakes and trails, and our professors are passionate and care about our students," Katie Alvino, CMO of the College of Saint Benedict and St. John's University said. "But if the product I am selling isn't coming through in the experience for the consumer, in this case students and their parents, it just falls flat, and then your reputation starts to unravel over a period of time because word gets out. It's like, 'Oh my gosh, they're promising this, but delivering on this. It's not the same.'"

Innovative experiences keep customers coming back and create novelty. New product launches and integration with new platforms—like Chipotle's partnership with virtual gaming platform Roblox (Chipotle, 2022)—lead to increased brand believability and customer engagement. D2C companies that launch new products create splash pages, social media promotions, and push alerts via SMS to alert customers with a sense of urgency to jump on an ethereal and exclusive opportunity to save money or gain access to a product available for only a short time.

"Our customers are crazy for our launches—when we launch something new, they are logged onto the system way before it goes live, and they're ready," Tammy Nelson, CMO of CONQUERing, says. "They set alarms so they don't miss our launches. Because they believe in us so much and they're so loyal, it really drives our growth."

The excitement that comes with product and service innovation carries over into the emotional category that builds a believable design and experience.

The Emotional Attachment of a Believable Design and Experience

Design and experience have a long, emotional tail, and live on beyond instantaneous encounters with a brand. Emotional attachment and brand love help to build brand believability by contributing to consumers' sentiments of satisfaction and loyalty, two concepts peripherally related to believability (Thomson et al., 2005; Ghorbanzadeh & Rahehagh, 2021). Emotional attachment can also lead to growth and profitability—and a brand's visual design is one of the first ways consumers encounter or feel anything relating to a brand at all (Magids et al., 2015).

"Most people typically have to experience the clinical effectiveness of a particular device firsthand before you're going to support its use," Darren Wennen, CCO of Caerus Corp., says.

When a customer experience is negative, that can erode believability without consistent and authentic commitments from the brand to pursue fixes.

"When I think about believability, I think about experience," BlueGrace Logistics CMO Mark Derks says.

> Can you build a smart supply chain strategy and can you execute it in a way that helps my business be better? If you can, then I believe in your brand, and I'll be loyal to that brand. If you can't, if you fail, if there are too many problems, too many issues, then no, and I'll have to go to a competitor. When we serve a customer, they have an expectation on the experience they should receive from the BlueGrace brand and every time that experience is positive, even if there's an issue and it's resolved in a positive way, our customers believe our brand can deliver them a positive experience. Each time we fail on our execution or we don't deliver a positive experience, that believability erodes. I'm a strong believer in brand loyalty, and it takes a long time to build brand believability and brand loyalty, and it takes very little time for that to erode if you're not providing a positive brand experience. So it takes a very long time to build up that believability and it can go away extremely fast based on customer experience.

The desire to connect in meaningful ways is a human inclination that brands can capitalize on through a consistent and engaging brand design and experience.

"We're humans, we're made to connect, and we're made to experience things," Jon Althoff, president and CMO of the Dakota County Regional Chamber of Commerce, says. "You can hardly find a brand where there isn't some kind of an emotional attachment because we want to have emotional attachment to things. We want to be attached to things. We want to have experiences that bring us happiness, joy, comfort, or save us from the opposite of those things."

Experiences with products and services can be positive or negative. Positive experiences, impressions, and perceptions keep consumers, clients, and employees coming back, while negative experiences can destroy a brand's believability. At the same time, negative experiences can be overcome with authentic, consistent, and quality engagements with consumers.

"Students can have a transformative experience on campus as the emotional attachment takes hold once the students become alumni, not before—I would argue to say ten years after," Katie Alvino, CMO of the College of Saint Benedict and St. John's University, said. "If you have done your job in both marketing messaging and delivering on your brand promise, students will become alumni who give back both financially and through participating in your brand for a lifetime."

Grocery stores are one example of how design and experience can work together. There is a logo on the front of the store; there is branded merchandise organized into an experience throughout; the customer service and wardrobe of employees reflect the brand personality.

Veterinary clinics and doctor's offices are other spaces and places where consumers experience emotional things relating to their own or loved ones' health. Intentional spatial design can contribute to believability in meaningful ways, as is the case for Ryan Companies, a construction firm that carries out end-to-end service for clients including hospitals.

Clare Scott, CMO of Ryan Companies, says,

> One of the things that we feel is a true differentiator as we think about who we are as a brand, as we think about how we go to market, is really that end-to-end service line. We can finance your building, we can design your building, we can develop it, meaning acquire the land and imagine it. We can build it; we can manage it at the backend. We can do all of these components. There aren't a lot of companies that do all of that. What

we say is, "We design better because we know management." Meaning, if you're designing a medical office building, we might put the thermostat outside the patient room. Why? Because if there's a temperature issue, you don't want to interrupt a doctor patient visit to adjust it. You want the tech to be able to come in outside and adjust it there. We say we're better at all of our services because of this.

Veterinary care in particular is an emotionally charged field given that animal owners care deeply for their pets. Intentional design choices help to enhance these emotional experiences in a way that builds believability.

"I think culture is something that you can't say, you have to feel, and that's where it comes in the experience," Amy Halford, CMO of Thrive Pet Healthcare says.

We're spending an awful lot of time thinking about what the client is going through, where their mind is in the specific moments and thinking about what we can do to add more value in that experience. We even think about pre-appointment and post-appointment, what are the touchpoints that we have that are going to really reiterate or remind people this is the experience that you are having or you're about to have, to show that care and support at every single touchpoint.

Communication design involves the quality of tangible touch points including social media messaging, websites, mobile alerts, and SMS messages. Beyond the design comes experience: Do the website and social media channels provide credible information? Is the content entertaining, educational, and engaging? Consistency comes in building emotional attachment and credibility through communication design and experience.

Amy Halford, CMO of Thrive Pet Healthcare, says,

What does our website look like? What does the experience of setting an appointment look like? What are the reminders that we send? What do they look like? What do they sound like? We have a membership program. How do we engage you in that in a way that is elevating care? With regard to communicating to consumers, they have to feel it and they have to experience it. Saying it doesn't matter. We really focus on the experience quite a bit. Emotional relevance is highly impactful for our brand and it is going to make or break us because emotions are what drive people and people have strong emotions about their pets.

Establishing Credibility Through Collective Insights and Data-Driven Metrics

Credibility of a brand's design and experience comes through consistent evaluation of customer engagement. Thrive Pet CMO Amy Halford says,

> We do a quarterly brand tracker where we're keeping tabs on where we're at in the marketplace, where the purchase intent is going, how behaviors may or may not be shifting given things that are going on in the economy, et cetera, so we're tracking that through the Net Promoter Score (NPS) and customer satisfaction. We're also social listening, keeping our ear to the ground in terms of what people are talking about, what they're saying, even with our employees. We watch all of the Glassdoor ratings and we watch Indeed ratings. We have to market to people who are in the industry so we can get them to come work for us but then, we also have to market to consumers, so we're watching any touchpoint we can to listen for feedback on that.

The Customer Satisfaction Score (CSAT) is a key way to measure customer satisfaction and is explained thoroughly in section 3.6.

3.4 Case: Chiro for Moms / Chiro for Kidz

Dr. Jesse Lillejord, founder and CMO of Chiro for Moms / Chiro for Kidz, envisioned a specialty chiropractic clinic for women—specifically mothers and their children—on a sketch pad during a continuing education conference for Webster-certified chiropractors. She'd been in general chiropractic practice for several years and, as a Webster-certified specialist capable of treating pregnant women and their children, was ready for a change after becoming a mother.

"I was in general practice for five or six years, and a lot of the OBs in the clinic below me were sending me their patients for chiropractic care. At the same time, I became pregnant and had my two babies," Dr. Jesse says. "I ended up leaving that general practice to be home with my kids for about three years, and in that timeframe, I continued to be passionate about the female care side of things. And I think without even realizing it, I had dreamt up my clinic."

When Dr. Jesse realized she could create her own brand design and experience from the ground up, she began to sketch logos and ideas for the clinic in a notebook. After spending hours and hours drawing every little detail up based on the things that she was learning at a continuing education seminar and capturing the excitement that she had, she knew that she was ready to launch a patient-driven, multigenerational clinic bolstered by a creative and innovative marketing plan.

"I loved the Celtic symbol for motherhood, which represents three generations—grandmother, daughter, granddaughter," Dr. Jesse says. "That night, I went home and bought all of the URLs that I could think of for Chiro for Moms—there were about ten other iterations—and saved them until it was time to start my practice."

Dr. Jesse sent her logo sketch to a designer who finalized and produced the Chiro for Moms / Chiro for Kidz logo—and a dream was born. Today, Dr. Jesse has a team that educates and connects with thousands of social media followers on a daily basis while treating thousands of patients in person.

Credibility for Dr. Jesse came first. She already had her Doctorate of Chiropractic degree and a Webster certification that made it possible for her to adjust pregnant women and their children.

"It's really important to have a specialist treating a woman's body, especially with pregnancy and postpartum, because you can do damage if you're not well-versed," Dr. Jesse says. "Everything we do is research-based, even down to the pillows we use, which are designed for women by a female chiropractor. Women's bodies are so different, and so much changes when you become a mother."

Dr. Jesse took her credibility and certifications from general practice into specialty care for women, mothers, and children as a professional and as a woman with lived experience through what pregnancy and postpartum chiropractic care required. Her credibility and lived experiences enabled her to create a brand experience set apart in the competitive space as a clinic that bridges the medical and natural/holistic gap.

Beyond the credibility of their treatment approaches for women and children, Dr. Jesse and her team prioritized emotional connection to their clients, emotional attachment, and inclusive design and experience.

A few policies that set Dr. Jesse's brand experience apart included treating only women and children, not doing treatment plans, and not having a cancellation policy.

"These were the things resonating in me as what would be really important for a patient-driven practice for women," Dr. Jesse says. "That, and a practice that caters to women so they could bring their kids. Because, at the time, when my kids were little, I really wasn't invited to bring my children anywhere with me. So, that was something that was really strong for me at the time. And here we are."

As Dr. Jesse began to navigate the waters of treating women and children—a traditionally underserved and underrepresented population in the medical profession—she found camaraderie, community, and credibility among peers and influencers in the women's health space.

Dr. Jesse's practice gained traction as she began to hear from local OBGYN providers and influencers that she had a gift for working with mothers and children. She began to be invited to and participate in community outreach events with well-established local providers who created referral networks for her and vice versa, which bolstered her practice's credibility further.

As Chiro for Moms / Chiro for Kidz moved from dream to reality, everything about the brand's design and experience was tailored toward mothers and their children. Inside of the office, Chiro for Moms / Chiro for Kidz's spatial design involves sensory experiences for patients through sight, smell, touch, and sound.

"Everything we do is visual. We design our apparel, so whatever our team is wearing complements what's on the walls in our clinic," Dr. Jesse says. "Smell is also a very important component of our brand and isn't something you'll see on social media, but it's a piece of our clinic that creates nostalgia and also memory. Smell is one of our strongest senses with regard to the things that we remember and feel. And so, smell and visuals in this clinic are big."

For smells, Dr. Jesse keeps essential oils running through the office and treatment areas—including eucalyptus, lavender, and peppermint. Choosing scents in particular is intentional, as chosen smells have numerous medicinal properties—in creams, ointment, and oil—and have been scientifically proven to ease muscle and joint pain, kill germs and bacteria, ease coughs and congestion, and heal wounds and infections. Similarly, lavender has medicinal properties proven to ease insomnia, anxiety, depression, and fatigue. Research shows that lavender produces slight calming, soothing, and sedative effects when its scent is inhaled.

For sounds, Dr. Jesse and her team have music playing in every room, tailored to the patients being treated at the time.

"There are times when we're doing craniosacral therapy and we decide individually for that particular patient that it's better to have it quiet, so we turn it off," Dr. Jesse says. "For other patients, some of my mamas or whoever we're treating at the time, might need something a little higher pep because they're going through something difficult, and they just want to feel good. We actually base the sound on our patients, which is interesting. But that has become a very big part of the experience for our patients."

Sound is an emotional element of Chiro for Moms / Chiro for Kidz's spatial design as children are welcome in the office both as patients and to accompany their mothers to treatment sessions. There are children's toys and play areas in every treatment room, and the staff are all hands-on when it comes to caring for kids who accompany their mothers for treatment sessions.

In addition to physical and emotional touchpoints with patients in the clinic, Chiro for Moms / Chiro for Kidz represents its brand design and experience through visual design on digital and social media platforms. Authentic, consistent, and innovative design and experience on social media is important to Dr. Jesse and her team. Chiro for Moms / Chiro for Kidz keeps things authentic, upbeat, educational, and innovative on social media with weekly videos that alternate between providing tips about chiropractic care, showcasing aesthetic and quality photographs of the treatment space(s), and entertaining dance videos that showcase the brand's personality for fellow practitioners and clients.

The brand also reaches out regularly to clients on digital and social media platforms with consistent and coordinated messaging to ensure patients know they are seen and cared for even and especially when they're outside of the clinic.

Visual branding across Chiro for Moms / Chiro for Kidz's platforms—in clinic and online on their website and social media channels—is consistent and intentional.

"The visual of what we wear and what our clinic looks like is very important because it's built-in marketing for us—we're always prepared to film. Sometimes it's planned but sometimes it's spontaneous."

In and through all of these spatial design choices, Chiro for Moms / Chiro for Kidz seeks to build and maintain a believable brand.

"Building believability with our patient base is of the utmost importance," Dr. Jesse says.

> Our patients need to understand and believe that we will listen to them because that's the very thing that creates the conversation that keeps them paying attention. So, they have to constantly believe in not just the way that we treat and the fact that they'll get relief, but the fact that we'll listen because the second that they don't, it's over. They stop showing up on social media and in our clinic.

Dr. Jesse hasn't seen too many competitors appear "because specializing in treating mothers and children is really hard."

Brand refreshes are always top of mind for Chiro for Moms / Chiro for Kidz, and Dr. Jesse is always asking questions of their patients and peers in person and online to evaluate whether their design and experience is as effective as it could be. For example, Dr. Jesse recently hired a specialist to integrate pelvic floor physical therapy—Pelvic Floor for Moms—to her practice to better care for patients experiencing challenges and dysfunction with their pelvic floor and the muscles surrounding it. As Dr. Jesse and her team pursue innovation in their practice, authenticity and consistency for Chiro for Moms / Chiro for Kidz is key.

"I'm honored to be able to show up every day and do this well, and do it beautifully," Dr. Jesse says.

> I think people underestimate the importance of personalization. I think that any company, big or small, should take personalization seriously, and should really home in on the individuality of the community base that they're talking to. I think we underestimate how much we can give back by listening and paying attention to our specific communities in person and in online spaces.

3.5 Application: Journey Maps

Journey maps are visual representations of the process a customer, client, stakeholder, or employee goes through to achieve a goal with a brand, product, or service. Journey maps are created to evaluate customer experience (CX), user experience (UX), or employee experience (EX) in the interest of optimizing a given brand's design and experience (Aguis, 2024). Journey maps can provide opportunities for brands to identify pain points and can also identify opportunities for gains or areas where the brand can improve the customer experience or capitalize on positive aspects to build believability.

Journey maps come in many shapes and forms, and can also be known as empathy maps, customer journey maps, experience maps, and service blueprints (Gibbons, 2017).

Internally, journey maps can provide alignment across teams and leadership by ensuring everyone across departments understands the customer or client journey; externally, it can enhance the customer experience of a brand by guiding the development of CX, EX, and UX strategies.

The first step to creating a journey map is to identify the persona represented. Are you evaluating a customer, employee, or client's experience?

- Persona: Identify and create a detailed description of the customer or user whose journey is being mapped, including demographics, goals, needs, and pain points.

The second step to creating a journey map is to identify a goal. Where is the customer, client, or employee going and what is the goal of their journey?

- Goal: Purchasing a product or service.

After the persona and goal have been identified, the third step of a journey map is to map out or illustrate an individual's journey. One way to map this journey is to apply the AIDA or marketing funnel—the persona's journey from attention to interest to desire to action, and beyond action, to loyalty.

Attention / Awareness

Innovation is key in the awareness stage of the customer journey. In the awareness stage, customers realize they have a problem. They begin searching for solutions to their problem, which is where brands come into play. Innovative brands—brands that use push marketing to provide new information to consumers and stakeholders—set themselves apart in the attention economy and provide value for consumers.

Driving Questions

- How does a customer become aware of a brand?
- What digital and physical touchpoints do they see or experience that bring them into contact with a brand?
- What pain points are they experiencing that lead them to search out this brand's products or services?

Interest

At this point, customers have moved beyond awareness into knowing they are interested in a specific brand, product, or service. In the interest phase, customers begin to compare brands and opportunities and to weigh pros and cons. Authenticity and consistency can help move consumers, clients, employees, and/or stakeholders toward a decision or action. Blogs, websites, ratings, reviews, and customer testimonials are key in this stage of the consumer journey.

Driving Questions

- How can a brand set themselves apart in the competitive landscape?
- What value can a brand provide to consumers or clients?

Desire

In the desire stage, customers have chosen a solution or option and are ready to take action. During the desire stage, a brand should deliver a seamless UX/CX/EX that removes barriers and obstacles to make buying products or services as easy as possible. Excellent and attentive customer service, promotions, and consistent, high-quality touchpoints contribute to customers taking action.

Driving Questions

- What touchpoints invite consumers or clients to take action?
- Is it possible for consumers and clients to have all of their questions answered?
- How easy is it for consumers or clients to take action?

Action

In the action stage, customers purchase or commit to this selected brand.

Driving Questions

- What is the purchase or partnership process like?
- What are the rewards for purchasing or partnering with a specific brand?

Loyalty

In the loyalty stage, consumers or customers become brand ambassadors who actively promote the brand to family, friends, and/or colleagues. At the loyalty phase of the AIDA funnel, brands should focus on providing a fantastic end-to-end customer experience. This should span from your website content to your sales reps, your social media team, and your product's UX. Most importantly, customers become loyal when they've succeeded with your product—if it works, they're more likely to recommend your brand to others; if it doesn't work, is the customer experience process consistent, authentic, and high quality? Loyal customers will also likely provide feedback and other solicited data to enrich your customer journey mapping strategy.

Driving Questions

- Are your brand's products or services sharable?
- Does your brand have a loyalty or referral program with discounts and/or perks for returning customers?
- Does your brand have data and/or metrics to quantify success?

The fourth step to creating a journey map is to consider or highlight the following elements in and through each step of the journey:

- **Touchpoints:** Specific interactions or points of contact between the customer and the brand at each stage (e.g., website visits, social media interactions, in-store experiences).
- **User actions:** Potential actions taken by the customer at each touchpoint (e.g., searching for information, making a purchase, contacting customer service).
- **Emotions:** The emotional responses of the customer at each stage or touchpoint, indicating satisfaction, frustration, delight, etc.
    - For example, at the awareness stage, consumers or clients may feel excited or desperate; at the interest phase, they may become curious or cautious; at the action phase, they likely feel confident and enthusiastic, but possibly frustrated; at the loyalty phase, they may feel relieved or satisfied.
    - You can create an Empathy Map to point out specific emotions users feel at various points of the journey process. Empathy maps are built on data from user interviews, surveys, and observations, and are often displayed in four quadrants: Says, Thinks, Does, Feels.
    - As an example: A brand is designing a new app for fitness enthusiasts. Brand researchers conduct interviews and observe users during workouts. An empathy map for one user might look like this, which helps the brand and app developer(s) better understand users' needs and frustrations:

- Says: "I wish I had a way to track my progress easily."
- Thinks: "I need to stay motivated to reach my fitness goals."
- Does: Uses a notebook to log workouts and progress.
- Feels: Frustrated with the lack of easy-to-use tracking tools.

- **Pain Points:** Challenges or obstacles that the customer encounters during their journey, which may hinder their experience or satisfaction.
    - For example, at the awareness stage, consumers or clients may feel overwhelmed by options; in the interest phase, they may feel confused by conflicting reviews; at the action phase, they may be confused by unclear warranty terms or unexpected shipping costs; in the loyalty phase, if there are difficulties in the product setup process or if they experience long wait times with customer service or a lack of personalized offers.
- **Solutions / Gains:** Opportunities for brands to turn pain points into opportunities for deeper connection with a brand through education and consistency.
    - For example, at the awareness phase, a brand can provide clear, concise product information; at the desire and/or action phase, they can simplify the purchasing process; in the interest and action and loyalty phases, brands can offer comprehensive setup guides and tutorials; at the loyalty phase, brands can implement personalized loyalty reward programs.

No two customers' journeys are the same—journey maps help to capture a persona's journey to and through a brand experience. Here are some examples of journey maps:

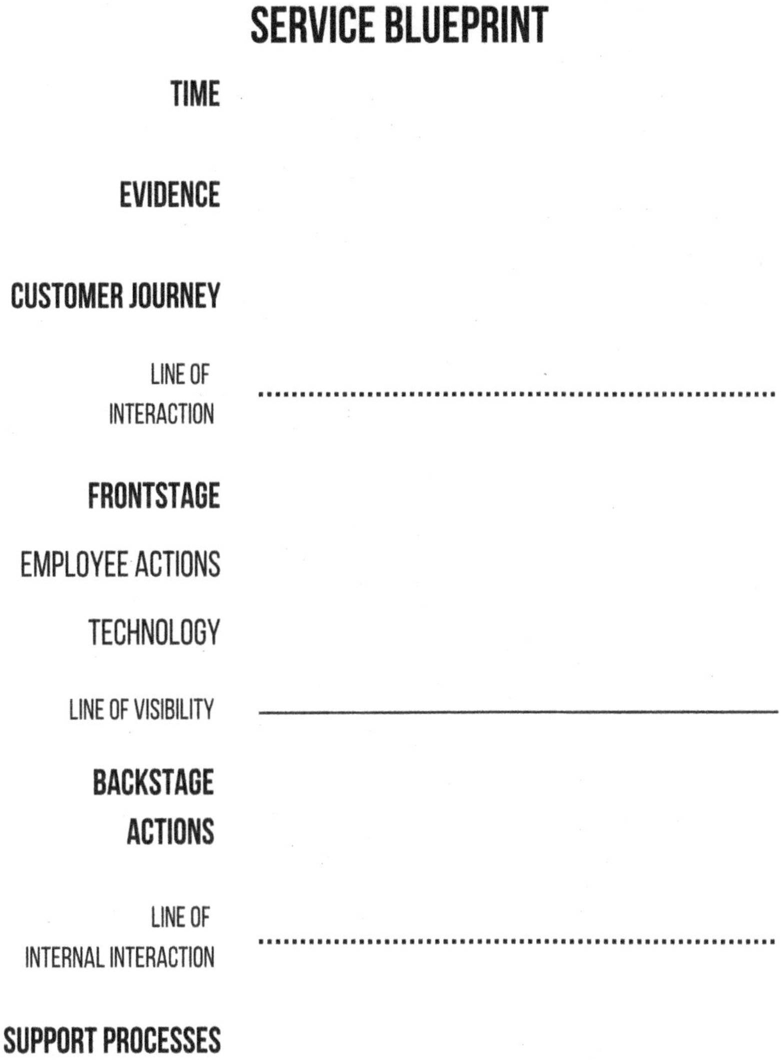

SERVICE BLUEPRINT

TIME

EVIDENCE

CUSTOMER JOURNEY

LINE OF INTERACTION ··

FRONTSTAGE

EMPLOYEE ACTIONS

TECHNOLOGY

LINE OF VISIBILITY ————————————————————

BACKSTAGE ACTIONS

LINE OF INTERNAL INTERACTION ··

SUPPORT PROCESSES

Figure 3.3 Service Blueprint Journey Map Example.

JOURNEY MAP

AWARENESS

Touchpoints	User Actions	Emotions

INTEREST

Touchpoints	User Actions	Emotions

DESIRE

Touchpoints	User Actions	Emotions

ACTION

Touchpoints	User Actions	Emotions

LOYALTY

Touchpoints	User Actions	Emotions

Figure 3.4 Customer Journey Map Example.

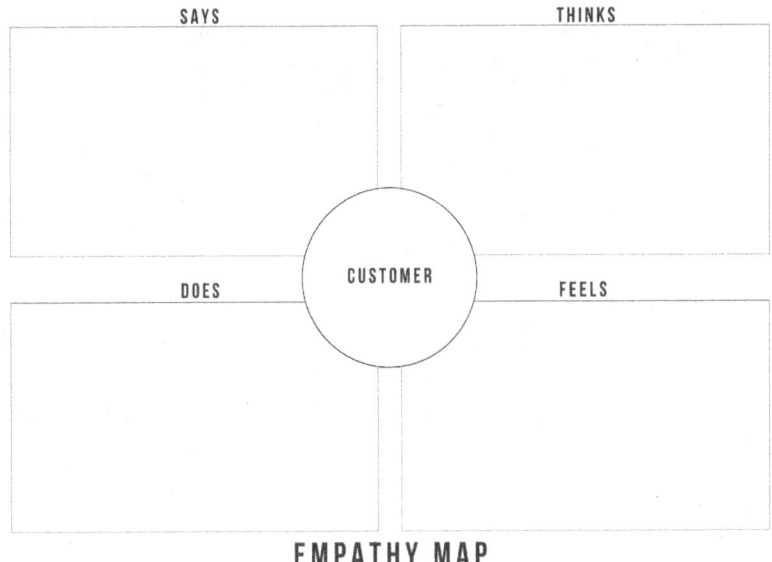

Figure 3.5 Empathy Map Example.

3.6 Metrics: Customer Satisfaction Score (CSAT)

CSAT, or customer satisfaction score, is quantified using survey questions about how satisfied customers are with a company's products or services. It's typically expressed as a percentage from 0 to 100 percent (Qualtrics, 2024a).

CSAT is calculated with a series of survey questions asking about a brand's products or services. For example:

"How would you rate your overall satisfaction with the [goods/service] you received?"

Respondents use the following 1-to-5 scale:

1. Very unsatisfied
2. Unsatisfied
3. Neutral
4. Satisfied
5. Very satisfied

CUSTOMER SATISFACTION SCORE (CSAT)

"How would you rate your overall satisfaction with the [goods/service] you received?"

1	2	3	4	5
Very unsatisfied	Unsatisfied	Neutral	Satisfied	Very satisfied

CSAT (% OF SATISFIED CUSTOMERS) = (# OF SATISFIED CUSTOMERS (4 AND 5) / NUMBER OF SURVEY RESPONSES) X 100

Figure 3.6 CSAT Calculation.

The CSAT percentage can be calculated with the following formula:

CSAT % = (# of satisfied customers (4 and 5) / Number of survey responses) × 100 = % of satisfied customers

To figure out if your brand, product, or service's CSAT is in line with competitors, the American Customer Satisfaction Index (ACSI) lists CSATs for a large variety of brands, products, and services (2024). If a benchmark isn't available, it's important to measure the CSAT consistently to evaluate whether or not the score is moving in an upward trajectory—if the score is moving from lower to higher, that's a great sign your brand is building believability.

Key Terms

Brand community
Brand experience (BX)
Brand guidelines
Brand identity
Brand personality

Customer experience (CX)
Employee experience (EX)
User experience (UX)
Journey map
Logo

Discussion Questions

1. Which is more important to brand design and experience: Authenticity, consistency, innovation, or quality? Why?
2. What brands have a believable design and experience and what makes them believable?
3. Are journey maps worth it? Why or why not?

Activity

Journey Map: Choose one type of journey map to map out the customer journey for a brand to identify pain points and opportunities for improvement. Choose a brand and research its customer journey from awareness to action using one of the following journey maps: Customer Journey Map, Empathy Map, or Service Blueprint. Be sure to include the following elements: Persona, goal, touchpoints, emotions, pain points, and opportunities/solutions.

Part II

Brand Growth

What is brand growth? The second section of this textbook discusses how to overcome market saturation with believable brand growth. Believable brand growth is built over time with market segmentation, channels and outreach, and communication. Creating and sustaining believable brand growth requires strategic planning and execution. A Responsibility Assignment Matrix (or RACI: Responsible, Accountable, Consulted, Informed) is an application that can help with this. Metrics to quantify brand growth include calculating market share and brand penetration.

Outline

II.1 Introduction: What Is Brand Growth?	108
II.2 The Problem: Market Saturation	108
II.3 The Solution: Believable Brand Growth	109
II.4 Application: Responsibility Assignment Matrix (RACI)	111
II.5 Metrics: Market Share and Brand Penetration	112
Key Terms	115
Discussion Questions	116
Activity	116

II.1 Introduction: What Is Brand Growth?

Brand Growth: How a brand gains and maintains competitive advantage in the market.

What is brand growth? We define brand growth as how a brand gains and maintains competitive advantage in the market. Brand growth is often a result of brands gaining awareness among audiences and cultivating loyalty from customers and consumers. Believable brand growth can be measured, or quantified, by market share, profitability, and product and service innovation.

Three pillars of brand growth include market segmentation, channels and outreach, and communication. These concepts will be defined and discussed in detail in the following three chapters. Before exploring brand growth in more detail, let's discover the problem facing brands seeking to grow: market saturation.

II.2 The Problem: Market Saturation

Market saturation is when the volume of a product or service in a marketplace has been maximized because there are no additional customers available or interested in investing in a product or service (Hargrave, 2024). When a market becomes saturated, brands can grow by introducing innovative new products or services; innovating to improve existing products or services; through taking existing market share from competitors with lower prices or premium offerings; and/or increasing overall consumer demand by moving into new segments to raise brand awareness through channels and outreach (Hargrave, 2024). Brands can create demand among their consumers to combat saturation by creating new categories and segments or designing their products and/or services to wear down or need replacement over time. Apple Inc. is one example of this, as they push out a "new" model of iPhone every year and offer incentives that encourage consumers to replace their "old" ones to stay relevant in the digital economy (Apple, 2024). Innovation is a major way to overcome market saturation and is a key value of building believable brands.

II.3 The Solution: Believable Brand Growth

To overcome market saturation and build believable brand growth, brands must grow with authenticity, consistency, innovation, and quality. Brand growth can only come after a brand has developed its belief system—its purpose, culture, design, and experience. As soon as a brand's belief system is established, brands can begin to get the word out about their value propositions, which leads to engagement with target audiences, clients, and consumers. As brands grow, they must continually revisit the believability building blocks presented in the Brand Believability Pyramid: Emotional attachment, credibility, authenticity, consistency, innovation, and quality. If there is consistency between outside and internal perception of brand values, a brand is perceived as authentic (Vallaster & Kraus, 2011).

Tactically, brand growth can be pursued in numerous ways. Performance marketing—defined as paying for results from marketing campaigns including sales, leads, or clicks through third-party channels including direct mail providers, search engines, and social media sites—is one way brands can pursue growth (Stengel et al., 2023). Drivers of brand growth include quality, personalization, and relationships (Huang & Dev, 2020). Brand growth is driven by customer value (Logman, 2007). Being a brand that communicates and demonstrates believability among its target consumer groups leads to sustainable brand growth.

There are two main ways to build brands. Brands can attract more people, and they can also penetrate more among new and preexisting audiences. Ways to build brand growth—also known as growth accelerators or strategies to pursue growth—include predisposing more people to a brand, being more present, and finding new spaces to grow (Kantar, 2024).

Predisposing people to a brand involves pursuing interactions and touchpoints with consumers in digital and physical realms. Interactions and touchpoints include exposures, experiences, advertising, and other content marketing activities. Brands people are strongly predisposed to are more likely to maintain a high proportion of market share and market penetration. Brands that value high-quality creative content and branding that is consistent over time present a positive disposition. Prioritizing diversified investments across categories, channels, and media outlets helps to get the word out as well—as long as brands are consistently assessing and evaluating the effectiveness of their touchpoints among consumers and categories.

A second growth accelerator is for brands to be more present. This can be accomplished in part by consistent and innovative owned, earned, and shared media among consumers and potential new clients, customers, or partners. Brand presence ensures availability and visibility to not only convert predisposed people, but to also capture customers from other brands when possible. According to Kantar, brands that are always present attract seven times more buyers than ones that aren't—the top 5 percent of brands have a category presence of over 80 percent (Kantar, 2024).

A third growth accelerator is to find or create new space by defining a brand category and finding spaces your brand can stretch into through innovation, expanded distribution, and compelling communications.

Once a brand's purpose and identity are established, they can be consistently distributed through market segments, brand channels and outreach, and across brand assets through brand communication. Integrating the brand identity across assets including marketing materials, packaging, website design, advertising campaigns, and social media is key to pursuing and maintaining believable brand growth (Mailchimp, 2024).

As brands grow, it's important to consistently evaluate brand purpose and brand equity—brand awareness, associations, meaning, and credentials—with consistent analysis and assessment (Avery & Greenwald, 2023). Concepts presented in Part I—including consistency across digital and physical touchpoints, a sticky and spreadable brand story, and innovation in owned, earned, and paid media spaces—continue to be important in cultivating believable brand growth. As brands grow, it's important to have accountability among stakeholders to ensure scalable growth. The Responsibility Assignment Matrix (RACI) is one application to ensure accountability. Beyond application, metrics to calculate brand growth include market share and brand penetration. Application and metrics are explained in detail in the following sections.

An intentional approach to brand growth involves the concepts presented in Part II of this book: Market Segmentation, Channels and Outreach, and Brand Communication.

II.4 Application: Responsibility Assignment Matrix (RACI)

To ensure sustainable and believable brand growth, teams can utilize a responsibility assignment matrix (RACI) to assign relevant individuals to various tasks. RACI stands for:

- Responsible: Who is responsible for the task at hand? This is the person or people doing the work to complete or create the deliverable—every task has at least one responsible person and could have several.
- Accountable: Who is the person in charge of this task? The accountable party is a single team leader who delegates responsible parties and reviews the work created, ensures the responsible person or team knows the expectations of the project, and makes sure work is completed on time.
- Consulted: Who is consulted before, during, and after the completion of a task or project to ensure consistency and quality? Project managers and teams identify and consult people and/or teams with a stake in the outcomes of a project to provide input and feedback

RACI MATRIX

TASK / STAKEHOLDER NAME & JOB TITLE	ALLISON: PROJECT MANAGER	HASEON: RESEARCH ANALYST	MARTY: CEO	SCOTT: CCO
TASK #1	R / A	R / A	C / I	C / I
TASK #2	A	R	I	I
TASK #3	R	A	I	I
TASK #4	R / A	R / A	C / I	C / I

Figure II.1 RACI Matrix.

on the work being done on a task or project. Consulted parties can be consulted by project managers and teams before getting started, throughout the work to check in, and at the completion of a task or project to get feedback on the outcome. A project manager should consider all possible stakeholders when creating a RACI chart and include as many consulted parties as is necessary and appropriate. Less is sometimes more.
- Informed: Stakeholders who are not decision makers in the task or project, but have a vested interest in the progress of the task at hand; usually outside of the project team and are often in different departments and/or senior leadership.

II.5 Metrics: Market Share and Brand Penetration

Market share and brand penetration are two concepts that drive brand growth. Market share is the percentage of an industry's revenue or comparable metric—web traffic, etc.—that a brand owns. Brand penetration is defined as the amount of a brand's product or service that is sold to customers compared to the estimated total market for that product or service.

These two concepts are sometimes used interchangeably but they are distinct—brand penetration is not market share, but brand penetration can drive market share. Increasing brand awareness across segments, lowering prices, and introducing innovative new products and services can help to increase market share and brand penetration (Zhukova, 2024).

Simple brand growth metrics can be measured by calculating profits and seeing whether or not they increase over time. Brand growth can

MARKET SHARE

(BRAND REVENUE / TOTAL INDUSTRY REVENUE) X 100

Figure II.2 Market Share Calculation.

also be measured with more complex metrics including the amount of market share a brand has, the amount of brand penetration within specific markets, the success of innovative new products or services, emergence into new markets and/or on social media platforms, an increase in the number of customers or potential customers that exist at the top of the marketing funnel, spreading awareness digitally and physically, and entering new geographic markets to increase the brand's footprint.

Market Share: Market share is the percentage of an industry's metric—revenue, web traffic, etc.—that a particular company owns (Riserbato, 2022; Romaniuk et al., 2018). To calculate revenue market share, take your brand's total sales revenue for a specific period of time and divide that number by your industry's total revenue during the same time period. Once you have this result, multiply the number by 100 to generate your brand's market share percentage (Riserbato, 2022): (Brand Revenue / Total Industry Revenue) × 100 = Market Share.

To calculate market share, you must first source market data. If you're calculating market share of revenue, you must collect your industry's revenue by leveraging market research tools and databases such as Statista and industry reports. If there isn't data on industry revenue readily available, you can download competitors' financial reports to combine their revenue figures with your own to get combined total market revenue (Dawes, 2016).

Relative market share is another way to measure brand growth as it compares any given brand's performance to industry leaders. Rather than using total industry revenue, you can divide your brand's market share by your top competitor's market share, multiplying the result by 100. The result will show you the portion of the market you own in relation to your most significant competitor: (Your Brand Market Share / Competitor's Market Share) × 100 = Your Brand's Relative Market Share.

RELATIVE MARKET SHARE

(YOUR BRAND MARKET SHARE / COMPETITOR'S MARKET SHARE) X 100

Figure II.3 Relative Market Share Calculation.

Beyond revenue, market share can measure a brand's market share of specific metrics including but not limited to website traffic, unit sales, and more. Market share calculations can apply to geographic areas, consumer demographics, etc. Some examples: A brand's market share in the United States or a brand's market share among Generation Z consumers (Zhukova, 2024). Metric-specific market share can be calculated in the same way as the market share and relative market share calculation—simply divide your brand's specific metric by the market metric × 100: (Company metric / market metric) × 100.

Brands that boast higher revenues than competitors have a higher market share. One way to increase market share is to enlarge the size of the customer base, with less emphasis on boosting loyalty and more on raising awareness and interest among light or infrequent buyers (Dawes, 2016).

Brand Penetration: Brand or market penetration is the amount of a product or service that is sold to customers compared to the estimated total market for that product or service (Baker, 2022). In other words, brand penetration calculates what proportion of the total addressable market (TAM) a brand has captured with a particular brand, product, or service (Jones, 2024).

A low brand penetration rate—meaning a product or service isn't sold to very much of a target audience—suggests there's room for brand growth. At the same time, a high penetration rate implies market saturation is near.

Measuring brand penetration can be calculated by taking the current sale volume for your product or service and dividing it by the total sale volume of all similar products available in the market: (Number of Customers / Target Market Size or Total Addressable Market) × 100 = Brand / Market Penetration Rate.

To identify the target market size or total addressable market (TAM), identify the total revenue your brand would generate if you had 100

BRAND / MARKET PENETRATION

(NUMBER OF CUSTOMERS / TOTAL ADDRESSABLE MARKET) X 100

Figure II.4 Brand/Market Penetration.

percent of market share. To calculate total market size or total addressable market, you can manually pull numbers from market research tools and databases including Statista and industry reports (Semrush, 2024). If data on total addressable markets are not readily available, you can download competitors' annual reports to combine their target market figures with your own to estimate combined total addressable market size.

To calculate your brand's total number of customers, determine the number of customers currently buying your product or service from your sales database or customer relationship management (CRM) system.

Frequently monitoring brand penetration is important in order to identify any increases or decreases in effectiveness of various campaigns. For example: It's helpful to calculate market penetration after every marketing and sales campaign you run to measure the effectiveness of various campaigns.

Conclusion

Part II of this book discusses the following concepts that unpack the concept of brand growth—how a brand gains and maintains competitive advantage in the market—in-depth:

- *Market Segmentation:* Dividing target markets into approachable groups.
- *Brand Channels and Outreach:* Matching brand values with appropriate channels to plan effective outreach to target audiences.
- *Brand Communication:* Connecting a brand with the market through paid, earned, and owned media.

Market segmentation is a tactic that lays the foundation for effective brand growth; brand channels and outreach are key components of improving the ways brands communicate with specific stakeholders and target audiences in digital and physical realms; and brand communication provides specific strategies to help brands connect with consumers, clients, and stakeholders across mediums, channels, and platforms.

Key Terms

Brand penetration
Competitive advantage
Customer relationship management (CRM)

Growth accelerators
Market saturation
Market share
Performance marketing

RACI matrix
Relative market share
Total addressable market (TAM)

Discussion Questions

1 Which is a more effective approach to brand growth: Beating the competition in an existing brand category, or creating a whole new brand category? Why?
2 Which metric is more important—market share or brand penetration? Why?
3 How can a brand use partnerships or collaborations to accelerate growth?

Activity

RACI Matrix: Your brand is expanding into a new global market. Select and define which global market this is, and use a RACI Matrix to develop a plan and identify opportunities for this brand to effectively approach international expansion. What tasks need to be assigned for successful entry into new global markets?

4

Market Segmentation

We define market segmentation as dividing target markets into approachable groups. Believable market segmentation is created by brands committed to effectively identifying and defining core and secondary segments with specific needs, desires, and expectations. Inauthentic and impersonal branding is a problem that can be overcome with commitments to authentic and high-quality segmentation. The Ansoff Matrix is presented as one way to ideate, illustrate, and execute a segmentation strategy. Different types of segmentation include demographic, psychographic, geographic, firmographic, and behavioral.

Chapter Outline

4.1 Introduction: What Is Market Segmentation?	118
4.2 The Problem: Inauthentic and Impersonal Branding	118
4.3 The Solution: Believable Market Segmentation	119
4.4 Case: Halara Cannabis	126
4.5 Application: The Ansoff Matrix	130
4.6 Metrics: Types of Segmentation	131
Key Terms	132
Discussion Questions	132
Activity	132

4.1 Introduction: What Is Market Segmentation?

Market Segmentation: Dividing target markets into approachable groups.

Market segments comprise groups with various characteristics, desires, or needs (Zhukova, 2023). For example, for athletic shoes, a core segment may include high-performance athletes, while secondary segments include casual athletes or those with an interest in athleisure.

Market segmentation inspires product and service development as it provides a clear road map for how products and services can be provided to specific segments by age, gender, socioeconomic status, hobbies, and more. Market segmentation can take numerous forms and approaches. Segmentation, targeting, and positioning (STP) marketing is one prominent and integrated consumer-centric approach that helps to deliver personalized content to target audiences. Market segmentation ensures that a brand can put its best foot forward to establish emotional attachment and credibility with its various audiences.

Anyone can participate in market segmentation, but to be done well, it must be deeply personalized and intentional. Branding sometimes comes across as inauthentic and impersonal, and authentic and believable market segmentation can help solve that problem.

4.2 The Problem: Inauthentic and Impersonal Branding

Inauthentic and impersonal branding is a result of brands, services, and products that attempt to appeal to everyone—and satisfy no one. Consumers want to feel seen and heard, and they want brands to align with social matters they care about in authentic ways. Consumers tend to prioritize word-of-mouth recommendations more than anything else when considering brands to follow and invest in—and word of mouth recommendations come from authentic and believable experiences with products and services (Park & Steinke, 2023).

When brands are inauthentic and impersonal, employees, stakeholders, and customers find it difficult to connect. When brands personalize content, consumers are more compelled to engage and partner with brands in the co-creation of believability.

Inauthentic and impersonal branding often involves a lack of personalization and is often a result of unclear data, lack of access to data, and/or lack of quality analysis of customer data. Data privacy laws and regulations can complicate the data-gathering process, as personal customer data are often protected by policies including the General Data Protection Regulation (GDPR) in Europe and the California Consumer Privacy Act of 2018 (CCPA) in the United States. These policies protect consumers, but can make it difficult to collect consumer insights efficiently.

Collecting fragmented data is a challenge. Depending on the industry and product or service, data must be collected through a variety of platforms and funnels including sales and marketing funnels. Validating, cleaning, and updating data on a regular basis is important, as well as integrating data from sources including web and social media analytics, customer service correspondence, and sales and marketing funnels.

Clean, accurate, and thorough data collection and analysis combats inauthentic and impersonal branding by helping to create high-quality market segmentation as follows.

4.3 The Solution: Believable Market Segmentation

Believable market segmentation is authentic and high quality. It starts with personalization through data collection and discovery. Market discovery can take place through surveys and other forms of market research including web analytics and social listening.

After data collection and discovery, brands can segment markets based on categories including but not limited to demographics, needs, priorities, behaviors, and common interests. Data to inform segmentation can be gathered via surveys and also via publicly available data including U.S. Census data and IP addresses for web visitors. No matter how small your company or organization, research can help refine market segments.

For nonprofits or brands and organizations with a small number of staff, market research can be collected through qualitative means including sales data, customer feedback and reviews, informal interviews, networking events, and social media analytics. Small or resource-constrained businesses might lack the necessary tools or skills that large Fortune 500 brands and organizations do, but it doesn't mean data collection has to lack quality.

With a staff of five, the Dakota County Regional Chamber of Commerce, based in Eagan, Minnesota, just south of the Twin Cities, utilizes data in many of their branding decisions. Jon Althoff, its president and CMO, says, "We don't have the budgets or the time to hire a firm to analyze our data, but our entire branding strategy is based on data—we run surveys with SurveyMonkey to ensure we know who our market is and that we are doing what our consumers and members want."

Likewise, other nonprofits or smaller organizations can benefit from continuous evaluation of their feedback and segmentation. Beyond surveys, consistent touchpoints with clients and consumers in person are key. The Chamber holds more than one hundred in-person events each year.

Segmentation also varies based on industry. For example, in the entertainment industry, market segmentation is also known as audience segmentation as brands evaluate what shows and services individuals are tuning into. Five major ways to segment markets are (Qualtrics, 2024b):

- Demographic Segmentation: Gender, education, socioeconomic status, occupation, nationality, race/ethnicity, age
- Geographic Segmentation: Geographic boundaries/regions
- Firmographic Segmentation: Industry, company size, company revenue, number of employees
- Psychographic Segmentation: Lifestyle, personality, traits, opinions, interests
- Behavioral Segmentation: Purchasing behaviors, consumption behaviors

To segment your market, it's important to first define your market, then select which categories to use from the above. Many brands use more than one category to create a segment—it's whatever works best for your brand.

Identify a Core Segment... and Others Will Follow

Many brands focus on building a core segment and stay niche, like chiropractic clinic Chiro for Moms / Chiro for Kidz, who focus on one core segment of women aged 25 to 40. They've found if the core is happy, other segments will follow.

Larger brands—including media organization CBS—diversify segments and identify hundreds—if not thousands—of audience segments or consumers.

Types of segmentation that will be most effective vary across sectors. When it comes to creating segments, behavioral segmentation works well for entertainment brands that have offerings across mediums and platforms. It's important to ensure segmentation is consistent across platforms.

"First, will our campaign engage and satisfy our core audience? Second, what will it take to attract other audience segments?" says Mike Benson, president and CMO of CBS. "Campaigns for entertainment products can sometimes be multidimensional. What interests our core audience might not necessarily attract other segments or drive viewing on different platforms. Once we understand how to position the content for our core audience and where and how they will watch it, we can be more strategic in designing each campaign to reach multiple target segments."

CBS's core audience loves its daytime dramas and various other programs, including *The Price Is Right, Survivor, 60 Minutes,* and *NCIS*—shows or touchstones that feature heroes, good guys, and memorable characters. When CBS considers new product or show launches, they consider staying true to a core audience that will bring in new viewers across multiple platforms.

"While we are always looking to grow audience share across our linear and streaming platforms, we start by thoroughly understanding what will drive our core audience to watch any given show," says Benson. "We then start to broaden and grow the audience from there."

Once a core segment is identified, defined, and prioritized, other segments will follow. Another way to segment consumers is digital vs. in-person. To expand a brand's footprint, investing in digital app development will likely increase market share and brand penetration if the app is developed with innovation and quality and drives awareness and action in the digital segment.

Market segmentation can be time-consuming and costly, but it is helpful in identifying and targeting products and messaging. Artificial intelligence (AI) is one way to segment markets in an efficient fashion—by using algorithms to segment a brand's leads, prospects, and customers into relevant segments. AI can also evaluate and analyze customer feedback and reviews to improve your products, services, and customer experience and to discover new behaviors and desires of consumers and clients (Digital Marketing Institute, 2023).

Market segmentation has become more focused over time. As technology has evolved, consumer behavior has become more integrated across mediums and platforms, making it more important for segmentation to be as specific and detailed as ever. Analytics and metrics can help define viewing behaviors and is key for entertainment brands to target consumers effectively and to create creative, differentiated, and diverse campaigns.

"When you try to serve everyone in the same way, you serve no one," Benson says.

> Even though we serve broad audiences with our diverse programming slate—and we have many shows that reach over ten million people a week—we tend to veer away from one-size-fits-all marketing strategies. We still aim to reach big and broad audiences, but with the high volume of product we need to market across CBS—and knowing how different audience segments discover and consume content across linear and streaming platforms—we must also be incredibly efficient to make the most effective use of our resources.

Two major ways to achieve brand growth include (1) attracting new clients and customers and (2) retaining existing clients and customers by cultivating loyalty. What are some ways to attract new customers? Creating innovative new platforms, touchpoints, and access points for customers, clients, and partners. Chipotle optimized their mobile app in the mid-2010s which enabled them to access new customers and, unbeknownst to them at the time, prepared them for a pandemic. This technological innovation enabled them to adapt and grow market share during a global pandemic while other brands faltered. "A lot of the consumers that we attract to the app are unique to Chipotle," Chipotle CMO and Chief Brand Officer Chris Brandt said.

Our digital users are not necessarily coming into the restaurant, and our in-person restaurant users aren't necessarily migrating over to digital. So, they kind of stayed in their lane, if you will. And so that was a big growth driver for us, even in 2019. Then when 2020 happened, fortunately we were ready. If 2020 had happened in 2018, we might have a different storyline.

Identifying accurate metrics and analytics for segmentation can be a challenge with fragmentation and limitations of consumer data due to data privacy. For example, it's important to ensure under Europe's GDPR that your brand has explicit consent from customers to use their purchase history and behavior data for personalization. It's also important to have a system in place for human oversight to review and potentially override AI-based recommendations and biases (Melinn & Boyd, 2024a).

Brand Profile: *Desperate Housewives*

Specific segmentation helps brands to market more effectively. Mike Benson, president CMO of CBS, spent time at broadcast network ABC where he helped to launch an innovative marketing and branding campaign for Emmy-award winning show *Desperate Housewives*—advertising on the side of dry-cleaning bags.

> One key insight was that there was a segment of women between the ages of 35 to 49, who are living quiet "lives of desperation"—as they are not living a charmed life, they're running daily family errands, including a frequent trip to the dry cleaners. Many of these women were miserable in their lives and looking for an escape. *Desperate Housewives* could become this for them. Our team uncovered this insight, which helped us design both our positioning and media strategy, including an idea to advertise the show on the side of dry-cleaning bags, which was a first-of-its-kind.

It was a media idea designed to target the core audience segment of the show in a way that was provocative and organic to the show. It also drove an unexpected amount of earned media and publicity for the show and ABC's marketing team.

"We learned that in a sea of other TV shows and movies being marketed, we needed to find new ways to get our show(s) noticed," says Benson.

> We placed our marketing in front of the core target audience in a way that resonated on a new level, and while the message on the side of the dry-cleaning bag, *"Everybody has a little dirty laundry,"* worked to sell

the concept of the show, the tactic also caught people's attention, since it was so unexpected. It created a new advertising platform for the dry-cleaning industry, but it also helped us see that we could get more value from our efforts when our marketing was authentically clever.

Prioritizing Segments

Higher education institutions share core audience segments of prospective students and, sometimes, prospective students' parents. Various other segments in the higher education sector include current students, alumni, donors, and faculty. Local businesses and organizations that support and partner with higher education institutions are a market segment as well, in addition to faculty administrators at other schools and, internally, faculty and staff.

"Our business community—the Minnesota business ecosystem if you will—is core to our value proposition, and this shows up across the enterprise: corporate donors who are philanthropic, companies that sponsor projects and hands-on learning experiences, professionals who serve as mentors and coaches, and recruiters that participate in our student career services," James Plesser, CMO of the University of Minnesota's Carlson School of Management, says. "While we have a variety of different segments that are important audiences to us—such as alumni, faculty, and staff—in my perspective the school is here to educate and support students—current students and prospective ones. That is who we are here to serve."

For health care institutions like Mayo Clinic, there are three distinct audience segments: patients, physicians, and platform users across apps and websites.

"We focus on three audiences, each with its own marketing strategy," says Sherri Gilligan, chief marketing officer, Mayo Clinic.

> The first is attracting patients who need specialized care, often those with serious or complex conditions that other medical institutions can't diagnose. The second is physician marketing, where we share our knowledge and connect with health care professionals who come to Mayo Clinic to learn. Lastly, we are transforming health care through Mayo Clinic Platform—an innovative initiative designed to transform health care by harnessing the power of data, advanced analytics, and

artificial intelligence. It aims to improve patient outcomes, enhance health care delivery, and expand access to quality care. By using vast amounts of medical data and cutting-edge technology, Mayo Clinic Platform helps accelerate the discovery of new treatments, facilitates more personalized care, and makes health care more efficient and accessible globally.

Brands that market to everyone serve no one—it's important for brands to be authentic about who they want to reach and to be able to say no if a customer doesn't fit the core segment to maintain consistency and quality deliverables. BlueGrace Logistics calls their core profile an "ideal customer profile" that falls within a certain revenue stream and industry vertical.

"There are so many companies that need shipping help and we're just not after all of them," Mark Derks, CMO of BlueGrace Logistics, says.

Segmentation is important because without it, brands can't create personas—profiles of target consumers that help align messaging and make it as effective as possible. For example, higher education institutions use demographic information to create personas for various student groups. Jaime Hunt, CMO of Old Dominion University, says:

> We really build out personas that give us a little bit of flesh on which we can hang our messaging. And then, we have to then go in and figure out how to assign a persona to somebody based on what we know about them. So we might look at zip code, gender, age, race, any high school activities that they're in, intended major, and so on. And then, craft communications that target those groups. We're in a stage of wanting to recruit more valedictorians and salutatorians, and also military-affiliated students. How do we craft messaging that will resonate with those two segments that are totally different?

Data and discovery can help convince senior leaders and key stakeholders of the importance of various approaches and types of marketing across segments.

"Senior leadership understands data and how important data is, so we had to use that to make the case for why we needed to roll out a marketing campaign that had different messaging geared toward the types of things that the surveys or the research showed our segments were interested in," Hunt says.

4.4 Case: Halara Cannabis

Halara Cannabis is based in California, one of the first states to legalize marijuana use recreationally in 2016. Halara segments their market for consumers ranging from college students to menopausal women, for recreational and medical use. Their segments range from recreation to medical use for cancer patients and those with chronic pain of various kinds.

Barriers to Halara's innovation include structural constraints from federal regulations and agencies to competition in an emerging market. Halara's core segment is frequent users—those who spend more money on products than secondary segments—and tends toward males ages 25 to 37. Secondary markets include medical patients and more casual users who want less potent options for sleep aids, pain relief, and relaxation. Because the cannabis industry is so new—as of this writing it is not yet legal in the United States federally, but is legal in several states including California and first became legal in 2012 in Colorado and Washington—it's an evolving market with opportunities for innovation in the midst of various regulatory and structural constraints.

Data collection and discovery is difficult for Halara. According to CMO Lizzie Spier, Halara leverages consumer data from multiple platforms within the cannabis industry that are available including point-of-sale systems, but the data received is incredibly fragmented.

"A lot of the point-of-sale (POS) systems that exist do not share data and do not integrate well with other systems," Spier says. "So a lot of the data that we get is rough at best. It often still provides a true scientific representative sample, but it's hard to extrapolate that to the larger state of California where there are seven-million-plus people."

The U.S. cannabis market revenue is forecasted to reach $42.98 billion in 2024, an 8.6 percent revenue increase over 2023, and the largest cannabis market in the world. The U.S. cannabis market is expected to grow 2.89 percent year over year through 2029, with a major focus on regulatory developments and market expansion.

Launched by a group of University of Minnesota alumni who moved to California to pursue their dreams shortly after cannabis became legal in the Golden State in 2016, Halara has grown to 158 employees. With approximately $3.5 million revenue per year, the brand is growing steadily.

Halara is a small business—Spier describes it as a life raft in the big ocean of California—where regulatory changes can be chaotic. Many cannabis companies in California are owned by larger ownership groups and market changes are evident through impacts on large sectors of business—as was the case in 2023, when California changed their tax collection process and many cannabis dispensaries collapsed due to defaulting on hundreds of millions of dollars' worth of loans. One large distributor in particular defaulted on $700 million worth of loans and represented eighty brands. They completely collapsed due to a negative effect of market regulation on market factors.

Within their product lines in general, Halara has a diverse set of customers. "It's like Coca-Cola, for example," Spier says.

> You have regular Coca-Cola, Diet Coke, and Coke Zero. Generally they're appealing, but they also have their very specific personas. I would say that even in my own case, I do consume products within all four of our product lines, but I'm doing so in a specific state of mind when I'm doing each. And I think that embodies what it can be for the consumer. You could enjoy all of our Halara products, but you'll probably use them at specific times in your life.

Halara seeks to diversify and expand their market share beyond the consumer groups above by appealing to environmentally and socially conscious individuals. As a registered B Corporation, Halara has set themselves up to eventually be certified once cannabis becomes legal at the federal level in the United States. Examples of environmentally conscious decisions Halara has made include compostable packaging. Halara also has a green facility that does multiple sortings of recyclable products.

"We sort nearly everything you can imagine—compost, paper, plastic, Styrofoam, wraps, silicone—and we properly recycle those products," Spier says. "And one of our new lines that is coming out is actually going to be launched in conjunction with our own recycling program. So we actually will be coming into dispensaries and offering them a recycling service so people can safely dispose of their vape products and e-waste in a closed loop system."

Socially conscious moves Halara has made include sourcing local materials from California suppliers and partnering with organizations for charity releases. Examples of these include partnering with a Compassion Program that donates cannabis products to veterans and cancer patients.

Halara has also partnered with Fire Relief and Restoration groups, the Humane Society, and has participated in local volunteer events, ocean cleanups, and highway cleanups.

Reaching users across channels and platforms is challenging as social media platforms including Meta ban Halara, given the fact that their products are federally illegal in the United States and in many other countries across the globe. Meta, for example, has censored Halara's product and won't let them advertise on their platform because Meta has users in other countries where cannabis is illegal. Beyond censorship, Halara's content is also shadowbanned. Shadowbanning is defined as a social media platform hiding or restricting a user or brand account's content from platform users without informing the user or brand that it's happening (Forsey, 2023). Shadowbanned accounts' content won't appear on anyone's feed, within search results, or on trending or hashtag pages unless they already follow the shadowbanned account directly or receive a post or content from another user directly.

"Their stance is, 'Well, we can't do it across the board, so we can't allow you to do it because someone in another country could still technically find your content,'" Spier says.

An illustration of the impact federal constraints has on Halara's operations is the U.S. Food and Drug Administration. Spier says,

> Right now, we are in the process of getting ready to launch a new product line, and we have hardware that's coming in to us from China, but we were just notified that right now, the FDA is apprehending 90 percent of packages that are coming from China because they're trying to find nicotine vape products that are getting brought into the United States from there. With that, they're apprehending products for seven to thirty days without warning, and they won't notify you. We're at this point of chaos because we are operating a legitimate business, but the product that we are using, at its core, is federally illegal. So every step of the way, there is this larger hand of the federal government as well the world working against us.

One way cannabis companies like Halara have found a way around these shadowbans is to be educational (Bartlett, 2021). For Halara, this is accomplished in part by providing users with new ways of consuming cannabis as a vape. Vaping is the third most popular form of cannabis consumption in the United States behind flowers/buds and edibles like gummies and cookies (Statista, 2024a). This positioning provides Halara an opportunity to not only acquire new audiences but also to convert existing ones to a new modality.

Beyond these challenges and limitations, Halara has segmented their market of existing and potential new customers in California as follows:

Segment 1 (Core): Frequent Users—Halara's core segment comprises frequent users that are sensitive to quality, sensitive to price, and are also very brand loyal. Halara thinks of this segment when designing and introducing new products. Halara's core segment tends toward males aged 25 to 37. This core segment is willing to spend more money than other segments and is interested in the heaviest hitting product: High potency, high quality, lots of flavor, frequent consumption. The product that aligns closest with this segment is Halara's high THC line, which is a proprietary Halara blend that provides a high-potency product with an alternate cannabinoid—a market differentiator.

Segment 2 (Secondary): Cannabis Connoisseurs—One of Halara's secondary audiences is cannabis connoisseurs. This segment of people has been consuming for a very long time, but are not necessarily the people that want a high-potency product. They're not necessarily the people that are smoking all day long, but they really care about the story, the craft, the strain, and the flavor of each product they consume. Halara's product that aligns with this market segment is in a gold box and is a crafted product with a 100 percent live resin. It's a premium price with premium hardware that makes the whole experience higher quality. This product does a lot of limited release strains working with different farms and highlighting certain blends to fit a live resin category/niche that has been growing rapidly. Halara has stood out in this space by winning some awards, which builds credibility among preexisting customers in addition to drawing new audiences in. This segment is a combination of preexisting customers and new audiences who want new products from a credible brand.

Segment 3 (Secondary): Casual Users—Halara segments casual users as a segment that doesn't want a high-potency product but wants a relaxed, eased feel, with the convenience of a discreet and portable vape. This segment trends younger and includes working students, blue collar workers, individuals with low amounts of disposable income but maybe higher consumption patterns and more frequent purchases with lower ticket value. This segment may potentially be seeking pain relief and may be a medicinal patient, but they may also be a mom or dad on the go. Halara's products designed for casual users are alternate cannabinoid lines—one in a darker bluish box and another in a lighter purple box. Each cannabinoid elicits different effects. The light purple box is the high-CBD line, and this is where Halara features more prominent ratios of CBD compared to THC. It doesn't smell like a joint, and that works well for a lot of casual users. It's also a very pure product.

Segment 4 (Secondary): Medical Patients (Chronic Pain, Insomnia, etc.)—The final market segment is medical patients who suffer from chronic pain, insomnia, etcetera. This product line for medical patients is in a darker blue box and is tailored to assist with sleep and to alleviate chronic pain and inflammation. CBN is the alternate cannabinoid that helps with sedative effects, inflammation relief, and pain relief. "For a lot of people, this product in particular is really geared and positioned toward those people that are coming to cannabis because they can't sleep at night, or maybe they have really intense pain and they just need something that will really calm them down at the end of the day," Spier says. "What's great about our product is that our vapes have a more instant effect than edibles and, therefore, a better delivery for a lot of people for the relief that they're seeking."

4.5 Application: The Ansoff Matrix

The Ansoff Matrix is also known as the Product/Market Expansion Grid. This matrix can help brands and organizations analyze and pursue growth across market segments in a strategic way (Ansoff, 1957).

Figure 4.1 The Ansoff Matrix.

When trying to figure out what products or services are most effective across segments, the lowest risk endeavor is *market penetration*, defined as the attempt to capture more of an existing market with an existing product offering through product innovation. A bit riskier of an approach is to take an existing product or service into a new market, a.k.a. *market development*. An equally risky approach is *product development*, the attempt to develop a new product to capture more of an existing market. The riskiest approach is to develop a new product or service for a new market—also known as *diversification*.

Brands should always be looking to innovate and create new products and services in line with their values and capabilities.

4.6 Metrics: Types of Segmentation

It's important for brands to identify a core segment, but first, they must identify all segments possible. As mentioned in this chapter previously, five major ways to segment brand markets are (Qualtrics, 2024b):

- Demographic Segmentation (D2C): Gender, education, socioeconomic status, occupation, nationality, race/ethnicity, age
- Geographic Segmentation (B2B/D2C): Geographic boundaries / regions
- Firmographic Segmentation (B2B): Industry, company size, company revenue, number of employees
- Psychographic Segmentation (B2B/D2C): Lifestyle, personality, traits, opinions, interests
- Behavioral Segmentation (B2B/D2C): Purchasing behaviors, consumption behaviors

To create a market segment, follow the following steps:

1 Define your market: Who is your target audience? Surveys and market research help define this.
2 Select which categories to use from the above, knowing you can combine more than one together: Is it demographic? Psychographic? More than one of these things? That is, U.S. users who wear athletic shoes to work out daily? Or users who purchase athletic shoes for fashion in Europe?

3 Identify who falls into this segment and how the segment is defined: Create personas to help illustrate who exactly you're targeting within the segment. Include as many details about their demographics, psychographics, geography, and behavior as possible, leveraging data and analytics from your brand's dashboards. If these metrics don't exist, create them and start tracking them regularly!

Key Terms

Ansoff Matrix
Behavioral segmentation
Core segment
Demographic segmentation
Diversification
Firmographic segmentation
Geographic segmentation
Market penetration
Psychographic segmentation
Secondary segment

Discussion Questions

1 What are the various benefits and limitations of using demographic, psychographic, behavioral, firmographic, and geographic segmentation?
2 How should market segmentation influence product development?
3 What is the most effective way to collect data for market segmentation? Why?

Activity

Market Segmentation Workshop: Select a brand or organization and use available data to evaluate how this brand or organization segments its market. Identify at least four market segments, define them, and explain which segments you think are most important and why. Present your findings and any improvements or blind spots you've identified in your chosen brand's current strategy.

5

Brand Channels and Outreach

We define brand channels and outreach as matching brand values with appropriate channels to plan effective outreach to target audiences. In order to communicate what's important to your brand to your target audience(s), deciding what channels your target audience will trust and engage with most often becomes especially important. Today's media environment provides information to consumers on numerous platforms amid a challenging trend of record-low trust in the media. The solution to this is to find which media channels work the best for delivering your brand values to audiences in an authentic and consistent manner. These decisions build believability. In this chapter, we will discuss how to build believable communication between consumers and brands by developing content across multiple channels in a coherent and value-centered way. Starting from defining the problem—today's fragmented media landscape—to presenting the solution—believable and effective outreach—this chapter explores how target audiences and personas can help brands attain meaningful metrics including reach, frequency, gross rating points (GRPs), and impressions. Chipotle's "For Real" campaign is introduced as an innovative example of a believable, value-driven multichannel marketing strategy.

Chapter Outline

5.1 Introduction: What Are Brand Channels and What Is Effective Outreach?	134
5.2 The Problem: Fragmented Media Landscape	136
5.3 The Solution: Believable Brand Channels and Outreach	137
5.4 Case: Chipotle	142
5.5 Application: Target Audiences and Personas	144
5.6 Metrics: Reach, Frequency, Gross Rating Points (GRPs), and Impressions	148
Key Terms	150
Discussion Questions	150
Activity	151

5.1 Introduction: What Are Brand Channels and What Is Effective Outreach?

Brand Channels and Outreach: Matching brand values with appropriate channels to plan effective outreach to target audiences.

What is effective outreach? Let's think about this from your own media experience first. If you take a count, how many media touchpoints do you encounter throughout a single day? It may start from the first time you check your mobile phone after you get up in the morning, and log in to your social media account to see what's new. Then, you will get ready for the day listening to podcasts, and walk along the streets to go to work—where you're very likely exposed to various kinds of banner ads placed on the bus stops, buildings, and magazine stands along the way. Any given U.S. media consumer is exposed to anywhere from a handful to hundreds of ad exposures across media channels every day (Anderson, 2023). Regardless of what the exact number of such ad exposures might be, the most important thing to understand is that we live with multiple brand interactions in a fragmented media landscape every day—or hour—and some encounters we might not even consciously notice.

Given that you, as a consumer, are exposed to various eye-catching ads from multiple media outlets, now let's think about the same experience again—from a brand's perspective. How do brands try to reach their consumers with multiple ad exposure opportunities they create along the consumers' decision journey, and what are the ways to effectively reach them while also targeting the group of consumers they are looking for?

Effective consumer outreach embraces the following components: (a) reaching out to target consumer groups your brand is aiming for, (b) engaging them to drive intended actions, and (c) through multiple media sources relevant to each phase of the consumer decision journey. Two powerful examples of implementing effective consumer outreach include influencer marketing and personalized recommendations informed by consumer data and analytics. We will explore these two examples throughout this chapter to dive deeper into the ways brands can utilize strategic approaches to reach a wider-yet-relevant audience through multiple media channels.

In an era of low consumer trust, leveraging the influence of social media influencers' authenticity and connections with audiences can serve as an effective marketing tool. Leveraging social media influencers as a trusted media source can help to achieve successful consumer outreach by targeting specific interest-based groups of consumers with a high level of engagement (Whitaker, 2024). The number of social media influencers across different market categories open up useful and cost-effective ways for a variety of brands to target and reach consumers interacting with them. Another great example of achieving effective consumer outreach is through personalized recommendations based off of real-time consumer data and analytics. Personalized advertising often utilizes third-party consumer data sources, including demographics, website usage history recorded through cookies, location, past purchasing history, or any other types of digital traces in order to expose right ads to the right group of consumers. Some consumers find personalized advertising "creepy," and this approach can put consumers' privacy concerns and perceived intrusiveness at risk (Segijn & van Ooijen, 2020). At the same time, when applied appropriately and ethically to your targeting strategy and with clear disclosures of how consumers' data will be used, data-informed personalized advertising can bring more benefits than risks to your brand by providing timely suggestions to your consumers.

5.2 The Problem: Fragmented Media Landscape

Today's fragmented media landscape brings several challenges to a brand trying to locate and engage the right audience with your message at the right time. Mike Benson, president and chief marketing officer of CBS, mentioned how reaching audiences is a combination of advertising, social media, partnerships, cross-promotion, sampling, and on-air brand experiences.

As Benson notes, cross-media communication becomes an essential part of reaching target consumers you are looking for in today's media environment. Television is not the only media outlet where people consume news—social media platforms including X (formerly Twitter), TikTok, Facebook, and Instagram are places where information is updated rapidly and in a way that is engaging global audiences. Just like that, your brand's target consumers are everywhere, but at the same time, they are nowhere—at least not staying in one single space. Therefore, the key to achieving effective target consumer outreach in this fragmented media landscape is knowing where target audiences are at the moment of influence, and how you can speak to them with a powerful message that resonates.

Another important characteristic of the current media landscape is an unprecedented low-trust toward media in general. Public trust toward *any* mass media has plummeted, facing historic and record lows among Americans. In 2024, Gallup's Trust in the Media poll results showed 36 percent of U.S. adults have "no trust at all in the media"—more than Americans with a "great deal" or "fair amount" of trust.

Unsurprisingly, such a low-trust tendency toward media messages has made it even more challenging for brands to get meaningful attention through multiple media channels, and then convert it to drive future purchases from their consumers. A survey of ten thousand U.S. consumers conducted by Qualtrics XM Institute (2024c) indicated that consumer trust toward brands has significantly decreased to reach its lowest point since 2016. The survey results shown below imply that over the course of particularly turbulent years where people got through the unexpected global pandemic of COVID-19 from the year 2019, societal, economic, and cultural consequences have followed, influencing how consumers respond to brand messages and develop lower levels of trust toward them.

Looking deeper into the specifics of the survey, the results reveal interesting differences across different age generations, showing that Generation Z consumers (18–24 years old) reported the lowest levels of brand trust where only 28 percent of them responded favorably, compared to 57 percent favorable responses from Baby Boomers (65 years and older). It is noteworthy that generational differences among consumers may hint at different expectations they have toward the brands they interact with by developing and maintaining varying levels of trust.

Industry leaders in advertising and public relations, in fact, have not only noticed the aforementioned challenges toward gaining consumer trust, but also realized the importance of making themselves believable through authentic and positive brand experiences. During our in-depth interview regarding brand believability with Mark Derks, chief marketing officer at BlueGrace Logistics, a third-party logistics provider in North America, Mark shared that it takes a long time to build believability, while it can erode incredibly fast when brands fail on execution or deliver negative experiences.

As Derks noted, establishing any level or any kind of brand trust takes a long time. It takes an even longer period of time when we are combatting the era of record-low trust toward companies. That being said, proactively addressing the fragmented nature of the current media landscape with a sophisticated, data-driven approach to accompany every step of consumers' decision journeys is critical to reach target audiences and develop trusted relationships. That way, facilitating consumer-brand interactions across multiple media channels will benefit both the people looking for believable products or services when they need them, as well as those who are trying to promote what they have to offer to the right people.

5.3 The Solution: Believable Brand Channels and Outreach

In order to understand how brands effectively communicate to their target consumers through multiple channels, it is essential to walk through each phase of what target consumers get to experience when they purchase a product. Traditionally, advertisers and marketers thought that sending promotional messages out to mass audiences would trigger interest among their target audience, which would lead to potential future purchases. This idea comes from the traditional one-way communication prevalent at the time, where your brand delivers a message to consumers without having an instant or real-time feedback available. With the increasing number of media and product choices consumers have in recent years, however, such traditional marketing strategies do not guarantee successful outreach as much as it did in the past—nor does it lead to desirable outcomes.

Now the question becomes, what does today's consumer-brand communication look like, and how is it different from the past? Today's fundamentals are centered on two-way communication, rather than traditional one-way communication. In two-way communication, your brand delivers intended messages to the target consumers, and those consumers receiving your messages may give instant feedback or responses to your messages—thus, real-time communication.

The AIDA Funnel

Keeping this knowledge of traditional one-way communication vs. recent two-way communication in mind, there are two dominating mechanisms that explain the concept of the consumer decision journey that we want to explore. First: A well-received and tested AIDA—Awareness-Interest-Desire-Action—purchase funnel rooted in one-way communication, categorizes where consumers are when considering your brand. The AIDA model suggests that consumers first become aware of your brand, then some of them may get further interested in what your brand has to offer and make efforts to find out more details. Then, even smaller subsets of those consumers will feel the desire for your product or service, developing some levels of emotional connections to it and, finally, making them want it. Consequently, those who feel the want and need of your brand will take actions to purchase. It is a rather linear process of how consumers experience each phase of awareness, interest, desire, and action to learn of, and use your brand. A fifth layer of the AIDA funnel is loyalty, or the stage at which consumers keep coming back to the brand and recommending it to others.

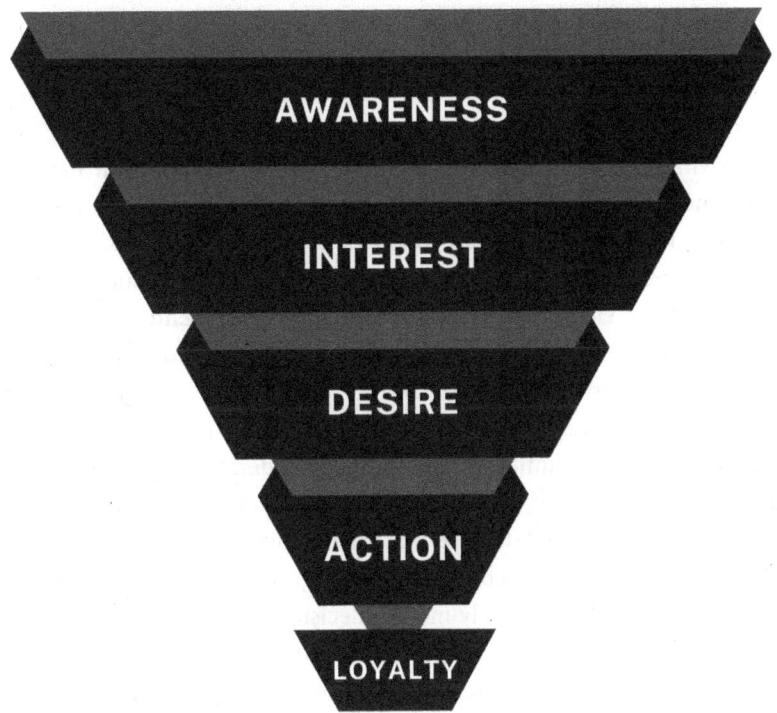

Figure 5.1 The AIDA Funnel.

McKinsey's Consumer Decision Journey (CDJ) Model

Another model is a comparably recent paradigm of the consumer decision journey that is more adaptive to technology development and media fragmentation. McKinsey's circular consumer decision model suggests a circular process by pointing out the limitations of understanding the consumer decision journey in a linear fashion (Court et al., 2009). McKinsey's model adequately reflects every logical step of a consumer purchasing journey in today's media landscape where two-way communication is more common. McKinsey's Consumer Decision

Journey (CDJ) model is primarily characterized by the circular nature of consumer-brand interactions these days, surrounded by various opportunities across multiple media channels to interact back and forth in real time with consumers.

Essentially, McKinsey's CDJ starts from a triggering event or moment where consumers feel the need or want of a product item. It could be as simple as the need for morning coffee, or something life-changing such as moving to a new state or city. After the triggering event happens, consumers will think of a typical or go-to set of brands as an initial consideration set. In this phase, digital and social media can significantly influence how consumers learn of any other relevant brands through advertising or electronic word-of-mouth by their friends or family, or other consumers who have used the brands and shared reviews online. Then, consumers will go on to dive deeper into the set of brands they consider and actively evaluate them so that they can make an informed purchase decision. Similar to the initial consideration set phase, digital and social media as well as earned media can play a significant role in helping consumers find detailed information about your brand. Once the active evaluation phase is completed, consumers will arrive at the moment of purchase when they finally make a decision to buy or not to buy your brand whether it's at the physical store or online.

McKinsey's CDJ continues to highlight post-purchase experience as a form of ongoing brand exposure, making this CDJ model distinctive to the traditional AIDA model. At the post-purchase experience phase, some of the consumers who purchased your brand may share how their experiences with your brand were by posting an online review about their direct interactions with your brand. This activates the power of positive or negative word-of-mouth recommendations—a form of earned media—for future purchases. An even smaller subset of consumers may enter the loyalty loop by becoming active or passive loyalists. Active loyalist consumers will remain loyal to your brand consistently no matter what, whereas passive loyalist consumers will show some level of brand loyalty, but still consider other competitor brands. This entire course of phases in McKinsey's circular consumer decision journey demonstrates the nature of consumer-brand interactions in today's media environment. By revisiting each phase to plan right messaging by matching what your consumers are looking for at the moment, your brand can get a step closer to meaningfully engaging your target audience and establishing successful reach.

Now, steering our attention back to how brands can overcome the challenges from today's media fragmentation, the ultimate solution to achieve successful outreach throughout the consumer decision journey is not only to find the right people at the right time, but also to deliver the right messaging in the right manner. In other words, brands must focus on a purpose- and value-driven approach to effectively locate and reach target consumers when interacting with them throughout the different phases of the circular decision journey. In doing so, several things need to be coordinated in tandem to achieve effective outreach by strategically planning communications through multiple media channels. Clare Scott, CMO of Ryan Companies—a real estate and construction company—noted that constant multichannel communications centered around the brand's single most important core value which, for Ryan Companies, is "delivering high-quality services with expertise," plays a significant role in building trust in what they do. Consistent multichannel communications make their consumers more likely to believe in the quality services Ryan Companies offer in the long run.

Jaime Hunt, CMO of Old Dominion University, a public research university located in Norfolk, Virginia, highlighted the importance of running promotions across multiple channels coherently so that target audiences can easily identify what is going on with the brand's communications and fully comprehend the overall meaning of it:

> We take an omnichannel approach, which is a very big shift for this institution. They've had to be very siloed, thinking about the channels and to the point that even social media and digital advertising was disconnected from the web. So if you're doing some digital campaigns on social media or on YouTube, they might go to our website and see nothing connected to that campaign, which is just mind-blowing. But there also has to be an understanding of those channels and what audiences are on those channels. For us, Facebook has really evolved to be for older alumni and parents of students. Whatever Gen Z is into changes every couple of weeks, it feels like, so you have to stay on top of that. But on the whole, TikTok is a great place to tell authentic stories.

Taken together, building believable brand channels and outreach strategy is based on understanding each phase of your target consumer's decision journey; selecting the most influential media channels that coincide with each phase; and centering your channels and outreach strategy around your brand's value-driven communications. This strategy will boost the effectiveness of your consumer outreach and will build believable relationships with your target audience.

5.4 Case: Chipotle

One successful brand showing off its purpose- and value-driven brand communication across multiple media channels is Chipotle. Chipotle is an innovative and leading player in the fast-casual dining category with a unique brand identity, reaching a record revenue of $9.9 billion in 2023, over thirty years following its first restaurant opening in 1993 (Chipotle, 2024). Behind the remarkable business success of Chipotle, there is a series of advertising campaigns showcasing what Chipotle cares about, and one of its core values: Food with Integrity.

The "For Real" campaign is an integrated marketing campaign Chipotle launched in 2018. The campaign's intention is to emphasize the brand's long-standing commitment to preparing real food made with only real ingredients.

Through a strategic and holistic media plan, several versions of the For Real ads were showcased across multiple different channels during the target period of the campaign, including Chipotle's own brand website, social media accounts, TV, digital and out-of-home, and print media. Interestingly, Chipotle went a step further and opened a second Instagram account solely dedicated to this campaign to educate its consumers about each of the fifty-three ingredients served in their products.

This campaign not only delivered a clear and purpose-driven message to Chipotle's current and prospective customers, but also helped the company increase their revenue, reviving the brand from a troublesome sales decline it had been experiencing since 2016 (Wohl, 2018).

Chipotle's CMO and chief brand officer, Chris Brandt, was the leader of Chipotle's marketing team at the time of the "For Real" campaign, and spared some time for an interview with us to talk about how Chipotle worked its way to build trusted relationships with consumers in part by casting an effective media plan. He started with a simple statement about the key to making your brand trusted and believable.

"I think whether it's being authentic, being believable, being transparent, just telling the truth and not trying to complicate things with bells and whistles and everything else, I think that's why our ads really work," Brandt said. "It's because we have our employees talking about it."

Brandt also shared a concrete example of how Chipotle approaches multiple media executions. One of the occasions was when the brand showed up at the Scripps National Spelling Bee, the largest and longest-running spelling bee in the United States. Chipotle engaged and entertained audiences with a value-driven messaging strategy:

> We showed up at the National Spelling Bee. One of our favorite creative executions of all time is when we had kids at the spelling bee spell a Chipotle ingredient like jalapeno or corn, and then we had kids spell a competitor ingredient like dimethyl polysiloxane. And so it was just huge fun. That was one of our favorite things. And that was a great experiment. We didn't know what we were going to get. So we said, 'Well, it wasn't expensive. Let's go down to the spelling bee and see what happens.' And we liked it so much we ended up putting it in theaters in the fall, because it was so charming and such a great and fun way to talk about what our ingredients are versus other people, and... it gave a little insight into our values.

Of course, while pointing out the innovative way of delivering Chipotle's core values, Brandt explained the value of breaking through traditional ad spaces like sporting events with creative marketing tactics:

> We also do conventional advertising. We're all over sports because those are big moments in culture, and some things we do are fun. We don't have a formal relationship with the NBA, but we advertise in the basketball championships. And we actually embedded codes in our ads where people could win a free burrito. So people are literally watching the show, stopping the ad, getting the code, and going in to win free burritos. And we usually give them away within a minute. The one we did in 2023 was for every three-pointer we gave away three hundred free burritos. "When they make a three, it's free" was kind of our little schtick. So we don't have a relationship with the NBA, but we're getting people to watch and to engage while they're watching. And so we're a part of that event, even though we're not official.

One common insight we can take away from these two examples of Chipotle's creative execution is that a brand can show up with value and grab the attention of its target consumers in unexpected ways. Such consumer engagement through media will eventually lead to authentic and enjoyable engagement and experiences that go a long way.

All in all, showing up with your brand's most important values and letting your consumers be a part of it is an effective and fundamental solution to achieve meaningful consumer connections and co-create believability in today's saturated media landscape. As Brandt said: "We want to show up. We try to show up in a little different way, in a fun way, in a way that reflects a little of the cheekiness of the brand."

5.5 Application: Target Audiences and Personas

Now that we have become more knowledgeable about the importance of multichannel integration for building believable consumer outreach, we can consider how to apply this knowledge to locate specific groups of target audiences for a particular campaign.

Understanding your target audience starts from understanding your brand first. An important set of questions you can ask to evaluate your brand's identity include:

- Brand Drivers: What is driving the acceptance or purchase of your brand? and
- Brand Barriers: What is preventing the acceptance of your brand?

The answers to these two questions can be drawn in part from earned media—also known as your existing consumers' user generated content. Assessing brand sentiment—or the feelings and opinions about your brand—and analyzing drivers and barriers to brand believability provide core insights into what your brand needs to improve on. As you consistently evaluate what your consumers have to say about your brand, you can adjust your strategic planning for the future.

Leah Larson, CMO of Madison Air, offered her organization's experience as an example of continuous analysis:

> Our sales process is relationship based. We're very consultative. We talk to customers, learning about the business, understanding business plans, priorities, pain points, etcetera, and then design our program and offering to that. And so it is potentially easier for us than a consumer brand that

has to rely on simpler messaging. We do adapt our lead message, it's not that they're not all applicable, but we carefully choose what lead message we use with this audience versus a different one.

Moreover, Jaime Hunt, CMO of Old Dominion University, added that making sure their current audience gets a positive, high-quality omnichannel brand experience—across digital and physical realms—should be the number one priority:

> When I was interviewing at a PWI and currently working at an HBCU, they asked in the interview, "Well, how would you help us recruit African American students?" And I said, "I'm not going to help you recruit African American students unless I know that they're going to have a positive experience when they come here, because if they're not, it's not ethical to me to try to get those students to come to a school where they're going to not feel a sense of belonging or part of the community."

Once you know more about your brand's barriers and drivers, and any other consumer opinions associated with your brand experience, you can begin identifying which group of people from the general population might fit your brand better than another. This process is what we call market segmentation. In order to locate a meaningful target audience that potentially leads to a longer-term relationship with your brand, you need to focus on finding a core group that matches with your brand's core values and purpose.

As a starting point of purpose-driven consumer segmentation, these four key questions are helpful:

- Who are your primary target consumers, and what important values do they hold?
- How and why do your target consumers choose your brand over the other direct competitor brands in your category?
- How do your target consumers tend to share their brand experiences with others, and what attributes of your brand do they mention the most?
- What media channels do your target consumers prefer to use the most often and trust the most for any brand-related interactions?

At the core of these questions, it is critical to acknowledge and address what is most important to your target audience, how your brand can tackle that by talking to the right people at the right time, and how they can talk with them in a believable way. Making sure that your brand has clear answers to the four questions above is one way for you to help your target audience feel genuinely connected to your brand's purpose. Value-centered, purpose-driven communication across channels can help clients and consumers find value in your brand's products and services.

Andrew Farrant is CMO of Global Jet Capital, a financial solution company that specializes in business aircraft. Farrant points out that segmentation can be helpful in taking a diverse global marketplace and organizing it—and your approach to it—based on what you see as your channels into that market and ultimately consumers. In Global Jet Capital's case, that is often high-net-worth individuals (HNWI) or corporations purchasing business aircraft:

> Direct contact with the ultimate decision maker in a business jet transaction can be difficult. By segmenting our access into a series of channels, often made up of key influencers, we can customize our behavior and messaging in ways that enhances our access. If we're dealing with a manufacturer, it's all about how we can help their end customer finance their next purchase. If we're dealing with a lawyer who specializes in business aviation transactions, it's all about how we can help their client while at the same time using our industry experience and expertise to make the lawyer's life easier. Ultimately, we are typically working through a third-party actor prior to the client—and in that context our access is often dictated by our ability to communicate and deliver what's important to them.

Practically speaking, there are also key target audience definitions that you can describe your target audience with based on their demographics, geographics, behavioral characteristics, or psychographics including daily lifestyles and values. Market segmentation is discussed in detail in chapter 4. Defining your target audience in the following ways helps you specify their needs and wants, and draws a concrete picture of what your target audience group may go through before and after your brand encounters:

- Demographic Segmentation: Gender, education, socioeconomic status, occupation, nationality, race/ethnicity, age
- Geographic Segmentation: Geographic boundaries/regions
- Firmographic Segmentation: Industry, company size, company revenue, number of employees

- Psychographic Segmentation: Lifestyle, personality, traits, opinions, interests
- Behavioral Segmentation: Purchasing behaviors, consumption behaviors

Once you have defined consumer segmentations by the above four factors, it is also helpful to narrow down these segments into personas, or individual examples that personify each segment. If consumer segmentation is about a group of people, a consumer persona is a living character of the target consumer group you defined. Here's an example:

1 Consumer segmentation—Busy Commuter Working Mom
    (i) Demographics: Between 25 and 40 years old, female
    (ii) Geographics: Living in a suburban neighborhood
    (iii) Behavioral characteristics: Commutes to cities, shopped at department stores more than four times in the last month
    (iv) Psychographics: Likes to shop online to save time, likely to buy name-brand clothes, heavy social media user, some usage of TV or Radio

2 Consumer persona of Busy Commuter Working Mom
    (i) Name: Jane Doe
    (ii) Age: 34 years old
    (iii) Gender: Female
    (iv) Location: Living in an upper-middle-class suburb
    (v) Job: Accountant commuting to Minneapolis metro area
    (vi) Hobbies: Shopping online usually at Nordstrom, Macy's, etc.
    (vii) Favorite brands: Coach, Michael Kors
    (viii) Media usage: Listening to radio when driving to work, using Instagram, Facebook, and X to share outfit-of-the-day posts, rarely watches TV

When you have outlined what your target audience and persona are like, supported by sufficient consumer or market data, that provides your branding and marketing team with information and data about who exactly you are speaking to and where they are primarily located when it comes to reaching them across media channels.

To go a step further, you may also want to explore what values and purposes your target consumers care the most about. That is when your brand's core values come in as you align your brand's values with clients' and consumers' in the interest of co-creating believability.

Merely implementing a clear-cut, one-way communication model will not work as effectively as it did a century ago. We continue to face a record low level of consumer trust toward media. Communicating in a way that aligns your brand's core values and purpose with that of your target audience takes time but will eventually get attention, attract interest and engagement, and build authentic relationships and loyalty over a longer period of time. And that's what having a meaningful impact through media channels and outreach means.

5.6 Metrics: Reach, Frequency, Gross Rating Points (GRPs), and Impressions

As much as it is important to effectively and strategically plan communication across multiple media channels, it is equally important to critically evaluate and assess what has been done well, and what needs to be improved upon for future campaigns. This is where applicable communication metrics, or Key Performance Indicators (KPIs), come into play. There are four fundamental metrics that media planners employ to measure audience delivery of a campaign: Reach, Frequency, GRPs, and Impressions. By definition, each of the four metrics are described as follows:

- **Reach** refers to the number of unique individuals who saw your content.
- **Frequency** refers to the number of times one individual saw your content on average. In some cases, reach and frequency should be considered together. What if one person gets to see multiple versions of your ad three different times across different channels while others may see it only once? To account for this duplicated number of exposures in media, there is another metric called:
- **Gross Rating Points (GRPs)**, representing the total audience delivery calculated as a relationship between reach and frequency (Reach × Frequency = Gross Rating Points).

- **Impressions** refer to the number of times an ad was delivered, displayed, or shown to the audience.

In a real-world setting where you understand and employ these metrics to assess your campaign results, each of the four metrics is used for gaining different insights. Reach, for example, will tell you the overall width of content distribution, indicating how widely your brand message has been shared with audiences. If your brand wishes to increase brand awareness with a particular campaign, you must aim for achieving more reach. On the other hand, frequency will tell you the depth of your content distribution, suggesting how frequently your audience was exposed to your content, potentially enhancing brand recognition or recall, which is a much more engaging response than simple brand awareness. Frequency is a good metric to boost if your brand desires a targeted, engaging influence while sacrificing the breadth of reaching the entire target audience. At the same time, if you want to reach more viewers, reach is the metric to boost. You might be asking: "Why don't we go for both higher reach and higher frequency?" While achieving both high reach and high frequency is a desirable and ideal outcome, in reality, agency budgets are very tight with their media campaigns, meaning that you may need to weigh the costs and benefits of your decisions to make the most out of what is viable. In that sense, will focusing on either reach or frequency serve your purposes? Gross rating points (GRPs) are considered to be a representation of the balancing act of pursuing reach and frequency: When one metric goes up, the other often goes down. Lastly: Impressions can be helpful to simply test how much traction your content gains in general.

Conclusion: Effective Outreach and Planning

As demonstrated throughout this chapter, measuring the success and failure of your brand outreach can be quantified with relevant metrics, which is very important to reach your campaign goals within a desirable timeframe. At the same time, no one single thing can guarantee the success of your brand's outreach. Even leading industry professionals with years of experience recognize that one single working strategy will never do the job every time. To build a believable brand channels and outreach strategy, there must be an authentic and consistent purpose-driven basis for every decision you make—ranging from multiple channel selections in order to target consumer segmentations to applying appropriate communication metrics so you can test desirable outcomes.

As Chipotle's example illustrates, effective consumer outreach can be achieved through new and innovative ways of thinking, sophisticated planning, and crafting value-driven messages. At the core of Chipotle's marketing strategy is their clearly defined brand value and purpose: Commitment to food with integrity. When planning every detail of their "For Real" campaign, there was one simple goal directing the brand activation: To communicate how Chipotle is devoted to keeping their ingredients fresh—purpose-driven, value-centered communication across channels.

Chipotle did not just put a few slogans out there and call it brand value. Believable brands that perform well in today's fragmented media environment strategically infuse their core values or purpose through every bit of their marketing campaigns through relevant channel selections, promotional content, and authentic targeting of groups of consumers that share their brand values.

Key Terms

Behavioral characteristics	Gross rating points (GRPs)
Brand channels	Impressions
Demographics	Outreach
Frequency	Psychographics
Geographics	Reach

Discussion Questions

1 What are some possible reasons why trust in the media has decreased?
2 Which metric do you think is most effective in measuring the effectiveness of brands' channels and outreach: Reach, Frequency, GRPs, or Impressions? Why?

3 In your own words, describe a consumer persona that you think fits well with Chipotle's "For Real" campaign.

Activity

Brand Storytelling: Choose a brand and a target audience. Create a series of messages for that brand tailored to a specific audience, writing the same message for a variety of communication channels including social media, email, and print. Compare and discuss how the messages adapt to each channel and the pros and cons of each message / platform.

6

Brand Communication

Believable brand communication is rooted in authenticity, consistency, and innovation, and is delivered seamlessly across paid, earned, and owned media channels. Every brand carries the responsibility of crafting a distinctive voice and tone—one that resonates throughout content strategies, editorial calendars, and social communities. Developing brand ambassadors and leveraging the power of user experience (UX) and SEO insights can help brands optimize their customer experience (CX). These are investments that build credibility and foster emotional attachment. In a world shaped by echo chambers and filter bubbles, believable brand communication faces significant challenges. Linear thinking can serve as a creative catalyst to set brands apart. Digital KPIs and analytics measure the effectiveness of brands' communication efforts.

Chapter Outline

6.1 Introduction: What Is Brand Communication?	154
6.2 The Problem: Echo Chambers and Filter Bubbles	155
6.3 The Solution: Believable Brand Communication	156
6.4 Case: Red Bull	165
6.5 Application: Linear Thinking	168
6.6 Metrics: Digital KPIs: Website and Social Media Analytics	170
Key Terms	171
Discussion Questions	172
Activity	172

6.1 Introduction: What Is Brand Communication?

Brand Communication: Connecting a brand with the market through paid, earned, and owned media.

What builds believable brand communication? Animals, nature, humor, and beauty don't hurt, and provocative messaging can be effective as well. It's also important to build communities and talk *with* people, clients, and stakeholders rather than talking *at* them.

Believable brand communication requires boldness and an awareness of your own vulnerabilities. Brand communicators must also fail fast, participate in social listening, and learn from competitors' mistakes. Consistent brand communication across all touchpoints and channels builds a brand's believability. Consistent and strategic communication with regard to products in particular has been proven to have a positive impact on a brand's reputation, which leads to increased brand equity (Dressler & Paunovic, 2021). Consistent messaging involves maintaining a unified brand voice and personality across all communication channels, whether advertising, social media, website content, or customer service interactions. This consistency builds credibility and ensures that a brand's personality, tone of voice, and values shine through in every interaction with the audience, which helps to cultivate a strong emotional connection.

A brand can push out consistent communication across platforms, but the co-creation of brand value means that it's important to socialize your brand across channels and platforms (Avery & Greenwald, 2023). When customers, employees, influencers, and stakeholders share brand stories, it enhances a brand's credibility and helps brands reach new audiences. It's important to identify which key gatekeepers, influencers, promoters, and communities will share brand stories to build this credibility—not all communicators and communities are a good fit to share brand stories, but associating with influencers who are a consistent and authentic fit provide opportunities to extend brand stories into new and innovative platforms.

Breaking through to consumers is the difficult part in an attention economy dominated by echo chambers and filter bubbles. Algorithms tend to keep consumers constrained to their interests and preferences, surrounded by those who like their content—but this can also be an opportunity to think innovatively about how to game the algorithm and break through to preexisting audiences and new consumers.

6.2 The Problem: Echo Chambers and Filter Bubbles

Echo chambers and filter bubbles are threats to brands, but can also be leveraged as opportunities. In some ways, echo chambers and filter bubbles have existed for centuries—humans tend to be drawn toward people and information they agree with and tend to avoid people and information they don't agree with. In the digital age, echo chambers are caused by algorithms, which are coded pathways the internet uses to direct viewers'/users' attention one way or another. Echo chambers are algorithmically bounded, enclosed media spaces that have the potential to both magnify the messages delivered within them and insulate them from rebuttal (Arguedas et al., 2022).

Similarly, filter bubbles are defined as a unique universe of personalized information that appears in individuals' search engine results and social media feeds. Filter bubbles have eroded lots of common ground as commercially driven algorithms are designed to target advertisements and messages based on user preferences, causing isolation and confirmation bias—whether they want it or not, digital and social media users are shown information similar to what they've liked or been drawn to before. Social and digital media users are increasingly shown more and more of things they "like," while things users don't "like" as often are hidden.

At their worst, echo chambers and filter bubbles can cause polarization as they reinforce individuals' views without challenging them or exposing them to differing perspectives and information. It takes intentional effort for individuals to seek out information they may not agree with, which presents a threat to brands in that it may be more difficult to reach new audiences. At the same time, echo chambers and filter bubbles can be seen as an opportunity for brands to publish authentic and consistent content that cultivates loyalty in existing customers by tapping into existing filter bubbles and echo chambers. Innovation can be a way that brands break through to new audiences by testing new messages.

6.3 The Solution: Believable Brand Communication

The first step in authentic, consistent, and innovative brand communication is developing a compelling brand voice and tone. The second step is to create content strategies and editorial calendars. The third step is to cultivate social media communities and create brand ambassadors. After implementing these concrete steps, it's important to quantify successful brand communication by monitoring data and analytics including but not limited to clicks, website visits, engagements, likes, and more. In and through all of these commitments, pursuing and upholding authenticity, consistency, and innovation are key.

Authentic Brand Communication: Developing a Tone of Voice

To develop an authentic brand tone of voice, make sure you gather input from employees and key stakeholders. Interview them, talk with them, and gather information about the brand—think back to the brand purpose chapter where sticky and spreadable brand stories ultimately uphold the building blocks of brand believability: Authenticity, consistency, innovation, quality, emotional attachment, and credibility. Beyond being sticky and spreadable, there are several storytelling frameworks brands can apply to create stories and develop a tone of voice from the ground up, including the "Three R's" of Relevance, Reach, and Resonance (Quesenberry, 2022); Hook, Pain, Solution, Call to Action (Dahl & Young, 2018); Erving Goffman's Dramaturgy (BBC Radio, 2015); and Freytag's Pyramid (Kakroo, 2015).

Beyond these storytelling frameworks, it's important to make sure your brand has clear value propositions and keywords.

Value Propositions: In addition to selecting a framework and creating stories in line with storytelling principles, brands can infuse their value propositions into their messaging and tailor them to resonate with specific market segments. What is your brand's unique selling proposition (USP)—why should consumers do business with you?

Additionally, how does your brand's value proposition set you apart from your competitors?

Consistent Keywords: Choosing consistent keywords is integral to developing believable and credible brand stories. Industry leadership recommends three to five keywords to center all brand communication around. To the best of their ability, every brand should push out and share at least one of these keywords in every web page, headline, subhead, story, blog post, photo caption, and social media post. In addition to going out in brand communication, brand keywords belong in mission statements and value propositions. To verify the effectiveness of keywords selected, brands can quantify the reach and saturation of their keywords using tools including Google Trends, SEMrush, and other industry-leading platforms. For a brand to identify keywords for the first time, SEMrush's keyword tools can be helpful to quantify the volume and keyword difficulty of various terms. Keyword volume is the number of searches occurring across platforms for any given keyword per month. Keyword difficulty is a percentage of how difficult any given keyword is to rank for in new content—100 percent is impossible, and the lower the percentage, the more likely it is for a brand to compete in that space or category. Selecting high volume keywords with a low keyword difficulty is the best approach for brands to take (Handley, 2024).

Beyond these tangible tools for developing a tone of voice, communicating authentically includes transparency and vulnerability about failures and negative brand experiences. For example, in the higher education sphere, student and alumni testimonials are an integral part of brand communication. Jaime Hunt, CMO of Old Dominion University says,

> We revamped the brand at Winston-Salem State while I was there, and part of that was publishing a series of very raw and real interviews with current students and recent alumni—it wasn't always this totally polished positive story. It also had those nuggets of ups and downs in their experience, but at the end, it was fantastic, and it changed their lives. That created a greater sense of believability because we weren't just putting the shiny stuff in front. We were telling the story in a more authentic way. We couldn't just say, "We're great," everybody has a great experience here. We had to be a little bit more raw to authentically acknowledge the breadth of experiences, and social media has a raw, believable, and authentic feel to it.

Creating Consistent Content Strategies and Editorial Calendars

In addition to authenticity, brand communication must be consistent and planned. Planning brand communication takes intentionality. Always remember to make stories as sticky and spreadable as possible in part by utilizing the Made to Stick SUCCESs principles (simple, unexpected, concrete, credible, emotional, stories). Also remember to set SMART Goals as you plan—specific, measurable, attainable, relevant, and time-based.

Building content strategies and editorial calendars involves first auditing the content a brand has on websites and social media. What sort of content is the brand producing and how is it reaching and resonating with audiences? This qualitative or quantitative analysis can be conducted through audits of existing content.

Website Audit

A brand's website is the first and foremost area or place where information can be provided to consumers about products and services. A brand's stakeholders must understand the current content landscape by conducting a website inventory that includes all assets—headlines, subheads, text, photos, and links. What content needs to be updated, rewritten, or deleted? What gaps are there in the content? Is there anything missing from the current website?

Social Media Audit

If your brands exist on social media, conduct an audit of the brand's existing social media accounts, too. Create a spreadsheet or table of existing accounts including key information: social media networks the company is active on, whether or not the social media accounts and profiles are fully optimized, number of followers, posting frequency, average number of engagements, reach, clicks, video views, and brand mentions that each component has, and whether or not it would be optimal to clean house or expand into new platforms accordingly.

Beyond auditing content that exists on websites and social media, is there a positive or negative sentiment about your brand on social media?

What are users saying? What are some pain points being discussed? What platforms are customers using the most? Are mentions going up or down at certain times of the day or year?

Social media KPIs can help quantify the success of a brand's communication and are listed in the metrics section of this chapter.

After identifying what type of communication a brand has going for it, it's important to create content calendars, templates, and plans based on what platforms your brand wants to prioritize. The digital marketing trifecta below is a helpful infographic to help brands identify what types of media are most effective:

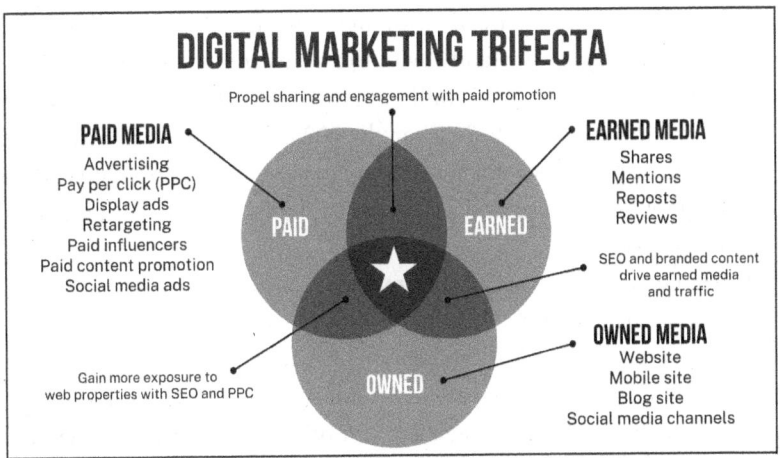

Figure 6.1 The Digital Marketing Trifecta.

Innovative Brand Communication on Social Media Platforms: Cultivating Social Media Communities and Creating Brand Ambassadors

Before sending content out on social media, brands must create innovative content to share. Four key content types to create and share include blog posts, which can be sent out on websites and social media platforms. Podcasts can be produced and published on YouTube and other leading social media sites. Infographics are a compelling way to tell stories with data, and video—prerecorded and live streams both work well—is another way for a brand to be innovative across platforms.

These four types of content—blog posts, videos, infographics, and podcasts—can be published on a brand's website or shared natively on social media sites including YouTube, LinkedIn, Facebook, and more.

Social media's role in the brand communication and consumer purchase journey has expanded as consumers search and make purchases directly through social media platforms themselves, a phenomenon known as social commerce. Social commerce is an affordance of social media apps including Facebook, Instagram, and TikTok, enabling consumers to buy and sell goods or services directly without leaving the app—consumers can make purchases almost instantly, with the swipe of a finger (Zote, 2023). Social commerce was an $89.4 billion market in 2020 and is projected to grow to $604.5 billion by 2027 (Charello, 2024). For these reasons, brand thinking is a more important framework than ever to help brands adapt and change with the rise and influence of digital and social marketing tools and platforms.

In partnership with social commerce, storytelling on social media also plays a crucial role in shaping perceptions and influencing decision making processes inside and outside of a brand. Social media empowers consumers to actively participate in brands and how they are developing (Lund et al., 2020). Ratings, reviews, and other forms of user-generated content can be used to co-create brands, and can also co-destruct them. Negative information and stories shared between stakeholders on social media in particular can harm brand value significantly (Lund et al., 2020). Content generated on social media can also have many different impacts on a brand ranging from creation to destruction—also known as a brand value continuum.

Beyond existing within and being consistent on social media platforms, it's important to consider what to delete, what to keep, and what to add; it's best to go deep, not wide when it comes to social media presence. One to two social media platforms are better than five to six, and you don't need to be on every social media platform all of the time or at all. Find your niche and stick to it—go deep and not wide. Also: Facebook continues to be the most used social media platform by audience size in the world, while YouTube is the second-largest search engine in the world (Statista, 2024c). If your brand isn't on these platforms, consider adopting them, if only for SEO advantages.

Leaning into the affordances of social media is important for all brands, and influencer marketing is a major way for brands to help get the word out about their value propositions and products/services. Matching influencers with your brand takes intentional effort.

Influencer Marketing

Market research shows the influencer marketing realm is growing by hundreds of millions of dollars year over year (Statista, 2024b). In addition to selecting a few social media platforms to be present on, brands can consider leveraging influencers to partner in their brand communication efforts. An influencer is defined as someone who has the power to affect the purchasing decisions of others because of their authority, knowledge, position, or relationship with their audience—influencers also have a following in a distinct niche, with whom they actively engage (Geyser, 2022). The size of an influencer's following depends on the size of his/her topic or niche. There are numerous tiers of influencers, including (Charello, 2024):

- Nano influencers—1 to 1,000 followers. This type of influencer is typically among the average social media user who can use their power to influence their close-knit followers like family and friends.
- Micro-Influencers—10,000 to 50,000 followers. These influencers hold a smaller reach with very high levels of engagements among their followers.
- Mid-Tier Influencers—50,000 to 500,000 followers. These influencers are between a micro and macro influencer, and are looked upon as an industry expert in their niche category.
- Macro Influencers—500,000 to 1,000,000 followers. These influencers have a very large reach and use their influencer status to generate income. Macro influencers often warrant representation from a talent manager.
- Mega Influencers—1,000,000+ followers. These influencers are typically celebrity influencers with a very large following. They often collaborate with brands on a paid-per-post basis. For example: Nespresso's partnership with mega influencer George Clooney is a foundational part of their global marketing efforts (Padula, 2023).

A common misconception is that social media influencers need to have millions of followers. The reality is that reach alone is not a requirement of being an influencer—authenticity and credibility are also important.

Some helpful facts about influencer marketing include:

- Influencer content delivers eleven times higher ROI than traditional forms of digital marketing;
- 54 percent of female consumers purchased a product after seeing it recommended by an influencer;
- 45 percent have followed a brand directly from an influencer's post;
- 70 percent of teenage YouTube subscribers trust influencer opinions over traditional celebrities;
- 86 percent of the most-viewed beauty videos on YouTube were made by influencers, compared to 14 percent by beauty brands (Charello, 2024).

For a brand interested in pursuing influencer marketing, it's important to also consider the downsides. For all of these highlights about influencer marketing, there are also some downsides. It's important to be aware of how the influencer industry can do better in the areas of diversity, inclusion, and representation in particular, in addition to protecting and addressing harassment and discrimination prevalent in the influencer marketing industry (Geyser, 2022).

There are several major factors that inform a successful influencer marketing strategy. Brands must identify the right opportunity; understand brand goals; identify talent; collaborate with talent; help to create content; edit content; publish content; engage and evaluate published content; and generate reports (Christine, 2024).

There are also many options as to how to leverage influencers—not all influencer partnerships have to be paid. Influencers can be unpaid, and can receive products as compensation. Paid influencers often participate in content development and event attendance—livestreams from influencers can be a major way that products and services are promoted online.

In addition to selecting and figuring out how to pay/compensate influencers, think about how you are going to manage the influencers—community management is a key part of influencer marketing. Someone needs to be responsible for the correspondence and feedback with influencers in addition to managing things if communication goes wrong. It's a best practice to be kind, transparent, and respectful with all influencers—you never know, but sometimes, correspondence with influencers could end up online!

When onboarding influencers, it's important to have a campaign brief describing goals and deliverables. A bullet list to keep on hand for influencer campaign briefs might include:

- Details of the brand
- Goals of campaign
- Key messages
- Expected timeline
- Usage rights and exclusivity
- Publication checklist
- Payment details

Don't be too restrictive in a campaign brief, though—it's important to not suck the fun out of influencer content.

Another important part of maximizing and codifying influencer partnerships is by implementing legal contracts. Brands should consult legal counsel or a lawyer to help them build influencer contracts to protect themselves and to ensure clarity in execution of the influencer agreement. Components to include in an influencer contract include but are not limited to:

- Influencer and brand details (address, etc.)
- Timeline of campaign and contract (some campaigns are shorter/longer than the contract—are you going to hire an influencer to execute more than one campaign during their contract period?)
- Rate and payment information
- Usage rights
- Exclusivity
- Deliverables
- Social media / brand guidelines

There is no set payment structure for influencers—sometimes it's best to ask a creator for their rate, other times it's helpful to present a rate based upon your brand's budget. To quantify a success rate for influencer content, help them think through creative directions or content angles and discuss the pros and cons of promoting content as paid media vs. creating organic, owned content. There is a balance for all brands here depending on platform—some platforms reward paid advertisements over organic content, so it's important to monitor the algorithms across platforms consistently. There is power in selecting the best times to post on social media, but there is also power in letting influencers choose those times organically depending on when they see the most engagement with their audiences, communities, and niches. A good practice is to let posts run organically for a week and then perhaps throw money at it if it's not gaining traction to meet your goals and objectives.

Some of the best KPIs for influencers include brand awareness, which can be quantified through impressions and reach; and engagement, which can be measured by adding together likes, comments, shares, and in some cases, clicks; divided by total reach. Screenshots of comments can be a helpful qualitative metric for engagement, too.

Influencers can be found on platforms including but not limited to Onalytica, Followerwonk, Buzzsumo, Traackr, Upfluence, GRIN, and Hootsuite. These platforms can help companies discover and map the influencers that are most influential, listen to what influencers are saying, interact with and develop relationships with influencer targets, and provide detailed reporting and ROI. If a brand doesn't have budget for influencer marketing, employees can conduct qualitative research to review tagged mentions and direct messages (DMs) on social media; can search for influencers by who is using popular hashtags within a specific brand niche; and can leverage Instagram or TikTok Creator Marketplace.

According to Christina Lampert of How Good Ratings, partnering with micro-influencers—or influencers with approximately ten to fifty thousand followers and a high-level of engagement with followers—is an effective way to progress sustainable product adoption while acquiring more consumers (2023). Lampert argues that awareness, education, exposure to alternatives, and behavior shift are an effective formula for product adoption with micro-influencers.

When choosing influencers to partner with, authenticity is key. According to Jessica Padula at Nespresso (2023), it's important for influencers to be fundamentally embedded with the brand: "Acquisition and retention have to be grounded in shared values!" One example of this is how Clif Bar partnered with skier Caroline Gleich, who connected her love of skiing with her love of nature to become an environmentalist (Beaubien & Gleich, 2023).

Advocacy also plays a role in sustainable branding. Cultivating a sense of community on social media is key. Nespresso has a saying: "Coffee is what we make, unity is what we create." Jessica Padula argues that "we're all connected through the coffee we drink." Pursuing this unity internally and externally with social media communities is key (Padula, 2023).

In any influencer marketing strategy, it's important to build lasting relationships. Maintaining influencer relationships makes it easy to identify opportunities to engage over time as trends evolve and develop and also allows influencers to speak to the pros and cons, strengths and weaknesses of your brand strategy.

Cultivating Engaging and Innovative Brand Content

Engaging digital content must contain images—90 percent of the information that comes into our brains is visual. Visuals can improve learning up to 400 percent; X posts with images generate up to 150 percent more retweets; and Facebook images generate approximately 2.3 times more engagements than those without (Charello, 2024).

Ratings and reviews can also improve brand engagement on social media platforms. Google reviews are a major way brands and organizations can rise to the top of search engine result pages (SERPs) (Gifford, 2024).

There are also better times of days to post than others, and better times of the week to post than others. Sprout Social has helpful guides on best times to post during the day/week across all social media platforms (Sprout Social, 2024).

Peter Morville's User Experience Honeycomb (2004) is a framework that brands can use to evaluate whether they are producing engaging content: Is your brand's content useful, desirable, accessible, credible, findable, usable, and valuable?

Beyond evaluating content using the components above, brands should leverage employees, who are the most important asset a brand has, to tell brand stories and to be brand ambassadors. Ultimately, customer experience is a reflection of employee experience, and employees are brand advocates and brand representatives, and without employees there would be no customers (Sullivan, 2023).

6.4 Case: Red Bull

Red Bull is the world's most popular energy drink. Created in 1987 by a collaboration between Thai entrepreneur Chaleo Yoovidhya and Austrian marketing professional Dietrich Mateschitz, Red Bull is a drink inspired by functional, syrupy tonic drinks from East Asia. Mateschitz discovered these drinks in his global travels as a marketing professional, and recruited

Yoovidhya to partner with him to launch a similar beverage for Western markets. Red Bull GmbH was born in 1984.

Yoovidhya and Mateschitz each invested $500,000 in Red Bull GmbH, and took 49 percent of the company's ownership with 2 percent given to Yoovidhya's son Chalerm. Mateschitz began to run the company, and it took him three years to master the carbonated drink formula comprising caffeine, taurine, B group vitamins, sucrose, glucose, and water. The Thai version of Red Bull is not carbonated and is called Krating Daeng, translated as red water buffalo. One of Mateschitz's friends came up with Red Bull's tagline: Red Bull gives you wings. Red Bull's mission statement is to Give Wings to People and Ideas, and another tagline it boasts is to tell stories that are "Beyond the Ordinary." Red Bull publishes a podcast by that same name.

At first, market research firms told Mateschitz that Red Bull as a product would be a disaster. Mateschitz proceeded with the launch anyway, and the product flew off of the shelves. Today, Red Bull makes up 43 percent of the market share of energy drink sales worldwide. Mateschitz created Red Bull as an alternative to coffee and, upon its introduction in 1987, created a completely new product category—energy drinks (Ridder, 2024).

When it was founded in 1987, the energy drink category did not exist globally—Red Bull created it (Dolan, 2013). Over the years, Red Bull the company has expanded to include numerous flavors and iterations in its portfolio.

Today, Red Bull rides the waves of the non-alcoholic (NA) beverage industry it helped create. The NA beverage industry is growing year over year with projections to hit almost $2 trillion by 2027. Energy drinks are a subcategory of the NA beverage industry, with revenue of $193 billion in 2023 with projected growth in coming years (Ridder, 2024).

Red Bull GmbH is the ownership company over Red Bull beverages and media properties. Founded in 1984 and headquartered in Austria, as of 2023, Red Bull GmbH operates in 170 countries worldwide. Red Bull GmbH achieved its highest global revenue to date in 2023.

In addition to the production and sale of energy drinks, Red Bull GmbH owns a variety of media groups including Red Bull Media House. In 2004, Red Bull GmbH entered sports ownership and now owns several football clubs worldwide. In 2007, Red Bull Media House was founded and became an award-winning, globally distributed multi-platform media company that publishes stories direct-to-consumer and also through brand partnerships across TV, mobile, digital, audio, and print mediums and platforms (Red Bull Media House, 2024).

Red Bull Media Group gets the word out about Red Bull on numerous social media channels and platforms, where they've amassed tens of millions of followers. Their content promotes their product, sponsored athletes, and branded events. Beyond social media, Red Bull Media House produces branded content through the following communication outlets:

- *The Red Bulletin*: An international magazine that covers topics like sport, culture, music, nightlife, and fitness. It focuses on people who are passionate about adventure and performance;
- *Servus in Stadt und Land*: Austria's best-selling monthly magazine;
- *Bergwelten*: An outdoor magazine that is popular in the German-speaking outdoor community;
- *Terra Mater*: A nature and knowledge magazine that is published in collaboration with an award-winning TV format;
- *Carpe Diem*: A magazine that provides inspiration for a good life and covers topics like nutrition, exercise, and recreation;
- *BÜHNE*: Austria's largest culture magazine that covers theater, musical theater, opera, and culture;
- SPEEDWEEK.com: A website for German-speaking motorsports enthusiasts; and
- Red Bull TV: An online television channel that focuses on live events and shows related to sports.

Red Bull Media House also produces and licenses live TV broadcasts and feature films. They also offer customized media worlds and content solutions for clients. Red Bull builds its brand through extensive marketing efforts—in 2013, the brand spent 30 percent of its revenue on marketing; for comparison, Coca-Cola typically spends approximately 9 percent (Dolan, 2013). Part of this marketing investment is in influencer strategy—Red Bull has invested in micro-influencers rather than mega-influencers and celebrities. Red Bull tends to invest in athletes and performers, and it sponsors eccentric sporting events including Flying Bach classical break dancing performances at opera houses, surfing competitions in Nova Scotia, skydiving out of a plane across the English Channel, the Red Bull Stratos Jump from outer space in 2012, the downhill ice skating event Crashed Ice, Soap Box Races, Red Bull Flugtag, and kite sailing in Hawaii—to name a few. Red Bull also sponsors extreme sports including Red Bull Rampage, an annual freestyle mountain biking event; Red Bull Cliff Diving; and on a more recreational scale, break-dancing contests, DJ competitions, and jam sessions.

Another innovative effort of note is a branded airplane hangar and restaurant called Hangar-7, located next to the airport in Salzburg, Austria. Hangar-7 houses the Flying Bulls, Red Bull's branded fleet of fifteen show planes that appear at air shows around the world. Red Bull also owns a Formula One racing team for $100 million a year—an investment that only generates approximately $70 million in revenue but is worth it to cultivate new audiences who follow Formula One racing worldwide.

These innovative brand communication ventures contribute to Red Bull's profitability and also brand awareness. In 2023, Red Bull boasted global sales of just over $7 billion. Beyond revenue, Red Bull's brand awareness is 91 percent among energy drink consumers. The United States has the highest energy drink sales of any other country in the world, and Red Bull ranks number one in sales ahead of Monster, Celsius, Bang, and Rockstar (Ridder, 2024).

Red Bull's brand communication revolves around extreme sports, adventure, and a high-energy lifestyle. Red Bull builds their brand authentically, consistently, and innovatively with a fleet of media, events, and influencers committed to these values. In these ways, the brand creates immersive, content-driven experiences that successfully blend entertainment with promotion of its product.

6.5 Application: Linear Thinking

Spotify hosts a "Hack Week" every year that facilitates innovation across teams by inviting Spotify staff members worldwide to gather physically and virtually to ideate and brainstorm together for new Spotify sub-brands, products, and services (Spotify, 2023). In a similar way, gathering employees from a brand for a day or week to brainstorm new brands, products, or services can be beneficial—and linear thinking is one exercise for teams to complete, dream, and innovate together.

Here is a linear thinking exercise:

1. Identify a brand, product or service your brand is promoting.
2. Describe this brand, product, or service in five words.
3. Identify a time of year, place, or other element that relates to the brand.
4. Describe this time of year, place, or other element in five words.
5. Match up one of the words from each column.
6. Draw an insight, pain point, or opportunity from the matched words.
7. Come up with an innovative idea or solution for your brand, product, or service.

For example:

- Product / Service You're Selling: Fried chicken sandwich
- Describe in five words:
    - Crispy
    - Spicy
    - Delicious
    - Messy
    - Greasy
- Time of Year: Summer
- Describe in five words:
    - Hot
    - Road trip
    - Pool party
    - BBQ
    - Beach
- Match up one of the words from each column:
    - Greasy food +
    - Beach
- Draw an insight, pain point, or opportunity from the matched words:
    - "Greasy food is really hard to eat at the beach."
- Come up with an idea:
    - "Create a box to hold the sandwich at the beach. Make the box better with fried chicken sandwich boxes that double as games, and provide wet wipes that include sunscreen or a playlist."

6.6 Metrics: Digital KPIs: Website and Social Media Analytics

Quantifying the believability of a brand can come from seeing the brand messaging multiply. Digital and social media metrics can be tracked over time by measuring follower growth on social media or subscriber growth on email lists; number of posts on social media platforms; likes on posts; comments on posts; shares of posts; total engagements with social media posts; total post reach; and/or clicks. Qualitatively, showcasing exemplars—social media posts that performed exceptionally well across platforms, including metrics of likes, comments, shares, reach, time posted, day posted, and topic—can be helpful.

Key performance indicators are most valuable when linked to goals, objectives, and metrics. For example: If your goal is to increase brand awareness online, objectives may be to grow your Facebook community by 100 percent; increase engagement by 50 percent per post; and to generate 50 percent more traffic on the website. Metrics to support these goals and objectives may be number of new fans or likes; number of likes, comments and shares; number of hashtags and/or brand mentions; and/or 50 percent growth in page views / visitors.

Additional KPIs include but may not be limited to:

GOALS, OBJECTIVES, METRICS

GOAL	OBJECTIVE	METRIC
Increase brand awareness online during Q1	Grow Facebook community by 200%	# of new Facebook followers

Figure 6.2 Goals, Objectives, and Metrics.

- Call to Action (CTA): The part of a social media message that attempts to persuade a person to perform a desired action; an example of a CTA would be "register today!" with a link to a registration form
- Clicks: How many times a person clicked on your post
- Open Rate: Email metric on what percentage of your email list opens any given email
- URL Click: How many times a person clicked on your call-to-action URL
- Engagements: How many times a person interacted with your content; includes likes, comments, shares, and in some cases, clicks
- Engagement rate: Percentage of your audience that has engaged with your content; to calculate engagement rate, divide the number of engagements by the total reach
- Followers: Total number of people who have followed, or liked your social media account and will see your posts show up in their news feeds
- Mentions: Number of times a person or business tags your business in a social media post
- Total reach (also commonly referred to as "impressions"): Number of people who have seen any activity from your social media account, including your posts, posts to your page by other people, ads, and more
- Return on investment (ROI): A measurement of the value from social media marketing, represented with a ratio between net profit and the cost of investment: (Profit / Total Investment) × 100.

Software that can be used to quantify these KPIs include Google Trends, Google Analytics, and analytics dashboards included with social media platforms including Facebook and Instagram.

Key Terms

Content audit
Content calendar
Echo chamber
Editorial strategy
Filter bubble
Goals

Influencer marketing
Key performance indicators (KPIs)
Brand ambassador
Linear thinking

Discussion Questions

1 What role does storytelling play in brand communication?
2 What KPIs are most helpful when it comes to measuring brand communication? Why?
3 How can brands effectively incorporate customer feedback into their communication strategy?

Activity

Influencer Marketing Campaign Brief: Select a brand of your choice and create an influencer marketing campaign brief for an influencer who would be a good fit to market your selected brand's products/services. Be sure to include the following: Details of the brand, campaign goals, key messages, expected timeline, usage rights and exclusivity, publication checklist, and payment details.

Part III

Brand Strategy

What is brand strategy? Building blocks of a believable brand strategy include research, assessment, positioning, and architecture. Believable brand strategy is built with consistency and innovation. Obstacles that impede believable brand strategy include stagnancy, which can be overcome with innovation. Figure storming is an exercise brands can execute to refresh brand strategy in innovative ways. Financial key performance indicators (KPIs) can help quantify the success of brand strategy.

Outline

III.1 Introduction: What Is Brand Strategy?	174
III.2 The Problem: Brand Stagnancy	174
III.3 The Solution: Believable Brand Strategy	175
III.4 Application: Figure Storming	176
III.5 Metrics: Financial KPIs	176
Key Terms	179
Discussion Questions	179
Activity	179

III.1 Introduction: What Is Brand Strategy?

Brand Strategy: Consistent analysis and evaluation of multiple aspects of a brand to identify where the brand is situated in the market.

What is brand strategy? Tactically, brand strategy involves thorough evaluation of multiple aspects of a brand to analyze and identify where the brand is situated in the market. Brand strategy includes research and assessment, positioning, and architecture. These priorities help align and identify internal and external expectations and perceptions.

Brand strategy enables brands to draw from data-driven insights to analyze the past, evaluate the present, and plan for the future. Data-driven insights can identify opportunities and solve problems related to brand performance, consumers' perceptions, unique selling points, and differentiation from competitors in the market. Brand strategy helps brands to align with their purpose, design, and experience to plan for future innovation.

What is one of the main problems or obstacles that can impede building a believable brand strategy? Brand stagnancy. The solution? Innovation.

III.2 The Problem: Brand Stagnancy

Brand stagnancy occurs when a brand's strategy becomes outdated or irrelevant. A brand stops evolving, innovating, and refreshing its identity in the face of evolving customer needs, industry trends, and technological advancements. Brand stagnancy leads to consumer churn as relying on traditional or past successes may not resonate with audiences and consumers. To avoid and overcome brand stagnancy, brands must invest in innovation by conducting regular market research, consistently assess their position in the competitive landscape, keep an eye on competitors, and ensure their brand architecture is optimized for products and services offered. Innovation can help brands to implement new marketing strategies that connect with current audiences and draw new audiences, consumers, and clients in.

At the same time, innovation can be intimidating when not pursued strategically. "Fail fast," "dream big," "adapt or die," and "the sky's the limit" are all mottos that have been utilized by brands and organizations over time. If a brand isn't innovative, it will inevitably succumb to industry pressures and fail to rise above the competition. Brands that innovate too frequently or without an authentic and consistent strategy are destined to fail.

Failures can be beneficial. Beneficial failures are sometimes called intelligent failures. Failure is intrinsic to innovation, and certain types of failure can be harnessed in intelligent ways (Hartley & Knell, 2022).

As mentioned throughout the first two sections of this book, to build a believable brand, a brand must be authentic, consistent, innovative, and must provide quality products and services. Emotional attachment and credibility are norms that drive and sustain believability. And, when it comes to brand strategy, innovation is key to reviving stagnant strategies.

III.3 The Solution: Believable Brand Strategy

Believable brand strategy comprises consistency and innovation. Consistent brand strategy involves clear communication between departments and brands from the top of the brand's organizational chart to the bottom. Innovative brand strategy comprises a symbiosis between the brand's value propositions and execution.

"There is a spectrum when it comes to a brand: does the brand drive the business strategy—or is it the other way around?" James Plesser, CMO of the Carlson School of Management at the University of Minnesota, says. "On the one hand, you might have your core brand value proposition and this drives the business strategy. On the other hand, strategic elements of the business—its product or service offerings, the organizational culture, the hiring practices, etcetera—may drive the brand."

One approach to creating an innovative brand strategy is an exercise called figure storming.

III.4 Application: Figure Storming

Creating and sustaining a believable and innovative brand strategy can be challenging. Figure storming can be a way to help spawn new ideas individually and with teams. Here's how to execute individually or with a team.

Pick three people, not in the room with you, alive or dead. How would they approach your marketing strategy or problem? For example: "How would J. Lo think about this campaign?" Write it down, think it through, be as concise as possible.

- Example: The holidays / marketing a product during the holiday season.
- Choose three figures: Michael Jordan, Lady Gaga, Claude Monet.
- Answer questions you ask from the perspective and positionality of your selected figures as best you can, with an emphasis on whatever element of strategy you're evaluating: Segmenting, targeting, positioning, tone of voice, and/or brand personality, etc.

III.5 Metrics: Financial KPIs

The successes of brands' strategies are often measured by financial key performance indicators (KPIs). The bottom line matters to employees and key stakeholders including shareholders in particular. Some strategic financial KPIs and their calculations include:

- **Revenue**: Revenue is also known as gross income or gross sales. For profit brands and organizations calculate revenue as the money generated from business operations, usually calculated as:
  - (Average sales price) × (the number of units sold)

Operating costs and expenses are subtracted from revenue to determine net income. Another way of understanding revenue is that revenue is the money brought into a company from its business activities over a specified period of time, such as a quarter or year, before subtracting expenses. Nonprofit organizations' profits are calculated by its gross receipts or donations from individuals, foundations, and companies; grants

REVENUE

(AVERAGE SALES PRICE) X (# UNITS SOLD)

Figure III.1 Revenue.

PROFIT MARGINS

NET PROFIT = TOTAL REVENUE − TOTAL EXPENSES

$$\text{PROFIT MARGIN} = \frac{\text{NET PROFIT}}{\text{TOTAL REVENUE}} \times 100$$

Figure III.2 Profit Margins.

from government entities; investments; membership fees; and profits from fundraising events. Government revenue is money received from taxation, fees, fines, intergovernmental grants or transfers, securities sales, mineral or resource rights, as well as any sales made.

- **Profit Margins:** Calculating profit margin is a clear, effective way to understand the profitability of a business. Profit margin is the portion of a company's sales revenue that is kept as a profit after subtracting all costs. For example, if a company reports that it achieved a 35 percent profit margin during the last quarter, it means that it netted thirty-five cents from each dollar of sales generated. Publicly traded companies are required to report their profit margins according to standard reporting time frames set by the market, typically quarterly and/or annually. Privately owned businesses may compute profit

margins at their own desired frequency, for example, weekly or monthly. Businesses that are running on borrowed money may be required to compute and report their profit margins to lenders, such as a bank, monthly. Brands and organizations can calculate profit margin using the calculations in Figure III.2.
- ○ For example, if a company has a total revenue of $200,000 and total expenses of $150,000:
  - Net Profit = $200,000 − $150,000 = $50,000
  - Profit Margin = ($50,000 / $200,000) × 100 = 25 percent
  - So, the profit margin is 25 percent.
- **Return on Investment**: Return on investment (ROI) is a performance measure used to evaluate the efficiency or profitability of an investment or to compare the efficiency of different investments. ROI tries to directly measure the amount of return on a particular investment, relative to the investment's cost. Key factors influencing ROI include the initial investment amount, ongoing maintenance costs, and the cash flow generated by the investment. The formula for return on investment is:
  - ROI = (Net Profit / Cost of Investment) × 100

RETURN ON INVESTMENT (ROI)

$$\text{NET PROFIT} = \text{TOTAL REVENUE} - \text{TOTAL EXPENSES OR COST OF INVESTMENT}$$

$$\text{ROI} = \frac{\text{NET PROFIT}}{\text{COST OF INVESTMENT}} \times 100$$

Figure III.3 Return on Investment.

Conclusion

There are three key components of building a believable brand strategy:

Brand Research and Assessment: Timely, insightful analysis that identifies a brand's competitive positioning while creating solutions that elevate the brand experience.

Brand Positioning: The space a brand owns in the mind of a customer and how a brand differentiates itself from competitors.

Brand Architecture: The relationship between brands within an organization and how they interact.

The following chapters will outline these elements of believable brand strategy in detail.

Key Terms

Assessment
Figure storming
Research
Positioning
Key performance indicators (KPIs)
Return on investment (ROI)
Revenue
Stagnancy
Strategy
Profit margins

Discussion Questions

1 How can brands avoid stagnancy?
2 How can failure(s) help brands succeed?
3 How can brands adapt their strategy to respond to changes in consumer behavior and market trends?

Activity

Strategic Innovation: Choose an existing brand and conduct a brand audit / SWOT analysis. After identifying key information including target audience; key competitors; and strengths, opportunities, weaknesses, and threats, identify two or three areas where this brand could innovate based on current trends, gaps in the market, or consumer pain points. Opportunities for innovation could include: Product innovation (introducing a new feature or product line); Service innovation (new customer experience strategies); Marketing innovation (unique storytelling, new channels, or influencers); and/or brand extension (moving into a new industry or target market).

7

Brand Research and Assessment

We define brand research and assessment as timely, insightful analysis that identifies a brand's competitive positioning while creating solutions that elevate the brand experience. Outpacing the competition in today's marketplace has become harder than ever before. Numerous media choices coupled with the exponential growth of technology have made it even more difficult for brands to establish effective strategies that find and retain clients and consumers. Conducting innovative and high-quality brand research and assessment is more important than ever for brands to execute and plan effective campaigns and communication efforts. Above all else, solving problems for target consumers that benefit their brand experience is the ultimate goal. To do so, we contend that brand value and purpose-driven research and assessment are what enable your brand to rise above the competition. In this chapter, we identify the problems that come with having excessive consumer data to analyze for brand assessment purposes, provide solutions to understand how to determine and utilize valuable data points, and conduct a case study exemplifying a successful case of believable brand research. Then, we suggest several ways to conduct brand research and assessment: with a brand value-driven SWOT analysis in addition to metrics including brand monitoring, social listening, and consumer perception analysis.

Chapter Outline

7.1 Introduction: What Is Brand Research and Assessment? 182
7.2 The Problem: Excessive Consumer Data   184
7.3 The Solution: Believable Brand Research and Assessment   186
7.4 Case: The College of Saint Benedict and Saint John's University   188
7.5 Application: SWOT Analysis   193
7.6 Metrics: Brand Monitoring, Social Listening, and Consumer Perception   196
Key Terms   199
Discussion Questions   199
Activity   199

7.1 Introduction: What Is Brand Research and Assessment?

Brand Research and Assessment: Timely, insightful analysis that identifies a brand's competitive positioning while creating solutions that elevate the brand experience.

It's important to do everything you can to build a believable brand experience for clients and consumers. Part of building believability is ensuring your client and consumers' brand experience stays positive, or at least maintains positivity while going through occasional ups and downs. There are multiple reasons for this. Your consumers will believe in your brand because of the quality of products or services you offer, or because they heard good things about you from influential people in their lives. Whatever their initial reason is for their first purchase or partnership, once they are in, it becomes all about their own firsthand experience with your brand. Regardless of what initially brought them into contact with your brand, their journey begins again with the experience they have with your products, customer support, refund, return, or exchange services, or just about anything that is related to brand use. If their own experience goes downhill for some reason and doesn't bounce back, your brand might not even appear in their initial consideration set the next time they are open to considering options, regardless of how many good things third-party sources say about you.

So how can brand leaders make their brand experience positive for clients and consumers? And how can you know if your clients' and customers' experiences are positive or not? CMOs often pursue partnerships with external research firms to qualify and quantify their brand's positioning in the competitive landscape. If your brand has an in-house group of researchers, that is another resource to examine how current clients and customers think about their brand experiences. Moreover: Technology contributes to assessing the sentiment or status of perceived brand or product experience and has the potential to bring influential and positive change. For example, in 2022, Unilever merged with an organic experimentation startup, "The Uncovery," a brand incubator that uses digital insight capabilities to test and launch new products as fast as thirty-nine days from idea to delivery (Tuchman, 2022).

Assessing and researching your consumers' opinions and sentiments, or feelings, about your brand experience brings several benefits to your brand's growth and future planning. Rather than playing a guessing game about what your consumers are experiencing, conducting market research periodically will ensure the effectiveness of your overall communication efforts, as well as allow monitoring any unprecedented events that might occur.

Chris Brandt, CMO of Chipotle, emphasized the importance of brand research and assessment during our interview. Brandt shared that Chipotle has an analytical culture. Measures tracked include consumer sentiment; digital engagement; and KPIs like clicks, brand trackers, and metrics related to ad spend and a variety of marketing mix models.

"We have different campaigns throughout the year, so we do a marketing mix model every quarter and are constantly measuring ourselves to see where we can optimize and what our return on ad spend is," Brandt says. "I'd do it more frequently if we could get the data faster."

Just like Brandt mentioned, brand research and assessment helps brands examine and optimize the cost efficiency of their ad spend. It also allows them to monitor the ongoing sentiment of their consumers and respond to any negative feedback promptly.

This chapter's next sections explore what factors should be considered to build believable brand research and assessment, provide a case of how a higher education institution carries out research and assessment, and apply this knowledge with a SWOT analysis and metrics including brand monitoring, social listening, and consumer perception.

7.2 The Problem: Excessive Consumer Data

Data is power. Data is what indicates a potential problem, gives evidence-based insights, and guides what action steps are needed. Mike Benson, president and CMO of CBS, emphasized the power of consumer data during our interview.

"You've got to bring data to the table to provide insights that will help [you] make better decisions, solve problems, or drive creativity," Benson said. "Data helps fuel discussion and debate and can lead teams to innovate. Sometimes, the problem you're trying to solve is not necessarily clear, and data can help to bring more clarity to the problem, or the opportunity."

Consumer data is what facilitates consumer-brand engagement and two-way interactions by allowing brands to identify untapped potential for their future communication and marketing efforts. Brands are not only meeting with their consumers at offline/online stores, but also across numerous digital, social, and mobile platforms. Regardless of what market category your brand is in, interactive consumer-brand communication across multiple platforms is considered essential to grab consumers' attention and stay in their minds. Rapid technological advancements including artificial intelligence, the Metaverse, augmented reality, blockchain, and more have opened up additional opportunities for digital consumer-brand engagement. As a result, brands are learning new platforms to find where they meet their target audience, and catching up with this fast-paced media environment to speak to them effectively. Katie Alvino, CMO within the higher education category at the College of Saint Benedict and Saint John's University, a private liberal arts college in Minnesota, shared an example of how her institution adapted to rapidly developing trends of communication to target college-aged students with increased awareness and conversions over time. After launching the brand's first ever integrated marketing communications campaign on digital platforms including Google, Bing, and social media, Alvino saw metrics including conversions increase almost immediately.

"We created a three-year strategic marketing roadmap, and had our growth—our top of funnel brand awareness year over year—grow by 25 percent," Alvino said. "We are starting to see it in down funnel conversions in partnership with admissions. This is classic brand building 101."

Compared to the past when brands launched their campaigns solely on websites and search engines, brands are now investing more dollars on Google, social media, and out-of-home and emerging media platforms including Spotify. Not only are there more media channels to populate with content, but there are also different types of consumer data points for use for targeting purposes, indicating how many impressions they got across social media platforms, how many views they attracted from Spotify ads, etcetera. It all builds into an abundance of consumer data that brand leaders have at their disposal for analysis.

Jaime Hunt, another CMO from the higher education category at Old Dominion University, affirmed the importance of leveraging consumer data. She shared how they use consumer data points to apply historic takeaways and current trends to future media plans:

> We hired a guy from an external agency called Honed. He takes all of our CRM data, all of our Google Analytics, all of this stuff including five years' worth of advertising spend information. And he ran an algorithm that pulled a report that is telling us, "You could spend more in this area to get more applications, but you could spend less in this area to get the same number of applications. This tactic didn't work. This tactic worked so well that you needed to put more money in it. This tactic worked great, but I don't think spending more money will make it work better." That report shapes how we do our media plan. Data is one of our priorities in our marketing maturity model.

As such, this trend of brands' consistent and high-quality efforts to stay connected with target audiences has expanded both the breadth and depth of consumer data that brands can access and analyze accordingly.

What do we mean by the breadth and depth of consumer data? Breadth of consumer data refers to the size of it. For instance, if we could only get a limited number of firsthand data points in the past, now we can easily obtain a wider range of other secondary, or third-party data points, in addition to an extensive range of firsthand data accessible for brands to use an optimal blend of data in targeting consumers. Depth of consumer data represents the extent to which data offers in-depth insights. For example, we could take the breadth of data provided by the number of impressions, likes, and shares on a brand's social media content combined with the depth of the data to analyze and evaluate what kind of social media users are interacting with your content, how they are connected to other users, and how to make use of the algorithms built in the social media platforms to facilitate consumer engagement.

As much as an abundance of consumer data can bring opportunities for brands to gain innovative insights, excessive data may ironically complicate analysis of the data as a whole. It can be challenging to pick and choose which data are most relevant and which analysis makes most sense to interpret the chosen data points. Deliberately selecting and assessing valuable data points is extremely important to build a believable brand experience.

In the next section, we will discuss strategies to determine which data points are most valuable to evaluate, depending on different communication objectives, and how to effectively analyze data.

7.3 The Solution: Believable Brand Research and Assessment

We no longer deal with just survey data to learn what clients and consumers think about your brand. Data is everywhere, and it's important brands learn how to capitalize on the information out there to build believability. Brands can incorporate multiple data points, including what social media channels tend to deliver the most impressions, which topics your consumers tend to talk about when they are a part of conversations about branded content, how positive your earned media comments are, etcetera. Rich consumer data allows advertising and marketing professionals to have a series of objective evidence to back up their strategic plans, and triangulating and combining relevant data points helps brand leaders avoid inherent human biases that blur insights from what consumer data is trying to tell you.

Jon Althoff, CMO of the Dakota County Regional Chamber of Commerce—formerly of General Mills, Nestlé, and Skyline Exhibits—

shares an exact example of how the role of consumer data can enhance branding efforts and help to minimize human biases in making strategic decisions:

> We're all humans and we all bring our own inherent and personal biases into everything that we do. Sometimes that's good, and sometimes it's not very good. We spent the last two and a half years driving an initiative that the research that we just conducted told us came in almost dead last of what our members want. So why were we doing that? We're not doing it anymore. What we're trying to do is make sure that what we are doing is based on the survey, which was fairly randomized by size of business, type of industry, age demography, and such. We feel that we know what they want, and that we can apply the programs and the help that they indicated that they need. So instead of doing things because we like doing it or have a passion for it, if it's not what the consumers want, we're not doing it. Our entire branding strategy is based on data, but I don't want to overplay the data. I mean, it's a SurveyMonkey survey. We haven't hired Booz Allen Hamilton or Accenture to do analysis for us or anything like that. You don't have to be big or have big budgets to make the right marketing calls. But it can certainly help!

Education, data, and experimentation help brands to be better. Coping with excessive consumer data begins with identifying what the most valuable data is for your brand at the moment, depending on the specific purpose of the analysis. While we can't overlook the long-standing value of firsthand consumer satisfaction surveys, it becomes particularly challenging for brands to understand how to approach the extensive range of digital traces of their consumers, and properly analyze the large-scale datasets for their own communication purposes.

To put it broadly, the first thing your brand needs to do is to solidify the "why" element of your data analysis: What are the primary reasons you're looking at consumer data? Once you have your purpose clearly defined, then you can pick and choose the most relevant sources from appropriate media channels where your brand is present. Now that you clearly know the specific purpose of the data analysis as well as where to look to get the relevant data sources, the next step is to find as much useful information as possible from the selected data sources. Likely, the data will be from multiple channels given that a multichannel or omnichannel approach is realistic and essential for today's consumer-brand interaction landscape. Each channel will tell you different "stories." Either the story will be about how receptive your target consumers are toward your promotional messages, how positive or negative the sentiment was, or which content did not reach a desirable number of impressions, engagements, or actions. Finally, taking a closer look at respective channels and analyzing the data with multiple measures will give you the "story." That's what ultimately helps your brand understand what is going on with your current communication strategy or specific tactics you are employing.

Chris Brandt, CMO and chief brand officer of Chipotle, also emphasizes that employing different measures, including a brand tracker for consumer sentiment, a marketing mix model to get the numbers, and digital engagement measures including clicks, are the building blocks of Chipotle's analytical culture.

In addition to what popular social media platforms can offer as a powerhouse of consumer data, Nielsen has published its own Brand Impact measurement to quantify how campaigns influence consumers' mindsets by capturing holistic coverage of digital, traditional, and hybrid media touchpoints (Nielsen, 2025). Acknowledging the need for finding a comprehensive measurement to account for the complicated nature of consumer targeting, Nielsen's Brand Impact measurement exemplifies how consumer data should be assessed to analyze multichannel brand communication—including brands' social and display content across different channels and how formats should be measured and analyzed—as if you are putting together jigsaw puzzles to make sense of the entire picture.

In the next section, we will dive deeper into a real-world example of how the College of Saint Benedict and Saint John's University leverages consumer data to help them tell their story and how they analyze it holistically to understand the dynamics between target audience and the brand.

7.4 Case: The College of Saint Benedict and Saint John's University

This case study is structured around the interview we conducted with Katie Alvino, CMO from the College of Saint Benedict and Saint John's University (CSB and SJU). The private university, located in Collegeville,

Minnesota, brings together St. Ben's, a female college, and St. John's, its male counterpart, into one cohesive unit.

According to her initial remarks on the role of marketing in the higher education category, she insisted that higher ed institutions should be treated as national brands because of their strong need for brand and reputation building to market themselves. This case, therefore, is particularly interesting to showcase the ways higher ed institutions advertise themselves and build brand reputation for their target audience—current and future college students and their parents. With this case study of CSB and SJU, we will uncover how to apply the step-by-step procedure of (a) how to assess the abundant amount of consumer data we went over in the previous section, and (b) how to validate your brand research and assessment results to successfully achieve communication objectives for your brand.

>Step 1: Solidify the purpose, the "why" element, of your data assessment.
>Step 2: Determine the most relevant sources of information across multiple media channels.
>Step 3: Conduct extensive and comprehensive research with selected data sources.
>Step 4: Analyze the data provided by each channel with several measures.
>Step 5: Conclude with the overall story that answers your question from Step 1, backed up by quantitative and qualitative evidence gathered from the data.

As background information for this case study, Katie Alvino was hired to lead CSB and SJU's rebranding initiative to integrate the two institutions into one. Her role was to build an integrated marketing communication team, do brand research, and get the first media campaign going for the two institutions integrated entirely as one.

Step 1: Solidify the purpose, the "why" element, of your data assessment

The purpose of the rebranding campaign for CSB and SJU was to (a) make target audiences aware of St. John's and St. Ben's as one fully integrated institution, and to (b) deliver their brand value as an authentic and believable brand to help students visualize their future dreams come true.

Alvino elaborated in our interview that her institution was looking for a strategic way to let the public know about the integration, as well as to plan for strong marketing communication that would help their target audience genuinely believe in what they were promising to deliver through the quality education they offer to their students:

> Especially with Generation Z and Gen Alpha coming up behind them you have to be authentic to who you actually are because they'll see right through that. That generation will see right through inauthentic brand messaging. So I could put forth all the beautiful advertising in the whole world, it has to be authentic and believable. And how it's believable is if your brand is able to deliver on that brand promise that you're promising in your marketing. So if what I'm selling isn't coming through in the product experience, if you will, in this case it's higher ed, that just falls flat. And then your reputation starts to unravel over a period of time because word gets out. It's like, oh my gosh, they're promising this, but delivering on this. It's not the same.

Step 2: Determine the most relevant sources of information across multiple media channels

The campaign planned to deliver messages through multiple channels in order to show up in every possible place where prospective students and their parents might be, Alvino said.

> Because we are two schools with two missions right now coming together and going to market fully as one, we can't be muddle in the middle. So I think it's a huge undertaking but an exciting one where it's going to be "rebrand." Going to market with our first large comprehensive media campaign this year. We're going to start to show up in places. I am dabbling in maybe some broadcasts. Local, albeit. We're doing OTT (over the top) television ads on Hulu. We're doing stuff on YouTube, digital. All the things we've never done. When I started, the last time we had checked Google Analytics on our website was 2016.

In this case, the most relevant sources of information for assessing their campaign effectiveness will be mainly local television, Hulu, YouTube, and their own brand website. Considering their target audience includes prospective college students who are likely to be heavy social media users, popular social media platforms could also be added to their data sources to examine potential electronic word-of-mouth going around.

Step 3: Conduct extensive and comprehensive research with selected data sources

Based on the information collected from those data sources, the next step is to understand what pieces of information will give you insights to develop a strategic plan for the next. Alvino elaborated more on how CSB and SJU's marketing team conducted extensive research and prepared comprehensive information for providing insights to its board members, particularly by learning more about the importance of public media buying data across all relevant media outlets.

> I think [it's] being prepared, showing the strategy of why we need to invest these dollars, also having competitive data. It's all public media buying data. I was able to do that and showed where we currently were and what we need and why we don't need seventy-five postcards anymore and we don't need to run ads in the *Star Tribune*. What's going to be relevant for this group? What's relevant for Generation Z? It's not about Gen X, which is me, or boomers, it's about the students. And really just continuing to say that over and over. Colleges and universities are brands, and the consumer is the student.

Step 4: Analyze the data from each channel with multiple measures

Data from multiple channels were then analyzed by looking at specific measures such as website traffic, social impressions, usage of visual elements in their content, etcetera. After that, she moved on to record and further investigate their campaign effectiveness by incorporating external sources, such as Sprout Social, Google, and social media platforms. The data points provided by the leading analytic tools/companies have helped her team to quantify the outcome of all their first-attempt tactics, which feeds more insights to strategize a longer-term roadmap for even better return on investment in the future:

We've had more visits to our website, and we've launched first-ever digital campaigns on Google, Bing, and social media. We've had Sprout Social for the first time to run social ads, ran our first out-of-home campaign starting last year, billboards for the first time outside of St. Cloud, doing some Spotify ads—I mean, just everything from soup to nuts that had literally never been done. We created a three-year strategic marketing roadmap—so we've had growth, as our top-of-funnel year over year has grown by 25 percent. In the Minnesota private school report that comes out each month, we are at the top for application activity. Either one or two behind St. Thomas. So it's been good, where we were down last year to being up on top of funnel activity. So it's having an impact. Using more photography, not having just words on paper. Creating that authentic experience and authenticity for the prospective student when they come to our social media pages and things like that.

Step 5: Conclude with the overall story that answers your question from Step 1, backed up by quantitative and qualitative evidence gathered from the data

Lastly, supported by the rich evidence and insightful data analysis, Alvino could finally see what narratives and stories worked best for her institution to deliver the core purpose of the first campaign, which was to communicate their brand value as an authentic and believable institution. She even shared a story about when students mentioned seeing their ad on a billboard, and how it spoke to them about their positive experience with the institution:

> We're seeing that relevancy and that believability in our current bridge campaign, so much so it's been mentioned in college applications from students at the top of the funnel. They're like, "Hey, I saw your billboard on 494. I totally get it. I met with the accounting professor, Boz Bostrom, and we've seen him all over the place." Albeit it's little. Right now little. It's inch by inch, where I'm like, "Wow, you saw our ad. That's awesome. And you're believing, and that's why you're here today." And we're seeing many more students. We had a packed house, I think it was just yesterday, at our first in-person student registration day that we've had in sixteen years. We're starting to build that momentum.

This case study of a higher education institution's rebranding campaign led by CMO Katie Alvino exemplifies that brand-value-driven messaging, constantly backed up by strong evidence and brand assessment, will speak to your target audience. Strong, brand-value-driven messaging across brand platforms builds believability and will bring clients and consumers back to you.

7.5 Application: SWOT Analysis

A SWOT analysis is a major step in building a believable brand research and assessment strategy. Fundamental questions you should ask in any brand research and assessment should include the strengths, weaknesses, opportunities, and threats facing your brand in addition to the market category your brand belongs to and defining characteristics of that category. Evaluating these factors in detail is what we call a SWOT analysis. In order to conduct an insightful SWOT analysis that goes beyond merely listing superficial facts about your brand and the market, you should first be clear and straightforward about how your brand's mission and core values are communicated to your target audience internally and externally. Ultimately, these four factors should align with what your brand aims to achieve in the purpose- and value-driven core communication efforts that speak to your current and prospective consumers.

Brand value-driven strategic planning through SWOT analysis has been undervalued despite its strong potential to guide a brand's way to believability. It's not just about putting a couple of introduction sentences in your "About" page or having an "Our Values" tab on your website. Instead, it is about authentic and consistent value-centered communications delivered to your target audience to draw audiences in because of the values and quality your brand stands for.

Andrew Farrant, CMO of Global Jet Capital, couldn't stress the importance and benefits of research and assessment enough. According to Farrant, the most important way to effectively manage a brand is to revisit consumer feedback regularly:

> We're in the market every two years doing an awareness and perception study, trying to understand how well the marketplace recognizes us and, just as importantly, what they recognize us for. When you start to see the fundamental tenets of your desired reputation or your brand platform

showing up in blind third-party research, that's when you know you're onto something. Having a customer or a key influencer read back your value proposition in the context of what's important to them and as a reflection of your brand is powerful. When that gets shared with the employee base, and they not only see their hand in it but they see that it's working, you're well on your way to brand believability. That feedback loop and the associated learning is critical to healthy brand management.

With a clearly defined brand value proposition, your SWOT analysis will provide a quality roadmap for where your brand is currently situated, and what future directions your brand should follow to achieve its goals.

Generally speaking, SWOT analyses can be categorized into two different factors: internal and external factors. Strengths and weaknesses are considered internal factors, while opportunities and threats are external factors. Internal factors demonstrate what's considered internal to your brand in and of itself, such as brand purpose/value, annual revenue data, profits and losses, R&D, employee staffing, etcetera. External factors, on the other hand, include what's outside of your brand but closely related to brand operation, such as global/local economy shifts, general trends of the market category, market shares, your competitors, etcetera. A template of a SWOT analysis is shown in Figure 7.1.

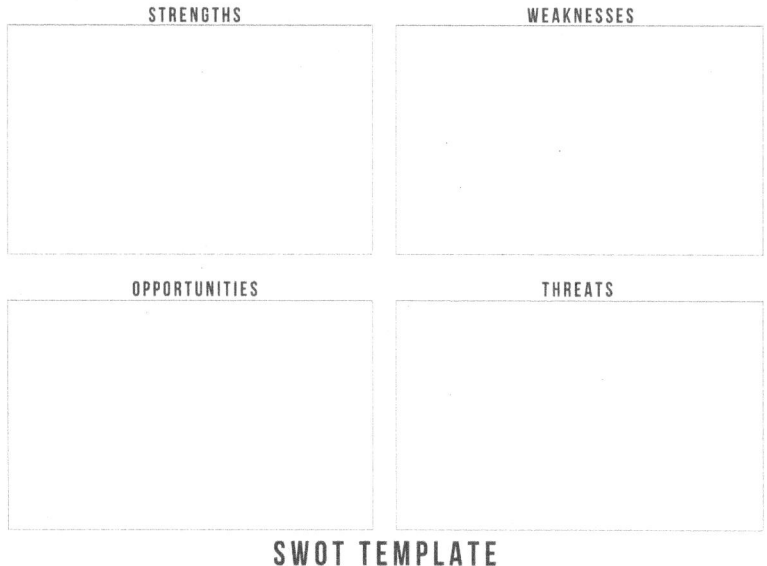

Figure 7.1 SWOT Analysis.

As you seek to fill in each element of this template, consider answering the following questions in each quadrant:

- Strengths: What is our strongest asset? What resources do we possess? What is our competitive advantage? What is our unique selling or value proposition?
- Weaknesses: What gaps do we have on our team? What resources are we lacking? What technology needs to be updated? What processes need to be optimized or improved?
- Opportunities: What needs in the market could we address? What trends are occurring that we could jump into? What could we offer that competitors don't?
- Threat: Are there any laws, policies, or regulations restricting our growth? What are competitors doing that we aren't? Are we dependent on one specific or narrow product or service or supplier? If we lose key stakeholders or brand leaders can we hire talent efficiently?

Now, to conduct a brand value-driven SWOT analysis, you should add value-centric perspectives to every element of your strengths, weaknesses, opportunities, and threats. For instance, let's say your brand's core value is facilitating inclusion and belonging through your products and services. Instead of revising already existing brand mission statements several times, you should turn your angle to really identify how many products and services actually reflect the values of inclusion and belonging, and report such data to locate where you see room for improvement. Instead of you stating that your company offers an inclusive environment for your employees, you should provide the actual number of employee resource groups you have at your brand or organization, or the number and the state of facilities available for employees who are differently abled and have accessibility needs at your workplace. Externally, instead of looking at the generic trends of your market category, you should focus on to what extent and how your direct competitors are implementing similar agendas in their operations, and figure out how your brand can win the competitive advantage in that aspect.

Once your brand is exercising these findings from the brand value-driven SWOT analysis in everyday operations, your consumers will see it. They will find you over the other competitors just because they see the authenticity and believability in your brand behaviors. In the following section, we will discuss how we can practically measure the responses from your consumers as you strategically plan for brand value-driven communications.

7.6 Metrics: Brand Monitoring, Social Listening, and Consumer Perception

To follow up on this chapter's earlier section on excessive consumer data, it's true that there is an incredible breadth and depth of metrics available to brands today, in addition to an abundance of media channels available for your consumers. There are many ways to effectively measure how your brand is communicating to target consumers, ranging from conducting consumer satisfaction surveys to digital and social media audits. Among the numerous options brands have to choose from, this section will focus primarily on digital metrics because of the fast-evolving nature of digital consumer engagement. We will go over three broad categories for understanding useful digital metrics based on relevance: Brand monitoring, social listening, and consumer perception.

Brand Monitoring: Online Visibility and Website Traffic

Brand monitoring is a very broad term. It may include monitoring your brand's presence in online and offline markets, tracking overall brand health related to how your brand is shared across different channels, or analyzing notable trends around your brand in general. In the digital realm, brand monitoring can be implemented by assessing online visibility and following website traffic regularly. Online visibility refers to the extent to which your brand is prominent on the Internet when your consumers are looking for you. You can keep track of online visibility with search engine optimization (SEO) or search engine marketing (SEM), Google Analytics, and a wide variety of third-party brand analytics tools. Website traffic is one of the handy metrics for you to track because it is the common firsthand data that your brand owns. You can track the total number of website visits, specific page views, clicks, or bounce rate—which refers to the number of website visitors leaving right after viewing only one page. There are several other ways to conduct brand monitoring such as distributing brand awareness surveys among consumers, and so on, but again, our focus is on how to conduct it through digital channels.

Social Listening: Likes, Shares, Comments, and More

Almost every brand, regardless of what market category they belong to, is on social media. Therefore, incorporating an effective social listening strategy is necessary to keep up with real-time consumer-brand interactions and to improve the quality of your brand's communication with clients and consumers. Social listening refers to the process of identifying social media content published by clients and consumers and analyzing what messages are communicated about your brand, competitor brands, or any relevant keywords you are interested in exploring. This type of brand assessment is increasingly powerful and significant as the breadth and depth of social media content being published and shared by users continues to grow. Not only are the number of likes, shares, and comments available to brand leaders, but the textual metadata associated with each post can be downloaded by using publicly available application programming interface (API) data accessible on a majority of social media platforms worldwide. Third-party social listening platforms with access to multiple social media platforms' APIs are another way to aggregate social data. Furthermore, higher-level analyses including social network analysis, computerized textual analysis, and topic modeling analysis are also available and widely used to better understand the conversations around your brand. These high-level analyses can also identify brand sentiment and engagement.

Consumer Perception: Sentiment, Keywords, and Themes

In digital spaces, perception can be measured by taking a closer look at what clients and consumers post online—also known as user-generated content (UGC), or earned media. This includes comments on your brand's content, reviews of your brand's products and services, or how consumers repost or share your brand's content. Social listening tools mentioned above can offer rich datasets for you to analyze the textual and visual content associated with your brand. Among others, analyzing the sentiment, or emotional values of digital content, is one way to assess consumer perception by looking at how positive, negative, or neutral users' responses are when discussing or engaging with branded content. Moreover, identifying primary keywords or dominant themes appearing from users' textual content can be useful to examine the topical side of the conversation. Are your consumers likely talking about your brand's products or services, or are they engaging with value-driven content? If so, what proportion of each keyword or theme exists within the analysis? Is the proportion aligning with the values your brand is trying to communicate? Likewise, there are multiple questions you can answer by conducting content analysis through social media data for brand assessment purposes.

Conclusion

Key takeaways from this chapter include (a) why brand research and assessment is essential to build an authentic and purpose-driven brand and develop a believable consumer–brand relationship rooted in shared values, (b) how to determine relevant data points from excessive consumer information, (c) the importance of a value-driven SWOT analysis and how this tool can provide your brand with useful insights to create a strategic roadmap, and (d) multiple ways to measure your brand's current believability through brand monitoring, social listening, and consumer perception research.

This chapter outlined what brand research and assessment means in purpose-driven brand communication, how to conduct a fundamental SWOT analysis centered around your brand's core value, and what digital metrics you should consider, highly dependent on your communication objectives. A case study of the College of Saint Benedict and Saint John's University walked through five actionable steps brands can take to conduct consumer data assessment, and provided a real-world example of how appropriate value-driven brand research and assessment can bring multiple benefits to target prospective consumers of your brand. This strategy can cultivate brand believability in the long term.

In conclusion, consistent, high-quality research and assessment is key. CMO of Global Jet Capital Andrew Farrant highlighted the importance of building a continuous feedback loop to build long-lasting believability with stakeholders and consumers:

"You need a continuous feedback loop to develop believability, and there's a lot of engineering that needs to go into that up front," Farrant said. "Engineering that needs to be like the old checklist for a value proposition. It needs to be relevant, it needs to be authentic, it needs to be credible, it needs to be enduring."

Key Terms

Brand monitoring
Brand perception
Consumer data
Consumer perception
Content sentiment

Feedback loop
Keywords
Social listening
SWOT analysis
Value-driven brand assessment

Discussion Questions

1 What is the most effective way to start brand research?
2 What is value-driven brand assessment, and why does it matter?
3 How can brands integrate consumer perception into their research and assessment?

Activity

SWOT Analysis: Create a SWOT analysis based on a brand of your choosing.

8

Brand Positioning

We define brand positioning as the space a brand owns in the mind of a customer and how a brand differentiates itself from its competitors. In this chapter, we cover how to position your brand among competitors in a way that gives you a competitive advantage above other brands in your category. We first identify the problem of ad and brand bombardment across media. Standing out from the competition is challenging, but not impossible, and we present several strategic ways to position your brand in a believable way. Creating a brand positioning map is one way to help brands differentiate from competitors. Market research and digital/social trend analysis are two metrics that can enhance your brand's positioning. Both metrics are introduced with several other important concepts relevant to building a believable brand positioning strategy.

Chapter Outline

8.1 Introduction: What Is Brand Positioning?	202
8.2 The Problem: Ad and Brand Bombardment	204
8.3 The Solution: Believable Brand Positioning	206
8.4 Case: Thrive Pet Healthcare	208
8.5 Application: Position Mapping	211
8.6 Metrics: Media Mix, Share of Voice, and Digital Presence Analysis	215
Key Terms	220
Discussion Questions	220
Activity	220

8.1 Introduction: What Is Brand Positioning?

Brand Positioning: The space a brand owns in the mind of a customer and how a brand differentiates itself from competitors.

This book has discussed how market saturation and today's fragmented media environment have made it challenging for brands to stand out from the competition. Beyond capturing audiences' attention, it's important to cultivate engagements and loyalty among target consumers. One way to tackle this large-scale problem is to strategically position your brand in the marketplace. Brand positioning is a marketing strategy necessary to establish your brand's place among direct competitors and to take up space in the minds of your target customers. The reason brand positioning is so important is because it helps brands recognize their strengths and weaknesses while placing themselves accurately within brand categories.

Brand strategist Andy Cunningham's "Get to Aha!" framework (2017) presents three types of brand archetypes that are helpful to consider as you evaluate and place your brand within the competitive landscape:

- Mothers: Customer-oriented companies are "mothers," and they win by building the best relationships with customers. Examples of mother companies are: Amazon, Adobe, American Express, and Accenture.
- Mechanics: Product-oriented companies are "mechanics," and they win by building the best products or services. Examples of product-oriented companies are Microsoft, Oracle, Apple, and Meta.
- Missionaries: Concept-oriented companies are "missionaries," and they win with creative vision, hoping to change human behavior on a fundamental level. Examples of missionaries are Tesla, Starbucks, FedEx, and Google (Cunningham, 2017).

Categorizing your brand within one of Cunningham's (2017) three categories—mother, mechanic, or missionary—can help to not only identify your brand's core strength and value, but to also identify your major competitors, which is helpful as you work to define your brand's unique value or selling proposition(s).

In addition to Cunningham's "Aha!" framework, thought leader Thomas Kolster argues that there is an "intention-action" gap in brand communication. He insists that every marketer should ask four purpose-centered questions to properly deliver on what their clients and consumers expect them to do. His four questions are:

1. What is it you do (i.e., the product or service you deliver, like running shoes)?
2. How are you unique in delivering your product or service (i.e., how your offering stands out, such as convenience)?
3. Who can you help people become (i.e., the personal transformation you enable, e.g., a mindful runner)?
4. When do you enable this change (i.e., a specific time of day, a situation, a life phase, or a state of mind)?

One of Kolster's main arguments is: Effective brands don't look at consumers, they look at citizens (2023). Take a moment and think about what it means to be an effective brand, and what it means to communicate purpose to your consumers in an authentic way. Once you connect those two dots, you've begun to build a believable brand positioning strategy.

Authenticity plays a significant role in developing and maintaining a believable brand in the mind of your consumers. Likewise, positioning your brand among its direct competitors should be an authentic process. We believe and suggest that purpose-driven brand positioning is how your brand can stand out from competitors. Therefore, positioning your brand centered on brand purpose and core values is a major way to acquire perceived authenticity in the minds of your consumers.

In this chapter, we will first discuss the current problem we face in positioning your brand effectively among a substantially crowded market. Then, we will identify solutions to help your brand stay in the minds of your target consumers. A successful brand case study, Thrive Pet Healthcare, shows how purpose-driven brand positioning works effectively and practically in the industry. Lastly, specific guidelines for believable brand positioning are provided for you to follow and practice. Along with that, the importance of conducting relevant market research and digital/social trend analysis is discussed.

8.2 The Problem: Ad and Brand Bombardment

Consumers are tired of being bombarded by advertisements. Ad bombardment—defined as excessive volume, repetition, obtrusiveness (when advertising interrupts what you're doing), and irrelevance—is the number-one negative driver—among other factors including data privacy and suspicious and unhealthy advertising—that prevents brands from gaining consumer trust toward advertising (Advertising Association, 2023).

Ad Age also pointed out a similar problem among U.S. Generation Z (Gen Z) consumers, stating that Gen Z consumers should not be considered "mindless scrollers" who only temporarily respond to short-form content and do not care what advertisements or branded content they see. Gen Z consumers prioritize word-of-mouth recommendations and TikTok trends or recommendations more than anything else when considering what brands to follow and invest in (Dunlavy, 2024).

Understanding the particular characteristics of digital native, and relatively younger groups of consumers, experts suggest that brands should avoid overwhelmingly loud and bright branded content in order to overcome the barriers of ad bombardment and get meaningful attention from young consumers in particular (Dunlavy, 2024). Considering the incredibly crowded state of advertising across media channels today, ad and brand bombardment has been an ever-challenging problem to tackle across generations (Sutcliffe, 2023). Brand trust and attitudes toward advertising comprise an individual's overall worldview, the core values they uphold in their daily lives, sustainability, privacy and consumption, and so on, covering a wider range of aspects in one's beliefs.

As multiple sources point out, simple and straightforward messaging will be key to beat bombardment and develop consumer trust over time. Believable positioning that connects with your brand's core values and purpose will stand out to clients and consumers. Mike Benson, president and CMO of CBS, recognizes the importance of brands rooted in a clear purpose: "Brands that stand for something become a beacon in a sea of choice, because if you don't stand for something, people will have a hard time understanding your value."

A great example that illustrates the power of purpose-driven brand positioning showcasing a brand "stands for something" is a plant-based food company, *Impossible*. The brand value and purpose they communicate to their audience is fairly straightforward: "Maker of high-quality, delicious, nutrient-dense meat from plants that's better for the planet." In March 2024, the brand announced its rebranding with a stronger focus on their sustainability mission by offering a fun way of dining experience serving a fully plant-based menu to their customers. Not only selling packaged plant-based meats at grocery stores, the brand showed its commitment to sustainability by announcing its new investment on the entire dining experience that minimizes environmental intervention but delivers similar high-quality "meats" that anyone can enjoy.

This revamp and strengthening of the brand positioning centered on their brand purpose has solidified the brand identity as both an environmentally friendly and nutritionally competitive player in the plant-based meat category. At the rebrand launch event, the president and CEO of the brand Impossible, Peter McGuinness, said: "We're the fastest-growing plant-based company in America, so it's a good time to evolve from a position of strength. We want to be inclusive to anyone who enjoys great food. It doesn't matter if you're a vegan, a vegetarian, an animal meat-lover, or somewhere in between" (Faithfull, 2024).

Another example of notable brand positioning from quite a different market category is Ferrari, a luxury automotive company. According to Kantar's (2024) extensive analysis on Ferrari's brand positioning, the brand Ferrari represents a powerful and unique positioning with its emotive personality. In its report, Kantar approaches "being different" as a fundamental driver for brand growth. In that aspect, Ferrari had a unique differentiation strategy by integrating the legacy of founder Enzo Ferrari's motorsport driver personality traits into the brand culture and image. Ferrari's long-lasting brand culture immersed with its bold uniqueness has built into the brand hero-archetype associations, including advanced engineering, Italian design flair, motorsport prowess, and exclusive luxury, thus contributing to believable positioning based in an emotive connection with its consumers (Horsley & George, 2024).

As Impossible and Ferrari demonstrate, believable brand positioning stems from your brand's purpose and values, and determines what core message your brand aims to deliver to your target consumers. Believable brand positioning lays a stronger foundation for brand growth and brand recall—the tendency of clients and consumers to remember your brand before others. If your brand has purpose-driven and value-centered positioning, your consumers can more easily co-create believability, loyalty, and trust that will last longer than the empty and temporary interactions that exist when consumers are bombarded by irrelevant and excessive ads and messages.

In this chapter's next section, we will cover ways brands can stay committed to consumers with authentic and consistent value-centered positioning that enables them to consistently connect over a long period of time.

8.3 The Solution: Believable Brand Positioning

What sticks in your consumer's mind for a longer period of time will take your brand the extra mile. Your brand's values and purpose are the significant drivers for achieving believable brand experience and subsequent consumer decision-making in the long-term. As one example, Global Jet Capital CMO Andrew Farrant shared interesting takeaways from their brand research and assessment in the past, pointing out that long-lasting brand perception and recall can overcome some of the disadvantageous aspects in your brand compared to the competitors excelling in a given category:

> Years ago, we conducted customer experience research at Bombardier focused on Bombardier, Cessna, Dassault, and Gulfstream customers. One of the most interesting findings related to the connection between customers' experience and the power of a brand. It turned out that, based on a series of functional factors, Dassault customers were having the best experience with their aircraft. But when it came to recommendations the brand Gulfstream, not Dassault, was at the top of the list. Clearly, Gulfstream—that American blue chip, bulletproof brand—was overcoming product issues.

What this story implies is that a strong brand perception cultivated with value-driven communication to target consumers over time can outweigh a brand's disadvantages. It is not to say that you can or should mask your brand's disadvantages—on the contrary, our research shows that being authentic about flaws and being consistent in pursuing quality fixes builds credibility and believability. Most importantly, brand perception is a key part of consumers' decision-making process, ranging from initial consideration to active evaluation, purchase, word-of-mouth intention, repurchase intention, and brand loyalty.

As discussed in Chapter 5: Brand Channels and Outreach, consumers go through a multistage circular journey when considering and purchasing from any given brand. While keeping each stage of the consumer decision journey in mind, this chapter pins our focus particularly on how to position your brand effectively to resonate in the minds of your consumers.

In order to identify what matters most to consumers when it comes to considering multiple brands positioned in the same market category, we conducted a series of focus groups among Generation Z consumers, and asked about their experiences and opinions. Quite a few consumers mentioned that they tend to support brands with shared core values they also hold, and often end up supporting those brands over other options. One consumer who agreed with the importance and significant lasting impact of brands' core values said:

> I definitely think of values that I support, but then also values that are important to me and my identities as well. For instance, just recently, I had a good connotation of the brand Bud Light because of their recent pairing with trans influencer, Dylan, as a queer person. Then, I have negative connotations with brands like Hobby Lobby and Chick-fil-A, which in the past and maybe present, I don't know, have been associated with their negative values toward the queer community. The fact that I don't know their current practices really shows that these things do have a long-lasting impact on people's conceptions of the brand and my conception of the brand, that it's hard for them to shake that. But I still don't go to Chick-fil-A and don't feel comfortable supporting them.

What's notable about this opinion is that once a negative brand-value association is established, it is hard to revoke or change it in consumers' minds due to its influence on whether or not they will still pay attention to any communication or updates from the brand in the long run.

On the other hand, when a positive brand-value association is developed with consumers, it could also facilitate active consumer loyalty since your consumers are assured that what's important to them aligns well with your brand's mission and values. Again, we need to understand that consumption nowadays is no longer just purchasing a product or service, but it reflects a much wider range of values and propositions an individual upholds in their life. Therefore, strong value-driven brand positioning could be a significant solution to help your brand stick in target consumers' minds in a positive way.

Brands communicating their brand values and purpose are important, and other important and related observations caught our attention, too. In addition to communicating about values and purpose, it's important brands communicate these things authentically. Are brands really serious about their commitments and do they follow through with actions? If brands don't follow through with their commitments and communication, their purpose statements are inauthentic. Consistency in following through with communicated commitments is directly linked to developing or deteriorating brand trust. As one Gen Z focus group participant said:

> I would like a brand to say their values or something like that, and then trust that me or reporters or someone will be able to parse the truth as well. I don't know about you guys, but there have been lots of times where I've seen a company say their values and I think I can tell when a company is being genuine versus not. There's something where sometimes it is really hard to fake that. So if they are faking that, then I'm going to see through it or someone somewhere is going to do their research. I think that sometimes putting your values forward can open up that conversation because it's like there might be a brand that you don't even think about associated with the environment or with social issues. But if they put out a statement, then that sort of cues in the public thinking, "Well, are they actually walking the walk when they're talking the talk?"

In our post-truth era of low brand trust, value-driven brand positioning is important to garner long-lasting brand trust and believability. Believable brand positioning must also be carefully thought through and strategically planned with consistent actions that prove authentic commitments to brand values and purpose.

8.4 Case: Thrive Pet Healthcare

In this section, we aim to understand how industry professionals approach brand positioning with the specific case of Thrive Pet Healthcare, a direct-to-consumer business in the animal care category. Thrive Pet Healthcare is a nationwide network of veterinary clinics, including emergency vets, urgent care vets, primary care vets, and specialty vets. Up to this point in her career, CMO Amy L. Halford has spent time in consumer branding and marketing at Best Buy, General Mills, and Self-Esteem Brands—the parent company of Anytime Fitness.

At Thrive Pet Healthcare, Halford's role has been to find and build out the company's marketing capabilities to operate on a much larger scale, moving from an exponential growth stage to running at scale. More specifically, Halford was tasked with building a unifying brand centered around a shared brand purpose for all of the pet hospitals affiliated with the company, positioning Thrive Pet Healthcare as a unique and trusted community of pet care professionals with a clear brand purpose.

Halford gave a comprehensive explanation of Thrive Pet Healthcare's positioning in our interview by describing what the brand believes in, what's important to their consumers, and, therefore, what their brand stands for from consumers' point of view:

> We exist to nurture people and pets through meaningful relationships and extraordinary veterinary care. When we were working on the brand promise, we were looking at the role that pets have in our lives and we were looking at this notion of an epidemic of loneliness and the United States specifically, that people more than ever are reporting that they have anxiety, more than ever are reporting that they're depressed and more than ever reporting that they feel isolated. Our brand and the reason that we exist is that we truly understand that and honor it, and we think about the relationship that we have with clients. That's one of the things when we look at clients, what's important to you in staying with a veterinarian? Number one every single time I've measured it is, "genuinely cares about my pet and me." That's about, "Do you listen to me? Are you partnering with me?" That's not about how much the service costs, it's not about how nice the facility is, it's not about any of those things, it's about, "Do you show that you care? Are you showing that you care and you're providing great care?" Our brand exists to deliver that. We exist to deliver that because we think it's important to humanity. We do that across different modes of medical care.

Three things struck us from her answers: (1) Thrive's brand purpose and core values are very clearly defined; (2) Thrive's values are based in brand and market research and clearly align with what their target consumers' values and purpose are; and (3) Thrive delivers their purpose and values in and through their communication and services they provide. These three factors exemplify what believable brand positioning should look like, and what desirable brand actions should come after you've authentically positioned your brand in a strategic way in order to sustain positive relationships with your consumers.

Moreover, Halford did not just touch on the abstract level of what brand value Thrive strives to achieve. Instead, Halford genuinely showed how a brand that actually cares about their core value and puts it into practice in their everyday operations would approach purpose-driven brand positioning.

Halford went on to describe Thrive's brand experience in detail to show how Thrive Pet Healthcare delivers on their promise to "nurture people and pets through meaningful relationships and extraordinary veterinary care:"

> A lot of times, people are very familiar with their general practitioner, and that's who they would go to for everything, but there are lots of different providers and there are lots of different specialties, so knowing how much people care about their pets and that they expect the same level of care for them as they do in human health, it's how do we bring this spectrum of care to people so that they see what they have available to them and their pet can get that level of care. The ones who do it really, really well are dedicated to the customer experience. Obviously, they're going to show that they love the pet, but one of the things that they do is that they're very in tune with the client, as well. They're thinking about things that are so subtle, but they make a difference. If you've taken your dog to the vet and the vet is examining the pet, the vet may just examine and then say, "Everything looks good," or the vet might talk to you while they're doing it and say, "Okay, I'm going to check Fluffy's ears right now. Oh look, they're all pink and healthy. Looks so good. Okay, now I'm going to feel right here. Yep, feels good, feels good. I'm going to check back here. Oh, those hips are sturdy." They explain to you what is happening. That's off the charts. People are like, "Oh, okay." Little, little things like acknowledging the pet when you come in, talking through the process. It really comes down to customer service and connection. That's why, even in our purpose, talking about building relationships, those veterinarians and the staff that look to connect with the client as much as they love the pet as well, they're the ones who do this really well. Then, what we'll see is really high ratings and reviews. What they'll say in the ratings and reviews is, "I felt cared for. They clearly cared about my fur baby as much as I do." That's the feedback that we get. It's all around care and listening.

As much as Halford emphasized the importance of purpose-driven positioning, she also consistently pointed out that every ounce of Thrive's attention prioritizes the customer experience—before, during, and after every brand encounter. What matters at the end of the day is whether or not your brand actually delivered what's been promised to consumers. You want your customers to come in with positive expectations, stay with you, and leave with positive experiences so that they come back again to continue their next experience in a positive way—and share those positive experiences with others. Likewise, Halford put it this way:

> We're spending an awful lot of time thinking about what the client is going through, where their mind is in the specific moments and thinking about what we can do to add more value in that experience. We even think about pre-appointment and post-appointment, what are the touchpoints that we have that are going to really reiterate or remind people this is the experience that you are having or you're about to have, to show that care and support at every single touchpoint.

This case study of Thrive Pet Healthcare illustrates and emphasizes the importance of brand purpose in positioning strategy and practicing it in everyday operations. The application section of this chapter will cover specific tools to help implement brand positioning effectively.

8.5 Application: Position Mapping

A position map is a visual representation of brands plotted out based on their defining characteristics or attributes. Position mapping is similar to perception mapping, an approach where brands are mapped out in a chart based on the perspectives or perceptions of their target consumers. Tactically, a position map is a two-axis scatter chart, where each axis represents a relevant brand attribute.

Position mapping is a way to differentiate a brand from its competition based on brand attributes that help identify gaps and opportunities for the unique positioning of a brand. Brands need clear and unique positioning strategies to stand out from their competition and to capture and retain the attention of audiences. Creating a position map can serve as a simple but intuitive way to differentiate your own brand from other competitors in the same market category. Creating a position map of your brand category provides insights for your brand for the following reasons: First,

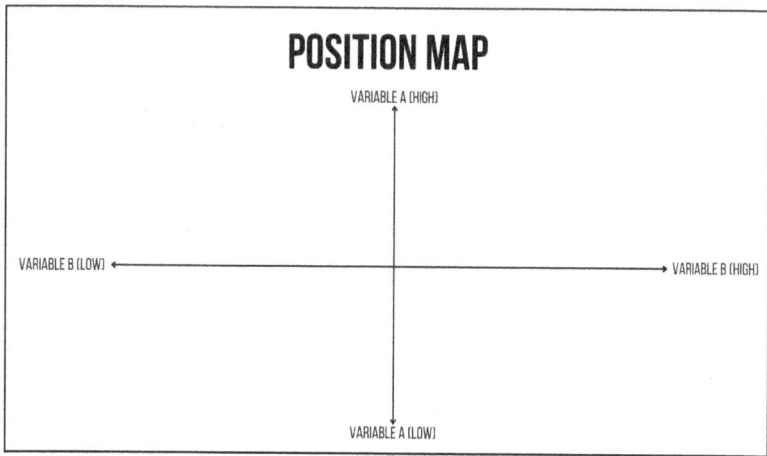

Figure 8.1 Position Map.

it helps you understand where your brand is situated in the market based on important attributes your target consumers value. Second, it identifies advantages and disadvantages your brand faces in comparison to direct competitors, and visualizes this information. Third, a position map helps you to define and clarify objectives and goals for your brand's strategies to help maintain or create your place within your brand category.

Now that you know the importance of a position map, here's how to create one:

1. Attributes: Determine two measurable attributes to focus on, with an emphasis on attributes your consumers find most important in your market category. Examples include price, quality, and other attributes pertaining to your brand category.
2. Competitors: List four or five major direct competitors in your brand category.
3. Rankings: Rank each competitor along with your brand based on the two attributes you identified in Step 1.
4. Create a Position Map of Step 1: Create a blank position map including an X-axis and Y-axis representing the two brand attributes you've identified, respectively.
5. Create a Position Map of Step 2: Place the brands you've identified on a scatterplot aligned with the X and Y axes you've created based on the rankings identified in Step 3.

To better understand each step of this process, here's an example of what a position map for automotive companies might look like:

1 Attributes: Two key measurable attributes for automotive brands are price and length of warranty.
2 Competitors: Four direct competitors in the automotive category for Toyota include: Nissan, Honda, Mazda, and Hyundai.
3 Rankings: Rankings of average price and length of warranty for each of the selected direct competitors and Toyota are tabulated below (Note: All the numbers and data are randomly created for demonstration purposes, and do not reflect the actual data from the brands):

Brand	Average Price	Length of Warranty
Toyota	$36,000	3 years
Nissan	$25,000	3 years
Honda	$38,000	3 years
Mazda	$28,000	3 years
Hyundai	$37,000	5 years

4 Create a Position Map of Step 1: Create a blank position map including an X-axis (average price) and Y-axis (length of warranty):

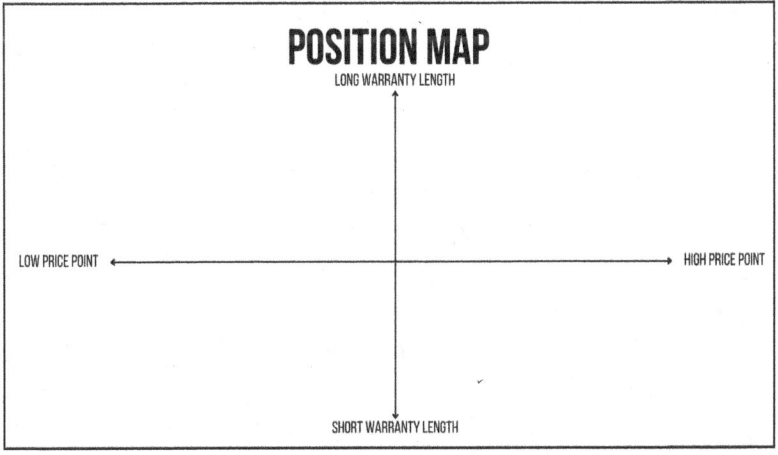

Figure 8.2 Position Map for Automotive Companies.

5   Create a Position Map of Step 2: Place all five brands—including Toyota, Nissan, Honda, Mazda, and Hyundai—on the map to finalize the positioning of Toyota in the automotive market category:

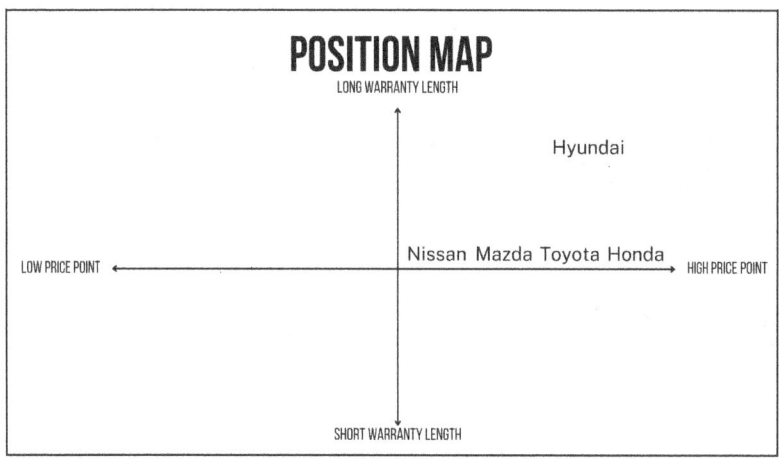

Figure 8.3 Position Map with Brands.

A position map shows where you are currently situated in terms of whichever two attributes you decide to evaluate. In the example above, you can see how each of these brands compares to its competitors with regard to average price and length of warranty. A position map is a visual representation of how your brand compares to its competitors and can also represent how consumers perceive your brand compared to its direct competitors.

Authentic and consistently communicated brand purpose is beneficial in every aspect of a brand's marketing efforts. Similarly, when you determine the attributes for a position map, you should not only consider the superficial facts about your brand and competitors, but more so it should include what attributes may be closely associated with your brand's purpose and values. Beyond descriptive attributes like price and length of warranty, purpose-driven position mapping can involve attributes like the proportion of employees hired from underrepresented groups or the dollar amount invested in sustainability.

In the long run, position mapping should be done frequently to best understand the shifting and changing nature of a brand's category as it is impacted by structural and market changes. Position mapping can help you identify new competitors and how your current competitors respond to changes in the market.

8.6 Metrics: Media Mix, Share of Voice, and Digital Presence Analysis

Conducting data-driven market research supported by consumer data across multiple platforms can strengthen your brand positioning. Without credible evidence supporting your analysis, the validity and reliability of the findings that have led to any suggestions you make in a brand positioning strategy will be lost.

Here are three fundamental analyses you can implement to leverage useful and relevant data that can be trusted for this purpose: Media mix and share-of-voice (SOV) analysis, digital presence/trend analysis, and social trend analysis. Though these three options are not mutually exclusive, the objectives of each analysis are to understand different aspects of positioning your brand uniquely in the market category.

Media Mix and Share of Voice (SOV) Analysis

Media mix and share-of-voice (SOV) analyses allow you to determine what percentage of media expenditure your brand owns across channels and categories. Media mix and share of voice compare your media presence with that of your direct competitors. Media mix analysis starts from analyzing your advertising spend as well as your direct competitors' advertising spend to expose the mix of paid branded content across media channels. How much money in total has your brand invested to get paid content out to your target audiences? Among the total investment across all media channels, how much money has been spent in each channel? What channel does your brand invest in most, and which one does your brand invest in least? After answering these questions for your brand, ask the same set of questions for each of your direct competitors. You might see some similarities and differences compared to your direct competitors in the same market category. By analyzing this data, you can adjust media spend according to what opportunities there might be for increased spend in certain areas and areas where you may be able to pull back depending on your position in the competitive landscape.

There are two types of pie charts you can create to provide useful insights: A media mix chart, and a share-of-voice chart. Both are illustrated below. A media mix chart visualizes advertising spend breakdowns by each media channel for a particular period of time, usually for a full year. For example: If all of your advertising expenditures totaled $110,000 last year, and your brand spent $34,000 on online advertising (for example, search engine marketing or SEM), $56,000 on social media (for example, influencer sponsorships), and $20,000 on out-of-home advertising (for example, billboards in a major metro area), your media mix chart should look like Figure 8.4:

MEDIA MIX

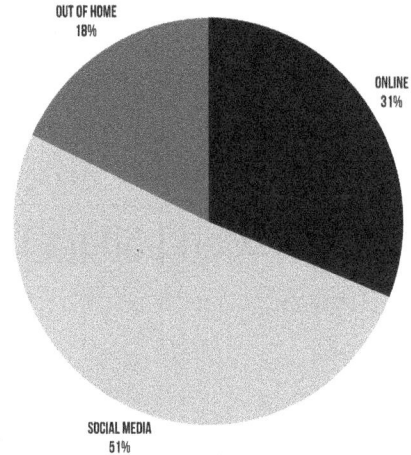

Figure 8.4 Media Mix.

On the other hand, a share-of-voice (SOV) chart can provide the relative amount you spend on advertising in total compared to your direct competitors. For example: If you conduct extensive research on your direct competitors' advertising spending in a particular year, you might find your competitors' total advertising spending data as follows: Brand

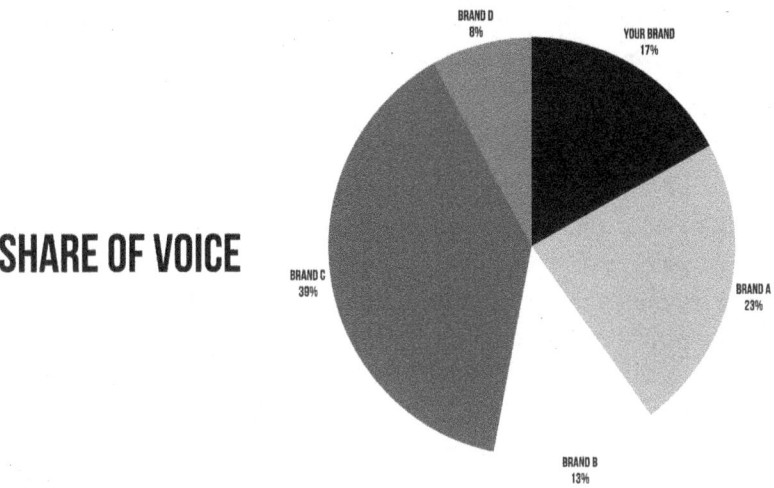

Figure 8.5 Share of Voice.

A ($150,000), Brand B ($80,000), Brand C ($250,000), and Brand D ($50,000). With this data, coupled with your own total advertising spend for last year, the SOV chart visualizing paid presence of your market category should look like Figure 8.5.

As demonstrated, analyzing media mix and SOV together provides complementary insights into how your brand is currently positioned in its brand category along with its direct competitors, particularly regarding its paid media presence. This information should inform any future media planning done for your brand to tackle comparable advantages—or disadvantages—and opportunities in a strategic way.

Digital Presence Analysis

All brands should incorporate some sort of digital media analysis into their communication plans. Examining the digital presence of your brand is an essential way for brands to develop and solidify your brand's position in the market, and can help brands identify additional factors to be considered and leveraged for future campaigns. There are four primary areas for brands to investigate in their digital presence analysis: Social media analysis, website analytics, online reviews and ratings, and user-generated content (UGC).

Social media analysis involves monitoring and managing your brand's official, or owned, social media accounts. Key questions to be answered include:

- Social Media Audit: Where is your brand active on social media? What handles do they own on what platforms? Are there any particular platforms where your brand's account is not as active or engaging as that of its direct competitors?
- Engagement: On what platforms is your brand particularly successful in facilitating conversations with consumers to hear what they have to say about your brand experience?
- Tone of Voice: Does the social media content your brand posts reflect your brand's core mission and purpose consistently?

The answers to these questions help brand leaders understand where your brand is positioned in relation to your direct competitors across different digital channels.

Website analytics are pretty straightforward. Typically, you should start with conducting a thorough audit of your own website by looking at your website's information architecture (IA) and structure. The hyperlinks your brand includes on its site and referral traffic are two concepts that inform potential connections with other parties. You may also analyze your website's overall traffic, including the number of unique visitors per day/week/month, and the number of specific page views, all of which are helpful to understand if your consumers are well aware of your website's usability and therefore come visit your website when they are interested. All of this data can be particularly handy because they are first-party data that your brand can obtain immediately without any other costs or processes involved, whether on its own content management system (CMS) dashboard or through a third party like Google Analytics.

Online reviews and ratings are also important because consumers refer to them and take them seriously, especially when they are negative. Google Reviews, third-party review websites, and comments on social media are accessible means for your consumers to share what they think and feel about your brand experience. Monitoring these reviews through social listening strategies and properly responding to them in a timely manner will show that your brand cares about your consumers' experience in an authentic and credible way. Engagement with negative reviews in particular can help your brand bounce back from negative sentiment.

Believable brands commit to authentic and credible engagement with clients and consumers even in the face of negative sentiment and adversity in the interest of winning back consumers and redirecting them to positive sentiment. As multiple CMOs have highlighted, it is the little things that brands consistently commit to with quality over time that convince clients and consumers that your brand is authentic and credible.

Ratings and reviews are one form of user-generated content (UGC). UGC can be curated through social listening tools and platforms or on a descriptive basis using observation of clients and consumers' engagements with a brand's owned media channels and/or earned media posted by users. Trends, themes, and topics posted by users reveal what your consumers care the most about at any given moment, and can help inform a brand's content strategies. Moreover, analyzing the overall sentiment of user-generated content with social listening tools available on social media platforms or through third-party providers can further enrich the insights you glean from UGC. Because what matters most is that the sentiment of your brand-related conversations is generally positive, not negative, it's important to dive deep into and engage with UGC in real time to help move conversations as much as possible toward a positive, favorable sentiment of your brand and its products and services.

Conclusion

Throughout this chapter, we talked about why purpose-driven brand positioning is important in the face of the ad and brand bombardment that characterizes client and consumer media experiences today. As a potential solution to tackle this problem, we suggested value-centered brand positioning to stay in the mind of your consumers. Impossible and Ferrari are presented as two examples of believable brand positioning. Moreover, the case study of Thrive Pet Healthcare explains how to integrate purpose-driven brand positioning strategies into the daily operations of your brand. To conclude, several applications and metrics are explored as tools to execute believable brand positioning including a position map exercise, media mix and share-of-voice charts, and digital presence analysis. We hope that the content from this chapter provides a useful guide for finding a believable and strategic focus for your brand's positioning—and specific pathways to achieve your goals in the end.

Key Terms

Brand bombardment
Media mix
Online reviews and ratings
Position map
Public trust

Reviews and ratings
Share of voice (SOV)
Social media analysis
User-generated content
Website analytics

Discussion Questions

1 What is ad bombardment and why is it problematic?
2 What are some ways brands can stay in the minds of consumers?
3 How can brands increase their share of voice?

Activity

Position Mapping: Select a brand. Determine two key measurable attributes to focus on, particularly considering what attributes consumers will find important to consider in the market category. List four or five major direct competitors in the market category. Rate each brand as well as your brand on the two attributes you identified in the first step, and compile the information in a table. Create a blank map including X-axis and Y-axis representing the two attributes, respectively. Put logos of the brands on the map based on the ratings in the table you created.

9

Brand Architecture

What is brand architecture? How does brand architecture help build brand believability? Brand architecture is the organizational structure of a brand and must be strategic. There are four types of brand architecture: Branded house architecture, house of brands architecture, hybrid brand architecture, and endorsed brand architecture. Each brand architecture model has pros and cons and must be consistent, strategically aligned, and informed by sentiment. Brands can expand through innovation, but innovation must be consistent with the brand's purpose and values. If brands expand too quickly without consistent strategy, brands can become misaligned and diluted. Research and data collection about brand positioning and brand sentiment can help brands quantify and maintain believable brand architecture.

Chapter Outline

9.1 Introduction: What Is Brand Architecture?	222
9.2 The Problem: Misalignment	226
9.3 The Solution / Case: Believable Brand Architecture at CBS	226
9.4 Application: Building a Strategic Brand Architecture Model	230
9.5 Metrics: Brand Sentiment	231
Key Terms	234
Discussion Questions	234
Activity	234

9.1 Introduction: What Is Brand Architecture?

Brand Architecture: The relationship between brands within an organization and how they interact.

What is brand architecture and what does brand architecture have to do with building a believable brand? Tactically, brand architecture is the organizational structure of a brand—often illustrated with a diagram—that helps to explain the relationships between a company's parent brand, sub-brands, products, and service lines (Qualtrics, 2024d).

Not only does brand architecture define the hierarchy of a company's branding strategy, but it also illustrates how various products and services are related to and distinct from each other. Brand architecture helps brands to build, scale, and grow in a strategic way. Brand architecture also provides transparency for employees and consumers with regard to how a brand is structured. Brand architecture is crucial because it helps manage a company's brand portfolio, streamlines marketing efforts, and ensures that new products and services are introduced efficiently and effectively.

There are four types of brand architecture: Branded house architecture, house of brands architecture, hybrid brand architecture, and endorsed brand architecture. Each type of brand architecture requires different strategies for sales, marketing, legal, and more. This chapter will define and explore the four major types of architecture, identify the main problem that obstructs believable brand architecture—misalignment—and give suggestions about how to build a believable brand architecture.

Branded House Architecture

Branded houses are also known as monolithic brands. Branded houses have a strong, dominant parent brand with sub-brands that match the parent brand's values and name. Within a branded house, all the brands in the portfolio share values with the parent brand and share their name. It's also likely that the sub-brands don't work independently of one another.

Brand Architecture

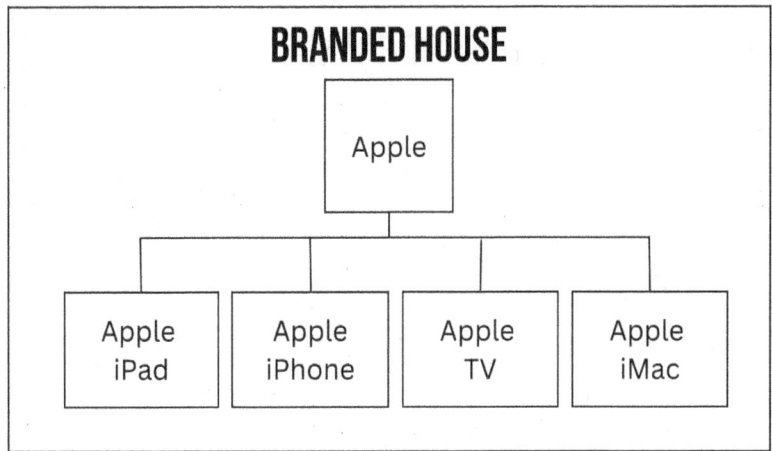

Figure 9.1 Branded House Architecture.

This style means all brands within the house are consistent in terms of look, feel, marketing messaging, and more. The intention of a monolithic or branded house is to create a strong and unified brand image, where the parent brand is dominant. Sub-brands within a branded house are consistent with the parent brand in terms of design, experience, and communication.

Apple is an example of a branded house. Apple is the parent brand with sub-brands that match, including Apple Music, Apple iPhone, and Apple AirPods. Another example of a branded house is FedEx. FedEx, the parent brand, has several sub-brands within its branded house including FedEx Express, FedEx Freight, and FedEx Ground.

House of Brands Architecture

A house of brands has a pluralistic brand architecture. In a pluralistic house of brands, each product or brand has its own distinct identity, with minimal association with the parent company. This allows each brand to operate independently, appealing to different audiences. A house of brands comprises a parent brand and multiple sub-brands that aren't necessarily related. Sub-brands in a house of brands may be in different sectors, with varying audiences, products, and identities. Procter & Gamble is an example of a house of brands. Procter & Gamble is the parent brand with

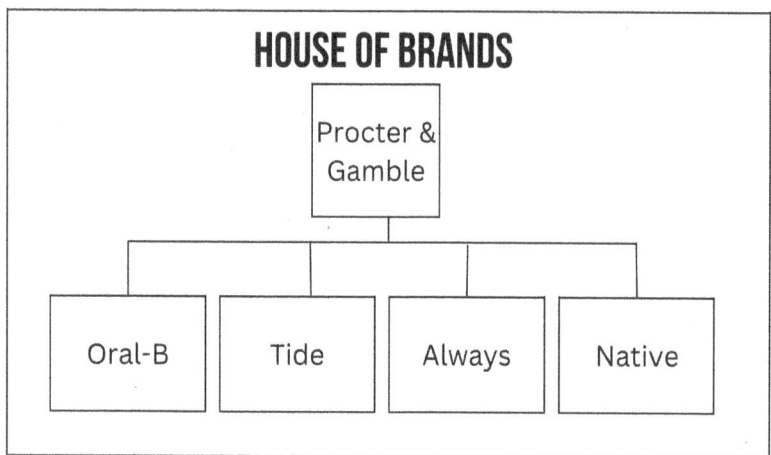

Figure 9.2 House of Brands Architecture.

sub-brands including Tide, Gillette, and Pampers. Unilever is another example of a house of brands. Unilever's house of brands contains several different brands including personal care brand Dove, food company Ben & Jerry's, and drinks brand Lipton.

House of brands architecture enables sub-brands to reach various segments and audiences without directly competing with one another for market share.

Endorsed Brand Architecture

An endorsed brand architecture model involves the parent or umbrella brand giving their endorsement to other brands that fall beneath them in the structure. In an endorsed brand architecture, the parent brand is also known as an umbrella brand that covers and lends the endorsed brands their credibility, which provides legitimacy and authority, often indicating that the other brands are of the same quality. All sub-brands in an endorsed brand architecture model will likely be within the same sector but have different audiences, offerings, and identities.

Endorsed brand architecture is common among hotel brands, including Hilton and Marriott. Hilton's sub-brands include brands like Hampton by

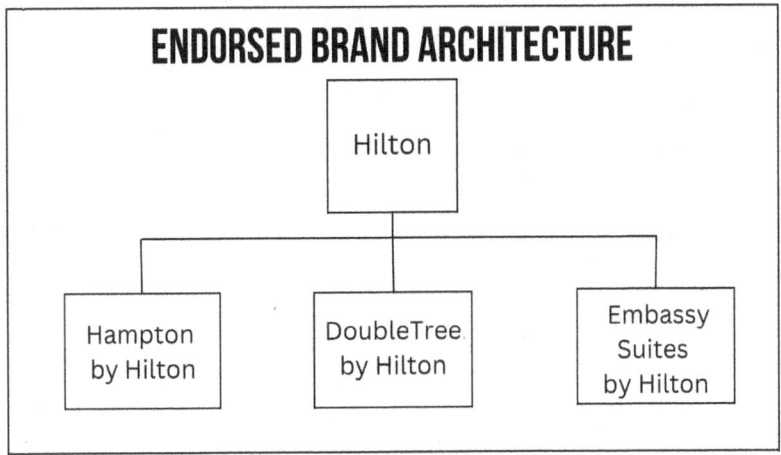

Figure 9.3 Endorsed Brand Architecture.

Hilton, DoubleTree by Hilton, and Embassy Suites by Hilton, which are all under and endorsed by the Hilton parent brand umbrella. Marriott offers its customers a range of brands for different tastes and price points, such as Residence Inn by Marriott and Courtyard by Marriott.

Hybrid Brand Architecture

Hybrid brand architecture includes brands that comprise elements of branded houses, house of brands, and endorsed brand architecture. Some products and sub-brands in a hybrid architecture are endorsed by the parent brand or closely tied to the parent brand, while others operate independently.

Coca-Cola is an example of a hybrid brand architecture with sub-brands including Coca-Cola, Diet Coke, Coke Zero, and Sprite. Coca-Cola, or Coke, is the prominent parent brand, with clear ties to Diet Coke and Coke Zero. At the same time, some sub-brands have independent identities, like Sprite.

Alphabet, Inc. is the parent brand over sub-brands including Google, which has several sub-brands including Google Play and YouTube.

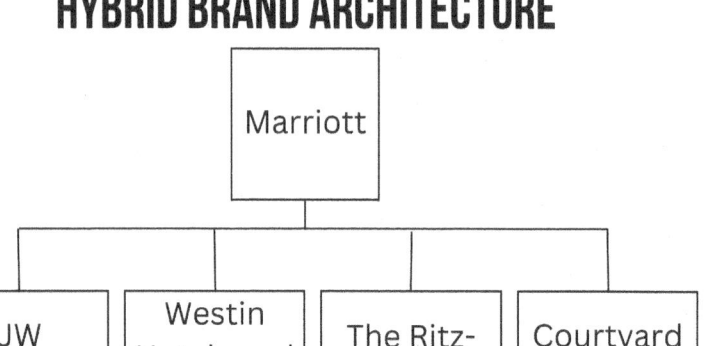

Figure 9.4 Hybrid Brand Architecture.

9.2 The Problem: Misalignment

Sometimes, brands expand beyond their capacity to scale. Brands may also have sub-brands that aren't aligned with the parent brand's mission, vision, and/or purpose. When a brand grows too quickly, or adds too many sub-brands through mergers and acquisitions, or creates departmental silos where teams don't talk to each other, there will be misalignment. Misalignment occurs between different departments and brands when communication breaks down about marketing, sales, positioning, value propositions, and/or product and service development. No matter which of the four brand architecture models an organization selects, what matters most is that the architecture is strategic, consistent, and believable. And, when innovative sub-brands, products, or services are introduced, innovation must be in line with the brand's purpose and values.

9.3 The Solution / Case: Believable Brand Architecture at CBS

CBS comprises a hybrid brand architecture as a parent brand of production studios including CBS Studios, See It Now Studios, CBS Media Ventures, and BET Studios. CBS's studios create content supplied to distribution channels and outlets including the CBS Television Network, Paramount+, Amazon, Disney, Netflix, and more. Additionally, CBS has three consumer-facing broadcast brands: CBS (Entertainment), CBS News, and CBS Sports. CBS, CBS News, and CBS Sports are all parent brands with numerous sub-brands and franchises of their own. For example, CBS Entertainment comprises franchises including *NCIS*. CBS Sports comprises franchises including the *NFL on CBS*, and CBS News comprises sub-brands and franchises including local news stations and *60 Minutes*, the award-winning news broadcast that appeals to consumers worldwide.

CBS has a unique opportunity to build believability with distribution partners and also with consumers worldwide. Its hybrid brand architecture model is fit for a global conglomerate that is constantly acquiring, building, and launching new brands, shows, and services. As brands expand, it can be challenging to maintain believability. President and Chief Marketing Officer Mike Benson is aware of this challenge and noted that CBS, founded in 1927 as a news radio station, has a strong core audience and is still evolving by acquiring new audiences and building believability with consistency and innovation. For CBS, consistency comes most notably in their understanding of and commitment to their core audience segment. Benson explained,

> We've been doing a lot of work to help put a fine point on the CBS brand. We know CBS is a trusted brand, but in today's entertainment marketplace, it needs more definition. Since its inception, CBS has always been a brand that offers a diverse range of entertainment, news, and sports programming for big and broad audiences, but we know that we need to clarify our brand for today's viewers who don't know or watch us. We want to leverage, but not dwell in our past, as we continue to provide fresh, new programming that ultimately unites audiences through story and characters that are unique, but still broadly accessible to viewers throughout the country. The CBS audience loves a good story, well-told. They love seeing new points of view, but in a way that is ultimately entertaining. They love seeing teams work together, mysteries being solved, and good people working together to do the right thing in our primetime dramas, as much as they love a romantic escape through our daytime dramas, to play along with one of our game shows, or laugh at one of our comedies. CBS audiences love the "comfort-food" feeling of our CBS shows. *The Price Is Right*, *60 Minutes*, *Survivor*, *NCIS*, *FBI*, *Ghosts*, *Tracker*, *Matlock*, and the *NFL on CBS* all deliver what our CBS brand does best.

Beyond understanding and prioritizing their core audience segment, Benson prioritizes values including unification, accessibility, and optimism. All of these values are held in high esteem as CBS innovates in the form of introducing new shows and/or franchises consistent with CBS's purpose with an appeal to the core audience segment. As the CBS brand evolves, Benson recognized that it's very important to combat brand dilution and maintain alignment underneath the brand's purpose by leveraging data and social listening to introduce new and innovative shows and sub-brands.

"We aim to be the most unifying media brand, bringing people together more effectively and on a larger scale than any other," Benson said. "This goal is largely driven by the popularity of CBS's programming, but it also ties into a broader sense of optimism, which feels right for our brand and is something the audience needs today."

A unique part of media brands' architecture is connections between the shows and the platforms they are broadcast or streamed on. Audience development across platforms is a key part of CBS's strategy as a media organization.

"Our marketing goals are twofold: keep our loyal CBS viewers engaged and attract new audiences. While many still watch CBS live, viewing habits are changing. People now watch what they want, when they want, and on various devices like TVs, connected devices, and mobile phones," said Benson. "We must create a compelling brand experience that resonates with different audience segments, no matter how or where they watch CBS. We want our viewers to feel like they are part of the CBS experience, which is central to our strategy."

In addition to building brands, CBS is distributing content across platforms. As the brand messaging goes out on various platforms, it's important to maintain consistency to avoid misalignment. In addition to misalignment, brand dilution is a danger that brands face when they expand too quickly or lose sight of their founder-inspired mission, vision, and purpose. Simplification is key to maintaining consistency and believability.

"Building our brand has become increasingly complex. We dedicate significant effort to understanding these complexities and finding ways to simplify and align," said Benson.

Our brand used to be limited to our network platform and traditional advertising. Now, we need to create a cohesive brand identity and personality that works across multiple business units and distribution platforms, including digital, social media, gaming, live experiences, merchandising, and countless other consumer and trade outlets. Managing continuity and consistency is challenging and resource-intensive, but it ultimately makes our brand more accessible and powerful.

Innovation must be strategic, and data driven. When creating new brands, sub-brands and franchises, it must be clear who is interested in what products and services. For a media company, to grow audience share, brands can consider distribution channels. Are you seeking to reach consumers and increase audience share on prime time? On an app? On a streaming service? Connected TV?

Data-driven social listening helped CBS to launch and build the audience for *Ghosts*, a quirky and accessible comedy series that resonated with CBS's core audience and also drew in a new segment of younger audience members interested in a quirky and accessible comedy available on primetime television and also on streaming services.

Benson said,

> First and foremost, we need to ensure we're satisfying our core audience. The second priority is, "Can we find other ways to attract other audience segments?" Our TikTok presence for the show *Ghosts* exploded, which was quite unexpected for a CBS show. However, it resulted in driving teenage audiences to sample the show, then talk about it through their own social media channels.

Fire Country is another example of innovation at an almost one-hundred-year-old network. The show features heroes and drama similar to that of a soap opera, values CBS's core audience segment prioritizes, and it became the most-watched new television launch of 2022.

"For *Fire Country*, we knew we needed to drive the core CBS drama-viewer, but the data told us there was more to this show," Benson said.

> Our team found that country music fans would also enjoy *Fire Country*. So, we tested our positioning against audiences who loved country music and created a campaign featuring country music artist, Kane Brown. We infused our campaign with a soulful but exciting country vibe, while at the same time, sold the characters and the storylines in a way that resonated with this segment, but also the CBS core. Our team did an excellent job using data to identify an opportunity that allowed us to go bigger, but also be more strategic and innovative.

9.4 Application: Building a Strategic Brand Architecture Model

Each type of brand architecture has benefits and drawbacks. To build a strong brand architecture from scratch or to evaluate whether or not your brand architecture is as strategic as it can be—brands can follow these steps:

- **Conduct a brand audit:** Assess your existing brands and sub-brands by evaluating their strengths, weaknesses, opportunities, and threats (SWOT). Evaluate brand performance and structure; if possible, draw on consumer insights to quantify and qualify consumer or market perception and sentiment.
- **Establish brand hierarchy:** A clear, structured brand hierarchy defines the relationships between separate brands, including parent and sub-brands. Developing, establishing, and/or evaluating an existing brand hierarchy helps to determine how each brand and sub-brand fits within a brand portfolio.
- **Identify which model of brand architecture your brand follows:** Based on your brand audit and brand hierarchy, is your brand a branded house, house of brands, hybrid, or endorsed brand architecture model?
- **Keep it simple:** Do not overcomplicate your brand structure. Overly complex brand architecture types can confuse both internal and external stakeholders regarding all the brands and sub-brands. A cluttered brand architecture model may lead to inefficiencies and complicate the relationships between the parent company and sub-brands. Consistency and clarity are key to believable and strategic brand architecture.
- **Create a visual brand architecture model:** If you don't have one already, create a clear and illustrative brand architecture model that showcases every brand and sub-brand and their relationships to each other.
- **Define brand positioning:** Identify the unique selling propositions for all brands and sub-brands; audience segmentation is a part of this.
- **Design visual and verbal identity:** This is discussed in-depth in chapter 3. A branded house strategy should include consistent

visuals and verbal messaging among related brands and sub-brands. Where there is stagnancy, create and develop innovative logos, color schemes, and design elements to unify multiple brands within your portfolio.
- **Implement consistent brand guidelines internally and externally:** Once you've successfully defined your brand architecture and created an illustrative hierarchical chart, create brand guidelines that ensure the brand is understood and consistently applied across all touchpoints. Internally, educate your employees on the parent brand and brand portfolio, defining their role in maintaining consistency. Externally, apply brand guidelines to all marketing materials and brand assets.
- **Consistent analysis and evaluation:** Consistently evaluate the effectiveness of your brand architecture by gathering customer feedback through qualitative and quantitative means. Qualitative data collection can come through social media, interviews, focus groups, and more. Quantitative market research can come through surveys and network analysis.

9.5 Metrics: Brand Sentiment

Brand sentiment is the overall feeling, tone, emotion, and/or attitude people have toward your brand. Brand sentiment is similar to brand perception, and can be measured in a variety of ways. Measuring brand sentiment informs brand strategy by identifying brand strengths, opportunities, and weaknesses across topics, products, services, and the entire portfolio. The steps to measuring brand sentiment include data collection, analysis, and calculation.

- **Data Collection:** The first and most important step in measuring brand sentiment is identifying word associations or keywords/phrases that employees, stakeholders, and consumers use in conversations and communication about and with the brand. To identify these word associations or keywords, collect data directly from your audience. Data can come from a variety of sources and channels, including but not limited to interviews, focus groups, surveys, feedback forms, social media platforms, third party reviews, blog posts, and customer service and sales contacts. Be sure to collect data from individuals across verticals and platforms to ensure you are gathering accurate information that will help segment your audiences and target your messages. Gathering feedback on customer experiences, perceptions, and emotions related to your brand across touchpoints is beneficial as well. For focus groups, surveys, interviews, and customer feedback forms, asking open-ended questions that encourage respondents to share their thoughts and feelings in their own words can help to provide insights into sentiment. Another way to collect data is by using social listening tools and software.

- **Use Social Listening Tools**: Social listening tools are platforms and technology that allow you to monitor metrics including, but not limited to: Brand mentions, keywords, hashtags, and conversations. Technology is always evolving, but current examples of these technology platforms include Hootsuite, Sprinklr, Brandwatch, Newswhip, Ipsos Synthesio, Sprout Social, Quorum, Quid, and Answer the Public. Subscriptions can be expensive but worthwhile. For smaller brands that need to conduct social listening in-house independently, it's possible to gather and observe engagements including mentions, shares, comments, and likes across social media platforms manually, natively on each app. Google Trends is one free tool that can be used for social listening as well. Manual sentiment analysis can be conducted by scraping data directly from social media sites and loading it into spreadsheets and with artificial intelligence to produce reports relevant to measuring sentiment.

- **Data Analysis and Brand Sentiment Calculation**: After gathering relevant data from interviews, focus groups, surveys, social listening, or other means, analyze and clean the data. Consider categorizing feedback and sentiment in buckets, including identifying what audiences the data came from—employees, consumers, etcetera. You can also categorize based on topic area, such as sales, experience, and so on. After categorizing the data, create labels and values to measure sentiment. At their simplest, these values might include positive, negative, or neutral sentiment aligned with each mention. Assign a numerical value to each score. For example: positive sentiment could be +1, neutral is 0, and negative is −1. Then, add up your brand's score and see where you end up as a total score. Is it positive? Negative? Close to neutral? What areas of improvement or opportunity are there? What threats are there to the score? Tracking your brand's sentiment score over time can help you measure changes in perception, track the effectiveness of your brand initiatives, and identify areas for improvement (Hootsuite, 2024).

- **Defining Sentiment:** Artificial intelligence (AI) tools categorize sentiment according to their algorithms, which are evolving and changing with time and technological advances. For those conducting sentiment analysis manually, positive sentiment indicates approval, satisfaction, joy, excitement, love, happiness, and the like. Negative sentiment involves dissatisfaction, complaints, criticisms, disappointment, sadness, anger, and similar comments or sentiments that come from bad experiences with the brand and its touchpoints. Neutral sentiment can be challenging to identify or differentiate from positive or negative sentiment, but generally lacks strong positive or negative feelings or emotions; neutral sentiment can include customers sharing or seeking information without expressing any personal feelings toward the brand.

Measuring brand sentiment can help brands understand if they are aligned well and allocating resources in proper ways across brands, sub-brands, platforms, and channels. If a brand has positive sentiment in a specific topic area or product/service line, that is a strength to be drawn on and leaned into. If there is negative sentiment arising in a certain brand, product, or service line, this could be an opportunity to get ahead of a crisis. Measuring brand sentiment can also reveal opportunities for new product or service development based on consumer preferences, needs, and gaps in the market.

As you develop a strategy for monitoring brand sentiment of your own brand, as time allows, be sure to keep an eye on competitor sentiment as well. It's helpful to identify and benchmark competitors' sentiment values to inform your own brand's strategy. How can you differentiate yourself and capitalize on your unique strengths and value propositions? Brand sentiment analysis and competitive benchmarking can also help you forecast ways to avoid decisions that may lead to negative sentiment.

Key Terms

Brand alignment
Brand architecture
Branded house / Monolithic brand architecture
Brand monitoring
Brand sentiment
Endorsed brand architecture
House of brands / Pluralistic brand architecture
Hybrid brand architecture
Mergers and acquisitions
Misalignment

Discussion Questions

1 What are the pros and cons of the four main types of brand architecture?
2 How do different styles of brand architecture influence the allocation of marketing resources and budget decisions including marketing strategy, resource distribution, and financial planning?
3 How can companies evaluate and adjust their brand architecture over time to ensure it remains aligned with evolving business goals and market conditions?

Activity

Mergers, Acquisitions, and Architecture: Select two brands who take part in a fictional merger or acquisition. Consider how to integrate or reconfigure the brands and sub-brands involved and present your internal and external communications strategy.

Part IV

Social Influence

Social influence is how brands contribute to the public good by implementing and supporting prosocial efforts and initiatives. All brands have influence among employees, clients, customers, stakeholders, and communities around the world. Sustainability, social responsibility, and brand resonance are all matters that build brands' social influence. One problem facing brands and organizations seeking to build believability is exploitation–within workforces and supply chains worldwide. Conscious consumers are driving change to encourage companies to become more sustainable economically, socially, and environmentally. Brand resonance is a concept that helps to bring all of these commitments together. B Corporations and Conscious Capitalism are two movements committed to helping brands influence society for the better. Brand awareness is a metric that helps to measure social influence.

Outline

IV.1 Introduction: What Is Social Influence?	236
IV.2 The Problem: Performative Activism and Exploitation	237
IV.3 The Solution: Believable Social Influence	239
IV.4 Application: B Corporations and Conscious Capitalism	242
IV.5 Metrics: Brand Awareness	245
Key Terms	247
Discussion Questions	247
Activity	248

IV.1 Introduction: What Is Social Influence?

Social Influence: How brands contribute to the public good by implementing and supporting prosocial efforts and initiatives.

All brands have effects on employees, clients, customers, stakeholders, and communities around the world. Whether or not these effects are prosocial—or positive and beneficial for individuals, groups, and society at large—is up to the brands' key stakeholders as they decide how to steward their brands' social, economic, and environmental responsibilities.

How brands stand with a social issue, or don't, is important to consumers who want to believe in brands that support and invest time and resources into socially responsible activities and organizations. Likewise, the way brands utilize accessible and inclusive mindsets both internally among its employees and externally to other stakeholders is considered vital to develop and maintain healthy relationships between consumers and brands.

We define social influence as how brands contribute to the public good by pursuing and supporting prosocial efforts and initiatives. Prosocial efforts that build social influence—and thus, believability—include commitments to environmental sustainability and social responsibility through accessibility, inclusivity, and philanthropic giving and service. Brand resonance is a concept that helps to bring all of these commitments together. Environmental elements of social influence include sustainability efforts in particular, ranging from brands' commitments to preserving natural resources, minimizing pollution, and reducing waste, to implementing renewable energy efforts and purchasing carbon offsets. Economic elements of social influence include creating systems and practices that generate long-term financial stability and growth without exploiting resources or people by implementing and supporting fair labor practices, human rights, access to education, health care, and inclusiveness.

Emotions consumers experience about cultural and social issues—including the climate crisis as discussed in detail in the sustainability chapter—are defiance and exhaustion. At the same time, experts note that consumers are "scared, not stupid" (Zhexembayeva, 2023). There is also hope that comes with solutions, especially purpose-driven companies that provide accessible and sustainable products. Consumers desire products that provide personalized solutions (Townsend, 2023).

Historically, in the Western world's capitalist economy, a majority of brands and organizations have failed to pursue sustainable practices and social responsibility as it has not been celebrated as profitable. As sustainable business practices gain traction, there are movements motivated by socially, economically, and environmentally conscious consumers that are leading to increased sales and profits.

As brands and organizations seek to jump on the bandwagon of social influence through implementing social, economic, and environmentally friendly policies and practices, some brands have been called out for pursuing inauthentic social advocacy, also known as performative activism or tokenism.

IV.2 The Problem: Performative Activism and Exploitation

Performative activism refers to actions that are more about gaining visibility or improving public image than about making meaningful change or supporting a cause genuinely. Performative activism implies a brand's superficial or insincere effort to engage specific social issues with a campaign, partnership, or messaging without substantial commitment. Human trafficking is one form of exploitation that is prevalent in global supply chains for consumer packaged goods and clothing in particular (Crane et al., 2019).

Federal law and policy are helpful frameworks and accountability mechanisms that help brands align with prosocial efforts and initiatives. In the area of human trafficking within the United States, the Victims of Trafficking and Violence Protection Act of 2000 (TVPA) was established in October of that year, and has been reauthorized several times since. The United States has passed additional anti-trafficking legislation since 2000, and defines labor trafficking as "the recruitment, harboring, transportation, provision, or obtaining of a person for labor or services, through the use of force, fraud, or coercion for the purposes of subjection to involuntary servitude, peonage, debt bondage, or slavery" (U.S.

Department of State, 2023). Forced labor occurs in developed countries as well as developing countries worldwide, and Western countries that are central to global production exploit workers within their own spheres quite frequently (U.S. Department of State, 2023). Illegal profits from forced labor in the private sector grew 37 percent from 2014 to 2024, and was quantified at $236 billion in 2024 (International Labour Organization, 2024). This rise in forced labor has been fueled by both a growth in the number of people forced into labor, as well as higher profits generated from the exploitation of victims. It is estimated that criminals profit up to $35,000 per victim from exploitation in supply chains, especially within developed countries like the United States (Crane et al., 2019).

Transparency laws—laws and regulations that require employers to disclose information to the public—are one way to hold countries, brands, and corporations complicit with trafficking to account. When corporations and brands are committed to transparency, whether by policy or law, and disclose what steps they're taking to address human trafficking in supply chains, this has been found to help to normalize ethical business practices; encourage companies to be more proactive; raise awareness among intergovernmental organizations, national governments, and nongovernmental organizations; and can pressure reluctant companies to act (Koekkoek et al., 2017; Limoncelli, 2017). At the same time, many brands and organizations are involved with and sometimes willfully blind to human trafficking crimes in their supply chains and labor practices to save money and increase profits by exploiting workers for low wages and poor working conditions (Pierce, 2010). On the other hand, American Apparel is one corporation that monitors their supply chains for trafficking and acts accordingly when transgressions appear (Pierce, 2010). Another example is Nespresso, a coffee brand that was found to be guilty of child labor and labor exploitation in their supply chain (Doward, 2020). As a result of these findings, Nespresso implemented a comprehensive sustainability plan to prevent and eradicate exploitation from their supply chain and production practices (Nespresso, 2024). Part of this effort was to become a certified B Corporation.

Human trafficking is one example of how brands' social influence efforts are integral: Stakeholders, employees, and consumers are becoming more aware than ever that there are exploitative practices in capitalistic economies in particular, and are backing up their decisions to commit to social, economic, and environmental sustainability with their spending practices.

IV.3 The Solution: Believable Social Influence

Believable social influence is co-created and validated by conscious consumers and consumer-driven change. Generation Z in particular is passionate about brands that are authentic when it comes to social influence in particular, but is aware when brands speak out in an inauthentic way. Brands should only speak out on social issues they are aligned with and invested in. Patagonia is one specific example of an authentic brand committed to fair working conditions and social and environmental causes that align with their brand's platform as an outfitter directly.

Our research shows that, when Generation Z looks for a brand to believe in, they look for brands that provide affordable, high-quality products. Biodegradable and compostable packaging is very important to Generation Z. At the same time, "green" products are more expensive than those that aren't ethically produced and sourced, presenting a sort of conundrum for those strapped for monetary resources yet wanting to invest in sustainable products and brands.

Our research shows that Generation Z consumers in particular appreciate when brands align with their own personal values, but that alignment doesn't make or break their investment; they will still spend money on a brand that doesn't uphold their values if the product is high quality and affordable. Keeping this in mind, pursuing and quantifying social influence is challenging, but when something matters, you have to measure it; if you don't, its value is zero (Aronson, 2023). This is the case in social influence, sustainability, and marketing. To this end, as much as possible, it's important to articulate social influence in annual reports and other company communications (Bakare, 2023). For example, Google publishes annual Sustainability Reports that provide an overview of their environmental sustainability strategy, including targets and annual progress toward them (Google, 2024).

Technology also contributes to impactful change. For example, Big Tech firm Google leveraged AI to quantify the energy footprint of their data servers. As a result of some AI experimentation, Google was able to reduce their output by 40 percent (Jay, 2023). And, using satellite data, artificial intelligence has been used to help predict floods up to a week in advance.

Industry leaders and executives agree that partnership and collaboration are key to sustainability and regeneration (Harrison, 2023). Emotion plays a critical role in brands' social influence, as well. According to Dr. Nadya Zhexembayeva of Reinvention Academy, providing emotional solutions to emotional problems goes a long way (2023). In many ways, sustainability is no longer optional; it's an obligation and social responsibility all brands, organizations, and corporations are subject to. Consumers—young adults in their teens, 20s, and 30s in particular—appreciate affordable brands that uphold sustainable practices and high-quality products. In addition to consumers desiring sustainable products, data shows they'll pay for them, too: 60 percent of American consumers are willing to pay more for products with sustainable packaging, and up to 78 percent of U.S. consumers say a sustainable lifestyle is important to them (NielsenIQ & McKinsey & Company, 2023).

Consumers are able to express their views on issues through their choices of which brands to support (Zhexembayeva, 2023). Because consumer choices fuel profits and market share, brands can see the efficacy of their sustainability efforts within traditional business metrics.

One example of this shows itself in U.S. consumer spending on consumer packaged goods (CPGs), which averages $14 trillion annually and comprises two-thirds of the U.S. gross domestic product (GDP). Sales of consumer packaged goods (CPGs) that advertise sustainable packaging include labels such as:

- Eco-conscious
- Environmentally sustainable
- Made with recycled materials
- Fair trade
- and more

Sales of sustainably packaged CPGs increased more than 30 percent in five years from 2017 to 2022: Annual profits were $268.9 billion as of July 2022 (NielsenIQ & McKinsey & Company, 2023).

For these reasons and more, our research shows that brand believability has grown for brands like Patagonia for their commitment to sustainability and donating large sums of money to organizations solving the climate crisis, and Target, because they sell sustainable products including Method cleaner which provides cleaning products in refillable glass bottles.

Not only is creating environmentally sustainable and socially responsible products morally imperative, but it is a sound business decision as shareholders continue to invest in sustainable products and businesses.

Consumer choices, especially for women, are ways they express their views (Townsend, 2023). In that way, profits and market share are a couple of ways brands can show their efforts to attain social influence in social, environmental, and economic sectors are working.

Liquid I.V. is a leading consumer packaged product sold worldwide with clear and concrete commitments to social influence in economic, social, and environmental sectors.

Brand Profile: Liquid I.V.

Liquid I.V. is a sustainable brand with clear and concrete social influence. A direct-to-consumer (D2C) company, Liquid I.V. sells an electrolyte drink mix distributed globally. Their key stakeholders segment social impact into four main pillars: Product donation, sustainability, grant making, and Confluence, which is their proprietary product donation program. In 2015, Liquid I.V. donated five hundred servings of its product to the Los Angeles Mission shelter to give hydration aid to its unhoused population. As of 2023, Liquid I.V. had established partnerships with numerous humanitarian organizations to distribute over 36 million servings to individuals in more than forty countries with a commitment to donate 150 million more servings by 2032.

In addition to social impact pillars, Liquid I.V. has four commitments to help create a healthier planet: Carbon reduction, water stewardship, zero-waste packaging and operations, and regenerative sourcing.

A key partnership for Liquid I.V. is with Map International, one of the biggest recipients of their product for worldwide distribution. Liquid I.V. also financially invests in some of Map International's programs in Burkina Faso and Liberia. This financial support adds to their commitment to community engagement.

Experimentation and incremental progress are key to Liquid I.V.'s sustainability efforts. Engagement with consumers, innovation, and product testing in various markets are key ways they experiment with their efforts with consumers and partners. According to Liquid I.V.'s VP of Impact, Sean Lavin (2023), "True impact is when you're actually connecting to the consumer… education is impactful!"

Liquid I.V. seeks to educate consumers by providing information on their packaging about the company's commitments to sustainability and social responsibility.

IV.4 Application: B Corporations and Conscious Capitalism

B Lab is a nonprofit organization based in Pennsylvania that certifies B Corporations, or "B-Corps." The B stands for "benefit," and refers to benefiting workers, the community, and the environment. B Lab was founded in 2006 in the United States "by three friends who shared a vision to make business a force for good." The first 82 Certified B Corps were certified in 2007.

As of July 2023, 7,113 companies in 161 industries across 91 countries qualified as B Corps. In order to achieve B Corp certification, a company must:

- be a for-profit entity;
- have an explicit social or environmental mission;
- have a legally binding fiduciary responsibility to take into account the interests of workers, the community, and the environment as well as its shareholders;
- amend its articles of incorporation to adopt B Lab's commitment to sustainability and treating workers well;
- pay an annual fee based on revenues;
- complete and publish a public-facing B Impact Report, or lengthy questionnaire that measures social and environmental impact, on a biannual basis;
- meet B-Lab's comprehensive social and environmental performance standards.

B Lab's ultimate goal is to change the nature of business in order to ultimately change corporate law. Currently, for-profit firms face legal pressure to forgo social goals (i.e., interests of workers, communities, and the environment) in favor of maximizing profits and the financial interests of shareholders.

To qualify as a B Corp, a firm must first pass an assessment that shows the company is meeting high standards of verified performance, accountability, and transparency on factors from employee benefits and charitable giving to supply chain practices and input materials. After becoming certified as a B Corp, all Certified B Corps share their B Impact Assessment overall scores and category scores on their public profiles on B Lab Global's website.

Conscious Capitalism

In addition to certifications, there are sustainability movements including Conscious Capitalism Incorporated (CCI), founded in 2010 as a U.S.-based 501(c)(3) nonprofit organization "to build a movement of business leaders improving the practice and perception of capitalism to elevate humanity so that billions of people can flourish, leading lives infused with passion, purpose, love and creativity; a world of freedom, harmony, prosperity, and compassion" (Sisodia, 2023). There are partners, chapters, and community sponsors involved with the Conscious Capitalism movement, most notably Whole Foods Market and Thrivent Financial. The movement provides educational opportunities and conferences for interested parties to invest in the movement worldwide.

Corporate Knights' Global 100

Corporate Knights is a Toronto-based media and investment advisory company that publishes *Corporate Knights Magazine*, a magazine focused on responsible business; operates an investment firm, Corporate Knights Capital, which builds indexing solutions and market-beating portfolios for institutional clients; and produces the Global 100, a sustainability stock index calculated by Solactive, a German index provider.

The Global 100 comprises the top 100 most sustainable publicly traded stocks in the world. The Global 100 is available on Bloomberg under the ticker <CKG100 Index> and on Reuters under the ticker <CKG100>.

The Corporate Knights' Global 100 has been one of the world's most valued and transparent rules-based sustainability ratings since 2005. The Global 100 shows the impact of a company's core products and services and is released every January with findings revealed at the World Economic Forum (Corporate Knights, 2023).

Every year, Solactive assesses all publicly traded companies with over $1 billion in revenue across 25 key performance indicators, including:

- percentage of sustainable revenue,
- percentage of sustainable investment,
- percentage of taxes paid,
- carbon productivity, and
- racial and gender diversity in the workforce.

The methodology is comprehensive and includes data on political influence, employee turnover, and more. The Global 100 disqualifies companies engaging in what they define as "red flag" activities, such as:

- using thermal coal,
- dealing in certain products or services including weapons and tobacco, and
- lobbying to block climate change-conscious policy.

All of the Global 100's Key Performance Indicators (KPIs) are linked to one or more of the United Nations Sustainable Development Goals (the UN SDGs).

One major benefit for brands and organizations included in the Global 100 is carbon productivity: Members of the Global 100 earn $384,077/tonne against the MSCI All Country World Index (ACWI)'s $173,600 on a weighted basis. Research by the McKinsey Global Institute and McKinsey's Climate Change Initiative finds that carbon productivity, defined as the amount of GDP produced per unit of carbon equivalents (CO_2e) emitted, must increase dramatically to mitigate the results of climate change, and members of the Global 100 are doing so at an impressive rate (McKinsey Global Institute, 2008). Another benefit of inclusion in the Global 100 is that the proportion of revenues that derive from clean sources increased from 26 percent to 37 percent from 2022 to 2023 (Scott, 2020).

IV.5 Metrics: Brand Awareness

Brand awareness is defined as consumer familiarity with a brand's identity, products, and/or services (Chandler & Munday, 2011; Gomez, 2024). Brand awareness is one of the foundational building blocks for brand believability. Consumers must be aware of a brand before believability is cultivated.

To build brand awareness, brands must establish credible social influence in social, environmental, and economic sectors. Brand awareness can be built through good or bad experiences. All press builds brand awareness, and it's up to the brand whether or not a negative event or experience can be redeemed with authentic, consistent, and innovative advertising and public relations strategies. Partnerships and alliances are another way for brands to build awareness.

There are several effective ways to measure and quantify brand awareness. Industry thought leadership from Statista, Mintel, Ad Age, and other sources include statistics and trends about consumer habits and brand awareness within specific sectors gathered through surveys, polls, and other mixed-method data collection measures. For example, Statista conducts a Consumer Insights Global survey with thousands of consumers across demographics. Questions relating to brand awareness ask consumers what specific sectors students pay attention to; favorite brands they follow; and similar (Statista, 2024c). If you want to create a brand awareness survey from the ground up, questions to include might include (Smith, 2023):

- How did you first hear about our brand?
- What do you associate with our brand?
- Did you buy or use our products or services?
- How is your customer experience with our brand?
- How likely is it that you will recommend our brand to your family and friends?

Brands can also conduct primary research to quantify brand awareness themselves. KPIs relating to brand awareness include website traffic; social engagements such as likes, comments, and shares across social media platforms; Google Alerts; brand awareness surveys that provide direct feedback from customers and audience members; and social listening, including comments across social media platforms (Decker, 2024). Google Trends and other platforms including Sprout Social and Hootsuite and Brandwatch can help brands quantify search volume: who is searching for your brand by name and what search terms are they using?

To quantify brand awareness, you can decide which KPIs relating to awareness you'd like to track and measure them over time. Is it social engagements? Website traffic? Total reach across website and social media platforms? Mentions online? Google Alerts? A combination? Choose and quantify and measure accordingly.

Conclusion

Social influence varies depending on the organization, but one thing is constant regardless of sector: Believable brands must be committed to excellence and equity in social, economic, and environmental practices. D2C and B2B companies often have different objectives and values, and social influence can be hard to quantify. According to industry thought leader Lola Bakare (2023), three questions that can reveal opportunities to leverage and attain influence include:

1 What are your brand's social debts? Past or present, in what ways has your brand, category, or industry contributed to social harm?
2 What functional benefits and emotional promises can align to meaningfully address relevant social debts? These are your impact insights.
3 How can addressing an impact insight deliver incremental commercial success?

Quantifying social influence is difficult, but brands and organizations are pursuing solutions including but not limited to renewable energy, fair trade certification, organic certifications, and LEED certifications. Two nonprofit entities seeking to transform capitalism include B Labs' B Corp certifications and the Conscious Capitalism movement. Global sustainability indexes like Corporate Knights' "Global 100" are also able to quantify the effectiveness of organizations' commitments.

Global sustainability indexes like the Dow Jones Sustainability™ World Index and Corporate Knights' Global 100 help quantify the economic impact of companies and organizations' sustainability efforts in particular.

The Dow Jones Sustainability World Index comprises global sustainability leaders as identified by S&P Global through the Corporate Sustainability Assessment (CSA). It represents the top 10 percent of the largest 2,500 companies in the S&P Global BMI based on long-term economic, environmental, and social criteria (S&P Global, 2023).

B Labs' B Corp certifications and the Conscious Capitalism movement are also dedicated to transforming corporate industries into socially profitable enterprises. Ultimately, the social influence aspect of brand thinking moves on to measure the results of the brand's core values and the impact it has on the society in terms of the financial benefit of the brand as well as the overall brand performance.

The following chapters address these elements of social influence:

- *Sustainability:* How brands act in environmentally responsible ways;
- *Social Responsibility:* Brands' commitments to promote well-being among employees, stakeholders, clients, customers, and communities around the world;
- *Brand Resonance:* A combination of emotional attachment and credibility brands develop and sustain with employees, stakeholders, clients, and consumers.

Key Terms

Brand affinity
Brand awareness
B Corporation
Conscious Capitalism
Core values

Corporate Knights' Global 100
Exploitation
Performative activism
Transparency laws
Social debts

Discussion Questions

1. Do you think brands have a moral imperative to create environmentally sustainable and socially responsible products and services? Why or why not?
2. For brands seeking to increase their social influence, which concept should be a priority: Emotional attachment or credibility? Why?
3. How can brands ensure their prosocial efforts and initiatives are authentic?

Activity

Believable Social Influence: Choose an existing brand and evaluate its social influence through analysis of its prosocial efforts and initiatives. Are this brand's prosocial efforts and initiatives authentic and aligned with its mission/vision/purpose statement and brand values? Why or why not?

10

Sustainability

What is sustainability and what does it have to do with believable branding? We define sustainability as how brands act in environmentally responsible ways. Sustainable branding has prosocial implications for economic and social sectors, as climate change has become a global crisis influencing and impacting companies, brands, industries, and organizations worldwide. Companies, brands, and organizations worldwide have a responsibility to operate in ways that are environmentally, socially, and economically responsible to help mitigate the effects of the climate crisis. Whether it be something as simple as encouraging employees to recycle rather than throwing everything away or something more hands-on, sustainability is an obligation and social responsibility that all brands, organizations, and corporations are subject to. Setting attainable goals, pursuing certifications, and making sustainable choices to support global climate policies can help. Climate solutions that brands, companies, and organizations are investing in include renewable energy, improved agricultural and sourcing practices, land restoration, conservation, the greening of food supply chains, and investing in carbon offsets like planting trees or building renewable energy projects. All of these efforts should be shared with consumers and codified with certifications and alignment with sustainable goals, value propositions, and key performance indicators (KPIs).

Chapter Outline

10.1 Introduction: What Is Sustainability?	250
10.2 The Problem: Climate Crisis and Greenwashing	251
10.3 The Solution: Believable Sustainability	255
10.4 Application: Context, Strategy, and Goals	258
10.5 Metrics: Certifications and Credibility	260
10.6 Case: Patagonia	265
Key Terms	267
Discussion Questions	267
Activity	268

10.1 Introduction: What Is Sustainability?

Sustainability: How brands act in environmentally responsible ways.

What is sustainability? Sustainability refers to the practice of meeting current needs without compromising the ability of future generations to meet their own needs. Sustainability is a concept that applies to environmental, economic, and social structures and processes, with the goal of long-term health and stability across sectors. Thousands of businesses, brands, and organizations are worsening the climate crisis with irresponsible operational, sourcing, and production practices. At the same time, there is a movement of forward-thinking, eco-conscious brands and organizations enacting sustainable practices, educating consumers, and putting pressure on other organizations and lawmakers to at least consider the planet while chasing profits. Activists, journalists, and watchdog organizations are keeping track of leading organizations' commitments in addition to calling out those participating in "greenwashing," or making products and/or commitments that appear to be more environmentally friendly or less environmentally damaging than they really are.

As United Nations Secretary-General António Guterres remarked at the 2019 Climate Action Summit, "The climate emergency is a race we are losing, but it is a race we can win" (United Nations, 2021). Winning this race depends on using current technological and nature-based solutions that can help mitigate more than 70 percent of greenhouse gas emissions: renewable energy, electric cars, improved agricultural practices, land restoration, conservation, and the greening of food supply chains. It is also essential for organizations, including corporations and nonprofits, to support the development of new solutions with an eye to the future.

10.2 The Problem: Climate Crisis and Greenwashing

Climate change has become a crisis in the twenty-first century. *Climate change* is defined as a "periodic modification of Earth's climate brought about as a result of changes in the atmosphere as well as interactions between the atmosphere and various other geologic, chemical, biological, and geographic factors within the Earth system" (Jackson, 2021).

The United Nations (2021) noted that the global population is collectively "producing greenhouse gas emissions at a record high, with no signs of slowing down." Further, the last four years were the four hottest on record; natural disasters including wildfires, droughts, typhoons, and hurricanes were prevalent; and 90 percent of global disasters are now classed as weather- and climate-related.

Economically, these disasters are costing the world economy $520 billion each year and are pushing twenty-six million people into poverty (United Nations, 2021). According to NASA (2021), climate changes observed in Earth's climate since the early twentieth century are "primarily driven by human activities, particularly fossil fuel burning, which increases heat-trapping greenhouse gas levels in Earth's atmosphere, raising Earth's average surface temperature."

NASA (2021) also notes that natural processes including cyclical ocean patterns like El Niño, La Niña, and the Pacific Decadal Oscillation, and external "forcings" like volcanic activity, changes in the Sun's energy output, and variations in Earth's orbit can also contribute to climate change. The National Geographic Society (2019) has found that, in polar regions, warming global temperatures associated with climate change have caused ice sheets and glaciers to melt at an "accelerated rate" from season to season which contributes to rising sea levels that have begun to damage coastlines "as a result of increased flooding and erosion."

Due to these adverse effects, almost one in four people in the United States are socially vulnerable and have low resilience to extreme heat exposure, according to U.S. Census Bureau data (2023).

For these reasons, and due in part to calls for action from activists and stakeholders worldwide, there are several ways brands and organizations are pursuing sustainable sourcing practices and social impact to help remedy the climate crisis and more. Brands and organizations that make inauthentic or inconsistent claims about their contributions to help remedy the climate crisis are guilty of greenwashing, a concept defined in the section below.

Greenwashing

Greenwashing is defined as the act or practice of making a product, policy, or activity appear to be more environmentally friendly or less environmentally damaging than it really is—or when a company is misleading about their sustainability credentials (Merriam-Webster, 2023). Red flags that signify greenwashing include but are not limited to weak goals, lack of transparency with consumers, and long timelines (*Wall Street Journal*, 2023).

In an attempt to align themselves with policies and treaties including the United Nations' Paris Agreement, many companies and brands are striving to achieve carbon neutrality, or net zero status (The Paris Agreement, 2023).

Carbon neutrality is defined as emitting the same amount of carbon dioxide into the atmosphere that you offset by some other means or that your carbon dioxide output has a net neutral impact on the environment. Carbon neutrality can help stem the effects of climate change. Net zero means a company or organization reduces all greenhouse gas emissions, not just carbon dioxide, across its whole supply chain (Kingsley, 2023).

One way companies and brands seek to reduce emissions is by purchasing carbon offsets—an action or activity like planting trees or building renewable energy projects—to balance their emission(s) of carbon dioxide or other greenhouse gases into the atmosphere (*Wall Street Journal*, 2023). Carbon credits or carbon offsets are seen by activists and environmentalists as short-term solutions to a long-term problem. They are also interpreted as controversial as their impacts aren't entirely clear and accountability is lacking. Longer-term solutions include but are not limited to converting organizations to carbon-free energy sources like wind and solar power.

Accountability for greenwashing is evolving as federal governments and regulatory agencies worldwide seek to impose measures including fines to companies who participate in unethical sustainability practices.

For example, the Federal Trade Commission (FTC) has imposed penalties on companies for deceptive green marketing practices. In 2010, the FTC started sending fashion retailers letters warning them against labeling clothes made of rayon as bamboo. In 2015, Nordstrom, Bed Bath and Beyond, JCPenney, and backcountry.com collectively paid $1.3 million in fines to the Federal Trade Commission (FTC) for continuing to mislabel clothes made of rayon as bamboo. Bamboo is the base material of rayon, but is not the same thing—bamboo is treated with toxic chemicals to turn it into the materials these vendors were selling (Federal Trade Commission, 2015). In 2022, the FTC went after Walmart and Kohl's for marketing some items as bamboo that were actually made of rayon. In addition to imposing $5.5 million in penalties, the FTC imposed injunctive provisions that require Walmart and Kohl's to change how they make textile representations and bamboo-related environmental claims in the future (Fair, 2022).

And, in 2022, retailer H&M faced a class action lawsuit from plaintiffs who argued that H&M's sustainable marketing for their Conscious Choice Product Line violated California and Missouri consumer protection laws, as well as the FTC's Guides for the Use of Environmental Marketing Claims / Green Guides. The case was dismissed in 2023, but instigated FTC's reevaluation of their Green Guides to ensure they are clear as possible when it comes to guidance for sustainable marketing claims (Ferris et al., 2023).

Another accountability mechanism is the U.S. Securities and Exchange Commission's (SEC) call for more transparency in companies' ESG disclosure requirements. For example, the SEC charged Goldman Sachs for violating compliance rules for their ESG fund research and marketing in 2022. Goldman Sachs neither confirmed nor denied the allegations against them but paid $4 million to settle the case (U.S. Securities and Exchange Commission, 2022).

Looking to the future, federal regulators in the U.S. and Europe insist that standardization of measurement for carbon footprints, sustainability for any given product, and standardization of information communicated to consumers would be helpful (BBC News, 2022). On a global scale, the European Union (EU) is developing a policy to require companies to back up their products' environmental claims with scientific evidence that would be individually verified. The FTC is looking to regulate environmental marketing claims and penalize companies for using deceptive language, and the SEC is proposing new rules for climate disclosures (*Wall Street Journal*, 2023).

Brand Profile: Asics

The fashion industry is notorious for their role in greenwashing and contributing to the climate crisis. According to The Ellen MacArthur Foundation, more than 70 percent of materials used to make clothing around the world are landfilled or burned (2023). In an attempt to help remedy the climate crisis and push back against this trend, running shoe brand Asics upholds a five-step circular approach to addressing climate change (Asics, 2023; Asics Global, 2023):

1. Design: Create products that use fewer resources.
2. Materials: Use recycled, bio-based and water-efficient options.
   - Polyester Fabric from Recycled PET Bottles: At least 70 percent of Asics' featured GEL shoes main upper portion is made with polyester fabric from recycled PET bottles.
3. Production: Source renewable energy and manufacture efficiently and cleanly.
   - Asics uses recycled polyester for more than 95 percent of new performance running shoe products.
   - In Europe, Asics sells products with fabric made of Ocean Waste Plastic sourced from PET bottles recovered from beaches in Sri Lanka. Local supply chain partner Hirdaramani processed the recovered bottles into new polyester.
   - Earth Day Initiative: In 2020, Asics used a circular manufacturing approach to recycle five tons of textile waste, the equivalent of

25,000 T-shirts, into new shoes. Also, the sock lining of the shoes was developed using a resource-saving technology called solution dyeing that reduces CO_2 emissions by around 45 percent and cuts water use by around 33 percent compared to conventional dyeing processes.
4. Use: Constantly improve quality so products last even longer.
5. New Life: Take items back for reuse and recycling.
    - ReAct Sustains: In 2020, Asics partnered with ReAct Sustains in The Netherlands to make sure defective items were being recycled rather than incinerated. For shoes returned to Asics shops, they set up a new process to make sure that items that cannot be reused or resold are instead recycled.
    - Asics's Road Tested Program: Asics accepts minimally worn returned shoes that they make available to consumers at retail outlets at a discounted price.
    - Give Back Box: ASICS has partnered with Give Back Box to provide convenient and free recycling for unwanted footwear and apparel. Asics allows consumers to reuse their online shipping boxes to donate gently used clothing, shoes, and accessories in the box your order came in with a prepaid shipping label to print and ship.

In addition to these five steps, Asics seeks to educate consumers by printing the carbon footprint, or total amount of greenhouse gases generated over a product's life cycle, on their product packaging. A detailed justification for their calculations printed on their packaging, including calculations for the carbon footprint of the GEL-KAYANO 30, are available on Asics's website with values shown on these products (ASICS Corporation, 2023).

10.3 The Solution: Believable Sustainability

Sustainability, accountability, and climate conscious consumers all play integral roles in building brands' believable sustainability efforts. Policy also plays a large role in holding corporations accountable for their role in advancing or helping mitigate the climate crisis by mandating transparency and climate action. Government and nongovernmental organization policies, including the United Nations' Paris Agreement and Sustainable Development Goals, play a large role in holding corporations accountable for their role in advancing or helping mitigate the climate crisis by mandating transparency and climate action.

In 1969, the United States' Environmental Protection Agency (EPA) enacted the National Environmental Policy Act of 1969, which committed the United States to sustainability, declaring it a national policy "to create and maintain conditions under which humans and nature can exist in productive harmony, that permit fulfilling the social, economic and other requirements of present and future generations" (U.S. EPA, 2014).

In 1987, the United Nations Brundtland Commission defined sustainability as "meeting the needs of the present without compromising the ability of future generations to meet their own needs" (United Nations, 2023a).

The Paris Agreement was adopted by 196 Parties at the UN Climate Change Conference (COP21) in Paris, France, in December 2015, with the goal to limit the world's temperature increase to 1.5°C. The Paris Agreement asks for greenhouse gas emissions to peak before 2025 at the latest and to decline 43 percent by 2030. Ratifying countries are held accountable through action outlined in their national climate action plans, known as nationally determined contributions (NDCs), and require cooperation from major brands and corporations worldwide to achieve those goals. Each successive NDC is meant to reflect an increasingly higher degree of ambition compared to the previous version (The Paris Agreement, 2023).

To help meet expectations and obligations outlined in policy agreements and mandates, industry leaders are attempting to create sustainable practices by pursuing transparency and educating consumers. The United Nations' Sustainable Development Goals provide a helpful framework for any brand, company, or organization to align with in a way that addresses a range of social needs including education, health, social protection, and job opportunities, while tackling climate change and environmental protection.

At the United Nations' Summit in September 2015, global leaders adopted the following seventeen Sustainable Development Goals meant to be adopted by industry leaders worldwide as part of the 2030 Agenda for Sustainable Development:

- No poverty;

- Zero hunger;
- Good health and well-being;
- Quality education;
- Gender equality;
- Clean water and sanitation;
- Affordable and clean energy;
- Decent work and economic growth;
- Investment in industry, innovation and infrastructure;
- Reduced inequalities;
- Sustainable cities and communities;
- Responsible consumption and production;
- Climate action;
- Life below water: Sustainably manage and protect marine and coastal ecosystems from pollution and address impacts of ocean acidification;
- Life on land: Urgent action must be taken to reduce the loss of natural habitats and biodiversity by supporting global food and water security;
- Peace, justice, and strong institutions that work with governments and communities to end conflict and insecurity; and
- Partnerships for the goals: Coordinating policies to help developing countries manage their debt and promote international trade.

The UN's SDGs are not legally binding, but provide a credible and practical application opportunity for any brand, company, or organization to align with in a way that addresses a range of social needs including education, health, social protection, and job opportunities, while tackling climate change and environmental protection (United Nations, 2023b).

Climate Conscious Consumers

While alignment with global policies is advantageous, industry research shows that sustainability is like "the frosting on the cake.... consumers prefer brands committed to sustainability... but there is a ceiling and a floor" to those benefits (Aronson, 2023). Consumers believe brands should help them change the world, and brands have a responsibility to educate consumers (Townsend, 2023). At the same time, consumers want to know more about solutions to the climate crisis beyond wind turbines and recycling. This is an opportunity for brands worldwide to communicate their priorities and values as educators of climate conscious consumers—like Asics does with printing their carbon footprint/emissions on product packaging. For these reasons and more, our research shows that brands Generation Z believe in include Patagonia, for their commitment to sustainability and donating large sums of money to organizations solving the climate crisis; and Target, because they sell sustainable products including Method cleaner which provides glass cleaning product bottles with eco-friendly refills.

A challenge in consumer industries in particular is that producing sustainable products is more expensive and time consuming than what has become normative in consumer-driven capitalism, and requires markup higher than market averages. In B2B businesses, sustainable practices can be more time consuming and expensive to develop. To combat these challenges from an industry perspective, leading executives in the sustainability space don't think much about competition. Rather, they see themselves as partners. As Raphael Bemporad, cofounder of BBMG, said (2023): "Our world is waiting: what kind of world do we want to inhabit? We need to create joy, community, and connection." Similarly, according to Mary Jane Melendez, chief sustainability and global impact officer at General Mills, "We will not compete when it comes to doing good.... We are all partners with Mother Nature" (2023). And, Scott Heid, vice president of Procter & Gamble, said: "There is no competition in sustainability" (Heid, 2023).

To this end, it is important for all brands and organizations to take inventory of ways they can combat the climate crisis, ranging from implementing a recycling program to becoming a B Corporation or similar. An application exercise for evaluating a brand's current context with tips for creating a strategy and goals is outlined below.

10.4 Application: Context, Strategy, and Goals

Sustainability KPIs will look different for many brands and organizations. No matter where a brand or organization is at in their sustainability journey, it's important to identify and quantify your brand's sustainability context, strategy, and goals. Here's a road map to get started (Cherel-Bonnemaison et al., 2021):

- **Context: How Good Can We Be?**
  - Determine the baseline: What is your brand/organization's sustainability context, strategy, and goals? If none exist, get started.
  - Competitive Analysis: To establish a sustainability benchmark for your brand/organization, evaluate what your competitors are doing in this area:
    - Conduct a competitive analysis and/or position mapping exercise to evaluate how you're doing in comparison to peers in the competitive landscape as it relates to sustainability efforts.
      - See details about competitive analysis and position mapping in Chapter 7: Brand Research and Assessment and Chapter 8: Brand Positioning.
  - Sustainability SWOT Analysis: Assess your brand/organization's strengths, weaknesses, opportunities, and threats as it relates to sustainability efforts.
    - See details about SWOT analyses in Chapter 7: Brand Research and Assessment.

- **Strategy: How Will We Get There?**
  - Create sustainability goals and KPIs: Create sustainability goals that align with your organization's value proposition(s).
    - See details about value propositions in Chapter 1: Brand Purpose.
    - See details about KPIs in Chapter 7: Brand Research and Assessment.
    - Ensure your brand/organization's sustainability goals align with the SMART framework: specific, measurable, attainable, relevant, and time-based.
  - Consistency: Set up policies and guidelines to meet regulatory, customer, organizational, and public sustainability expectations and demands in the present and future.

- **Goals: Take Action**
  - Implement principles and initiatives for conscious consumption and production in line with your brand/organization's goals and objectives.

- Are there gaps to fill or areas to improve on?
- Pilot innovative initiatives. How can your brand/organization pursue:
  - a zero-carbon supply base?
  - waste reduction in supply chain, on-site, etc.?
  - zero tolerance on human-rights violations at suppliers?
- Consider certifications: What areas do you want to develop/improve on? Are there certifications to pursue in:
  - Organic, Fair Trade, B Corp, LEED, etc.?
- Continuing education and expansion: Would your organization benefit from:
  - new employee hires in the sustainability space?
  - more frequent visits from consultants in the sustainability space?
- Deploy at scale: Are there collaborations or partnerships with sustainability organizations/efforts that your brand/organization can pursue?
- Communication plan: How can you clearly articulate your sustainability goals and objectives with internal and external audiences and constituents?
  - See tips on developing a compelling content calendar in Chapter 6: Brand Communication.
- Track performance against targets: Measure your sustainability efforts with attainable KPIs.
  - See tips on developing and selecting effective KPIs in Chapter 7: Brand Research and Assessment.

10.5 Metrics: Certifications and Credibility

Certifications can provide an extra layer of credibility for brands. B Corp, Fair Trade Certified, and Organic certifications play key roles in consumer industries.

Emerging C-suite positions like chief purpose officers (CPO), chief mission officers (CMO), and chief sustainability officers (CSO) are responsible for setting the mission, vision, and metrics behind the brand's commitments to sustainability and social responsibility. Oftentimes these executives are responsible for ensuring brands are aligned with sustainable processes and values that matter to key stakeholders, and for pursuing and maintaining various certifications in the marketplace.

Sustainability looks different for brands across the board. For a direct to consumer (D2C) company like General Mills, Seventh Generation, or Nespresso, paying attention to supply chains, ethical sourcing of products from farms to fulfillment and distribution centers to stores, and product quality are key. Innovation is key to ensuring sustainability in supply chains. Sustainability in supply chains is challenging, expensive, and takes time. Some brands leading in this space include Gap's activewear stores Athleta, where you can send in your clothes to be recycled back into their product lines. Another example is Beautycounter, a beauty brand that has a "mission team" that carries out a five-step screening process and twenty-three safety checks for each product before it gets past the "innovation team" to consumers. Luana Bumachar notes this makes the innovation team's job harder, but that it's all worthwhile for the brand's value proposition (2023).

Growth in the organic and fair trade markets is very difficult to plan for, especially when a brand upholds transparency back to the source. For companies like herbal tea brand Traditional Medicinals that source their products from farmers worldwide, it takes time to cultivate deep relationships that are necessary to support farmers because certifications can be difficult to attain and are very expensive. Traditional Medicinals invests in creating a compostable infrastructure. The brand also seeks to provide opportunities to educate and engage consumers in the advocacy process. To engage consumers, they help customers connect with local compost companies and encourage customers to engage in political advocacy by writing to their local reps to support the compostable act (Horst, 2023).

Industry researchers have found that environmental claims and commitments benefit products more than social ones do. On the other hand, social claims and commitments benefit companies more than environmental ones do (Aronson, 2023). Some experts argue that providing sustainable products is more important than consumer education (Townsend, 2023).

For business to business (B2B) companies like a construction company, supply chain management and certifications including U.S. Green Building Council's Leadership in Energy and Environmental Design (LEED) certifications are integral to proving a commitment to sustainability (U.S. Green Building Council, 2023). Beyond LEED, there are hundreds of new certifications emerging across sectors on a regular basis.

In the corporate realm, Environmental and Social Governance (ESG) emerged in the 1960s as an investment strategy based on brands' and companies' commitments to a set of environmental, social, and governance standards (Atkins, 2020; Napoletano, 2023). ESG commitments are quantified on a 100-point scale: Companies and ESG rating firms including Bloomberg, S&P Dow Jones Indices, JUST Capital, MSCI, and Refinitiv use various metrics and weighting schemes to evaluate annual reports, corporate sustainability measures, board structure, management of resources, employees, compensation and finances to help guide investors to socially responsible brands, companies, and organizations.

Sustainable ESG funds—investments that consider environmental, social, and corporate governance factors—exceeded $350 billion in net assets in 2021 (Hale, 2022). This shows that it is becoming increasingly profitable for companies to produce sustainable products and to lower their carbon footprints: Because investors and consumers alike are demanding it.

Fair Trade Certification

Consumer-facing and B2B brands can both benefit from fair trade certification as it ensures their commitment to sustainable and safe working conditions and supply chains throughout the development, sourcing, and manufacturing of a product. Fair Trade USA was founded in 1998 and certifies that a company is following these social, environmental, and economic standards (Fair Trade USA, 2023):

- Ensuring safe working conditions
- Participating in environmental protection
- Providing sustainable livelihoods
- Contributing to community development funds

Fair trade brands and organizations pay community development funds directly to Fair Trade USA, who then invests it directly back into marginalized communities in line with needs identified through a Fair Trade-issued needs assessment in sectors including water, education, housing, and/or health care.

Fair Trade Certification aligns with the UN's SDGs, so companies who are certified can message their support for these sustainability goals to their consumers and stakeholders.

Fair Trade Certification contributes directly to upholding the UN's SDGs. Consumers can also become fair trade certified as "conscious consumers."

USDA Organic Certification

The U.S. Department of Agriculture (USDA) implemented national organic standards on organic production and processing in October 2002, following more than a decade of development (Greene & Kremen, 2003). According to researchers, organic farming is a significant step in mitigating the climate crisis because it reduces pollution, conserves water, reduces soil erosion, increases soil fertility and health, and uses less energy (Mullen, 2021). Organic farming does so by following federal regulations for sustainable soil quality, animal raising practices, pest and weed control, and biologically based farming methods like regular crop rotations. Additionally, to achieve organic certification, organic producers must:

- rely on natural substances, without most conventional pesticides, bioengineering, or ionizing radiation;
- not give animals antibiotics or growth hormones, or feed them animal by-products;
- not use genetically modified organisms (GMOs);
- only use pesticides made with natural ingredients.

According to the USDA website (2023), the National Organic Program (NOP) develops the rules and regulations for the production, handling, labeling, and enforcement of all USDA organic products. There are five basic steps to organic certification:

- The farm or business adopts organic practices, selects a USDA-accredited certifying agent, and submits an application and fees to the certifying agent.
- The certifying agent reviews the application to verify that practices comply with USDA organic regulations.

- An inspector conducts an on-site inspection of the applicant's operation.
- The certifying agent reviews the application and the inspector's report to determine if the applicant complies with the USDA organic regulations.
- The certifying agent issues an organic certificate.

To maintain organic certification, farms and businesses go through an annual review and inspection process. Businesses and brands not located in the United States can also attain USDA organic certification but must go through a separate approval process. American consumers are willing to pay up to 116 percent of the market price for an organic product (Chimata, 2023), so pursuing USDA organic certification and marketing that certification on product labels and in content marketing materials including websites and social media is advantageous.

Brand Profile: Clif Bar & Company

Clif Bar was founded in 1992 by Gary Erickson, a cyclist who was inspired to create a better tasting energy bar (Sustainable Brands—Clif Bar & Company, 2023). Clif upholds responsible sourcing goals, practices, and policies including the following CORE commitments (Clifbar, 2023b):

- **Connecting:** With the farmers who grow their ingredients to create a traceable and transparent supply chain.
- **Organic:** Clif became USDA Organic certified in 2003, and 76 percent of everything Clif has bought since 2003 is certified organic, over one billion pounds of organic ingredients. By sourcing organic ingredients, Clif supports agricultural practices that support soil health and carbon sequestration and encourages restorative agricultural systems, such as crop diversity and rotations.
- **Restorative** practices: Clif became climate neutral by offsetting the carbon footprint of their offices, business travel, bakeries and delivery to distribution centers by investing in wind energy. They've also partnered with environmental organizations including American Forests to plant five thousand trees to offset their employee commutes. Clif also switched to 100 percent recycled paperboard for their packaging, generating an environmental savings upstream of 14,000 trees and 6 million gallons of water every year.

- **Ethical** sourcing and fair labor practices: Clif's suppliers go through an extensive screening process for quality ingredient selection and enforces a supplier code of conduct modeled after International Labor Organization (ILO) conventions that uphold legal, social, and environmental responsibility.

Certification: In 2023, Clif Bar's CLIF Kid snack bar brand became Climate Neutral Certified, the leading consumer label for climate neutrality. Carbon labeling has become increasingly vital for brands to demonstrate accountability, provide education about greenhouse gas emissions and earn consumer trust (Clifbar, 2023c).

10.6 Case: Patagonia

Patagonia is an outdoor outfitter with a mission statement committed to sustainability: "We're in business to save our home planet." In 1973, Patagonia opened its first outdoor outfitting store. In 1985, Patagonia began to pledge 1 percent of their sales to the preservation and restoration of the natural environment. In 2002, Patagonia's founder Yvon Chouinard, along with the owner of Blue Ribbon Files Craig Mathews, created "1% for the Planet," a nonprofit corporation/alliance of businesses that align over concern for the social and environmental impacts of commercialization. Participating organizations in 1% for the Planet contribute 1 percent of their total annual sales to grassroots environmental groups. In return, members receive the satisfaction of paving the way for more corporate responsibility in the business community and the recognition, support, and patronage of conscientious consumers who value serious commitment to the environment (1% for the Planet—Patagonia, 2023; Chouinard, 2023).

As of 2023, Patagonia had awarded over $140 million to domestic and international grassroots environmental groups making a difference in their local communities (Patagonia, 2023).

B Corp certification is one way Patagonia shows and certifies their commitments to sustainability. In January 2012, Patagonia was the first California company to sign up for B Corp certification, joining more than 500 certified B Corporations in 60 different industries. As of 2023, fewer than 6,000 companies around the world are certified as B Corp businesses.

B Corp members must meet strict environmental, social, and governance standards and benchmarks set by B Labs to gain certification in addition to paying annual fees. Patagonia publishes their annual benefit corporation reports on their website, which is a requirement of all certified B Corps (About B Lab, 2023).

Ownership is another way Patagonia signifies their commitment to sustainability and purpose. In 2022, Chouinard announced that, instead of "going public," that Patagonia would be "going purpose." In 2023, Chouinard wrote:

> One option was to sell Patagonia and donate all the money. But we couldn't be sure a new owner would maintain our values or keep our team of people around the world employed. Another path was to take the company public. What a disaster that would have been. Even public companies with good intentions are under too much pressure to create short-term gain at the expense of long-term vitality and responsibility. Truth be told, there were no good options available. So, we created our own. Instead of "going public," you could say we're "going purpose." Instead of extracting value from nature and transforming it into wealth for investors, we'll use the wealth Patagonia creates to protect the source of all wealth.

Chouinard gave away ownership of Patagonia to a climate-focused trust—the Patagonia Purpose Trust—and a group of nonprofit organizations called the Holdfast Collective. Chouinard noted that this decision was intentional after weighing every option, and is a choice that allowed him to give every dollar that is not reinvested back into Patagonia to be "distributed as dividends to protect the planet" (Chouinard, 2023).

As of September 2022, Patagonia's non-voting stock was worth close to $3 billion, and the company expected they'd be giving away $100 million per year (Gelles, 2022).

The Holdfast Collective is a 501(c)(4) not-for-profit organization that can "advocate for causes and political candidates in addition to making grants and investments in our planet" (Chouinard, 2023). According to Patagonia (2023), the Holdfast Collective is funded by Patagonia's profits: "Each year, excess profits—money we make after reinvesting in the business (including money we want to save for unforeseen events, like a pandemic)—will be distributed as a dividend to the Collective to be used for its work."

The Holdfast Collective "uses every dollar received to fight the environmental crisis, protect nature and biodiversity, and support thriving communities, as quickly as possible" (Chouinard, 2023). In addition to running off of Patagonia's profits, the Holdfast Collective owns 98% of the company and all of the nonvoting stock—nonvoting stock carries economic value but not decision-making authority.

The Patagonia Purpose Trust owns the remaining 2 percent of the company, and was "created solely to protect our company's values and mission" (Chouinard, 2023). The Patagonia Purpose Trust owns all of the voting stock of the company, which gives it the right to approve key company decisions, like who sits on the board of directors and what changes can be made to the company's legal charter, including its reason for being and B Corp commitments. The Patagonia Purpose Trust is directed by the Chouinard family. The Chouinards elect and oversee leadership and own 2 percent of the company, including all of the voting stock. Because voting stock has both economic value and decision-making authority, the Patagonia Purpose Trust—guided by the Chouinard family—also guides the philanthropic work performed by the Holdfast Collective (Chouinard, 2023).

Key Terms

Carbon neutral
Carbon offset
Climate crisis
Environmental and Social Governance (ESG)
Eco-conscious

Fair Trade
Greenwashing
Organic
Sustainability
Sustainable Development Goals

Discussion Questions

1 Define sustainability and provide 3 examples of brands leading the way in this area. Why do these brands stand out as leaders in this space?
2 Describe the differences between fair trade and organic. What type of companies would benefit from a fair trade or organic certification?
3 What are various ways D2C / B2B companies can become more sustainable?

Activity

Sustainability Social Media Campaign: You are a digital marketing specialist tasked with creating a social media campaign to promote your brand's commitment to sustainability with the goal of raising awareness of your thought leadership in this area. Choose a brand to represent, then create a blog post, video, podcast, and infographic for publication on a social media platform of your choosing.

11

Social Responsibility

We define social responsibility as brands' commitments to promote well-being among employees, stakeholders, clients, customers, and communities around the world. Two pillars that support social responsibility include diversity, equity, inclusion, access, and belonging (DEIA+B) efforts and charitable giving. This chapter provides practitioners with hands-on guidance for incorporating socially responsible initiatives and priorities across operations and in consumer interactions. This chapter also identifies miscommunication as a prevalent and noteworthy problem regarding social responsibility initiatives, and provides solutions for communicating the value of these initiatives to consumers and customers. Potential solutions include creating a purpose-driven approach, exemplified by the case of an accessible jewelry brand and Ben & Jerry's social activism. Metrics for measuring social responsibility include employee experience and charitable giving and philanthropy.

Chapter Outline

11.1 Introduction: What Is Social Responsibility?	270
11.2 The Problem: Miscommunication	272
11.3 The Solution: Believable Social Responsibility	274
11.4 Case: CONQUERing	277
11.5 Application: Conscious Consumers and Brand Value Co-creation	280
11.6 Metrics: Employee Experience (EX), Charitable Giving, and Philanthropy	283
Key Terms	288
Discussion Questions	289
Activity	289

11.1 Introduction: What Is Social Responsibility?

Social Responsibility: Brands' commitments to promote well-being among employees, stakeholders, clients, customers, and communities around the world.

Brands' social, financial, and environmental commitments all play a role in building believability. Socially, brands implement and uphold various initiatives relating to diversity, equity, inclusion, accessibility, and belonging (DEIA+B) internally through ethical production practices and fair treatment of workers, and externally through partnerships. Financially, brands promote well-being for communities around the world through charitable giving and philanthropy.

Environmental and social governance (ESG), corporate social responsibility (CSR), and corporate social advocacy or activism (CSA) are all acronyms to codify brands' social responsibility with implications for brands' prosocial commitments, which inform their social influence. Brands' stakeholders and leaders decide how to steward their resources to promote well-being among employees, stakeholders, clients, customers, and communities within their organizations and around the world. Well-being begins as a part of a believable brand culture among a brand's employee base and, from there, can expand externally to influence believable branding and messaging.

Two social responsibility commitments we explore in this chapter include diversity, equity, inclusion, accessibility, and belonging (DEIA+B) initiatives; and charitable giving and philanthropy. Consumers are actively looking to buy goods and services from authentic and consistent socially responsible companies. This chapter takes a dive into how authentic and consistent commitments to DEIA+B and charitable giving and philanthropy can help brands build believability.

One way brands pursue social responsibility is through establishing comprehensive corporate social responsibility (CSR), corporate social advocacy, or corporate social activism (CSA) agendas that involve intentional charitable giving and partnership efforts with prosocial brands and organizations. An increasing number of socially responsible brands and organizations began to build explicit DEIA+B mission(s) in the 21st century. Our research and industry trends show that the implementation of DEIA+B initiatives occur with varying levels of effectiveness. Research shows that authenticity is key to success with these initiatives and that such initiatives have increasingly served as an effective means for brand management by allowing brands to express their identity that aligns with their consumer values (Ferraro et al., 2023). Consumer markets are now exponentially growing to embrace and appeal to global audiences, calling for deeper understanding across real and perceived differences between individuals with regard to their race, age, physical or mental abilities, socioeconomic background, sexual orientation, and more (Rynarzewska et al., 2024). Likewise, industry leaders highlight the increasing importance of addressing DEIA+B in an appropriate manner to boost brand trust, loyalty, and purchase intention among consumers. According to consumer research conducted by Wong (2024), consumers are more likely to support brands that show commitment to diversity and inclusion values in their marketing. This is especially true for Latinx+, African American, and Millennial consumers (Wong, 2024).

Believable brands integrate their promotional activities with the values they stand for. Authentic and consistent commitments to DEIA+B are an important component of building brand believability. As more companies realize the critical role of integrating DEIA+B into their day-to-day operations, we recognize brands need timely and practical guidance on how to do this in a believable way. Consumers are more conscious of brands' commitments to social influence than ever, and DEIA+B is one area where brands have experienced major setbacks due to inauthentic and inconsistent efforts and initiatives.

Addressing the needs for strategic guidance on communication centered on DEIA+B, this chapter walks you through the major problem facing brands attempting to implement effective DEIA+B initiatives—miscommunication. Additionally, this chapter explores solutions to anticipate these potential setbacks by redirecting brands' focus to their purpose. The case for this chapter is the inclusive and accessible jewelry brand CONQUERing. The chapter concludes with application of these strategies and metrics that can help show the effectiveness of DEIA+B initiatives and purpose-driven communication. By providing concrete examples and step-by-step solutions to tackle potential problems in implementing DEIA+B in brand operations, current and future professionals in the fields of advertising, branding, communication, and marketing will have tools to revisit and reinvent their status quo in DEIA+B.

11.2 The Problem: Miscommunication

Despite the prevalence of straightforward communication regarding brands' social responsibility efforts in environmental, economic, and social sectors, consumer skepticism toward such missions is increasing. Brands' authenticity is of the utmost importance when it comes to DEIA+B initiatives in particular. Driving profit is the number one priority for many brands, which makes it harder for consumers to be convinced and persuaded of the authenticity behind brands' DEIA+B efforts. Our research shows how this skepticism has manifested itself. Gen Z consumers in particular call out brands' DEIA+B efforts as unethical when emotion and sentiment are used:

> Sometimes it's not ethical… you never really know anymore. I would say it's like a brand capitalizing on—they have these ads that are super sentimental, they make sure to include diversity and capture emotion and have like, "Oh we're connecting people, connecting cultures."… I think that is a way a lot of brands try to capitalize on social impact or make a social impact by being like, "We are contributing," or "We're making a social impact with our brand."

Consumers often express concern over the authenticity of brands' social responsibility commitments due to brands' prioritization of driving profits which, according to consumers, comes into opposition with quality social responsibility initiatives:

> Just like we're trying to buy a product, they're trying to sell a product. They're trying to make money, and that's their main goal. So no more responsibility than any other person would have…. Their top priority is making a profit, nine out ten times. There are some, of course, that are actually good like Patagonia, for example, but nine out ten times, their number one concern is profitability.

There could be some generational differences in this point of view that driving profit is inconsistent with social responsibility initiatives, given that these focus group participants are all from the Generation Z age group. Nevertheless, it is noteworthy that overall consumer expectations toward brands taking social responsibility seriously are low or nonexistent. On the other hand, if brands are *mis*communicating their social responsibility values, the magnitude of backlash to such missteps will be bigger than that of what brands will gain by doing it right.

One example that demonstrates the significant and negative impact of brands' missteps toward DEIA+B communication is Lululemon. Founder of Lululemon, Chip Wilson, who left the company back in 2015, has faced a significant amount of backlash and criticism from the public regarding his comments on the brand's mission toward diversity, equity, and inclusion at an event in 2023 (Mordowanec, 2024). Chip Wilson publicly expressed his distaste for Lululemon's diversity and inclusion mission, stating that the diverse appearance of models featured in its advertisements looks "unhealthy, sickly, and not inspirational." Wilson stepped a mile further, saying that "I think the definition of a brand is that you're not everything to everybody.... You've got to be clear that you don't want certain customers coming in." Though Lululemon later debunked his comments by explicitly detaching him and his comments from the company, it is inevitable to admit that the original founder of the company has disrespected a large portion of its own consumers as well as prospective consumers.

Such brand missteps regarding social responsibility value communication, however, are not uncommon among other big corporations. Target, for instance, has faced a continuous stream of boycotts and criticisms against its Pride Month LGBTQIA+ merchandise displays since 2023, and suffered significant backlash and threats from some of their customers. In 2025, Target continued to face backlash and protests from consumers and communities for rolling back some of their DEIA+B initiatives. Similarly, Bud Light triggered extreme hostility from some consumers with its DEIA+B initiatives in an attempt to broaden its reach through partnerships with Dylan Mulvaney (*Guardian*, 2024). Target and Bud Light's examples in addressing DEIA+B values through day-to-day brand operations don't always land with consumers—especially if those efforts aren't authentic and consistent with a brand's mission and values. These two examples, in particular, have also appeared in some of the focus groups we conducted among Generation Z consumers. In the case of Bud Light:

> I feel like [Bud Light's] pitfall with that, which is sad, because there's not many transgender influencers being incorporated, they are trying to be inclusive, but the way they did that wasn't.

Well, it was weird because Anheuser-Busch, Bud Light's parent company, a couple days after that thing, put out this super pro-America, patriotic, guy riding a horse in the mountains, stereotypical beer, heart of the country ad. People saw that as responding to the backlash for having a trans influencer on their can and whatever. So I guess, from that example, you could argue that it worked at some point at least for that. But in the long run, I don't think it worked.

I think with going off of that, diversifying the ways that people are seen in marketing, diversifying the group of people that are consuming a product is a good way that brands are messaging consumers. Like we had talked about, it's important to see yourself in a brand for you to want that brand. So if you are seeing an advertisement from a brand with someone that you identify with, that you can relate to, I think that's a good way that a brand can entice me.

Taken together, the aforementioned examples illustrate major problems that even bigger brands are facing when communicating their social responsibility missions. Brand value miscommunication may lead to significant consequences for losing brand reputation that takes a long time to build and solidify, and agitate its consumers who may not be coming back to purchase it any more. At least for the younger generation of consumers, such as Generation Z groups, the overall reactions to the *mis*communication regarding social responsibility agenda are twofold: (a) They want to see it implemented appropriately, and they do think it's important to see themselves and the values they hold on to in a brand, and (b) They do not see clear connections between a brand advocating for DEIA+B and its clear and positive impact on brand communication in general. Taking these noteworthy problems into consideration, the next section discusses how to direct the focus of social responsibility—with an emphasis on charitable giving, philanthropy, and DEIA+B.

11.3 The Solution: Believable Social Responsibility

This solution is twofold: Brands that are committed to charitable giving and philanthropy and authentic and consistent DEIA+B initiatives co-create believability with employees, stakeholders, clients, and consumers. This work is hard work, as it involves innovative connections with these groups and a commitment to working through miscommunication with credible strategy.

We define diversity, equity, inclusion, accessibility, and belonging as brands' creation of inclusive cultures by cultivating fair, representative, and welcoming commitments to clients, customers, employees, and stakeholders of all abilities, identities, and backgrounds. Given that consumer skepticism toward brands' DEIA+B value communication is quite prevalent and can become problematic, it is fair to ask who bears, or is supposed to bear, the burden of social responsibility: Consumers, brands, or both? Among the 20 CMOs we interviewed, many of them and their company leaders see their organizations as lagging or behind in the DEIA+B space, and are actively thinking through how they can infuse DEIA+B values and priorities into their company/organization's purpose(s) without being inauthentic. They often actively build and pursue partnerships to uphold commitments to diversity, equity, and inclusion, including minority mentoring programs and contracts with minority-owned businesses. The problem we see, however, is that these companies' approaches do not always align with what their consumers are expecting from them. We asked the same question to our consumer focus groups, and found one way consumers are aligning with brands they can believe in is by doing their own research to gain knowledge of employees' working conditions, wages, and whether or not the brands and organizations they follow and believe in have equitable and accessible labor environments. While many brands rank well on the sustainability front, they may not boast high-quality employee labor relations conditions. Consumers believe employees' working conditions are some of the most important criteria brands should build quality efforts in to prove they have an authentic DEIA+B mission.

If there is a disconnect between what company leaders, including CMOs, consider important in their DEIA+B value communication and what consumers value, there is a significant and long-term risk for miscommunicating what both parties expect from each other. A practical solution to avoid this discrepancy and subsequent negative setbacks is to redirect the focus of DEIA+B communication efforts back to its cause: Brand purpose. CMOs we interviewed consistently stated how important it was that their teams "ladder up" to the brand purpose in and through their day-to-day operations. For example, Mark Derks, CMO of BlueGrace Logistics, a B2B third-party logistics company, pointed out that communicating purpose leads to proper brand understanding which helps boost brand awareness, trust, loyalty, and overall brand growth:

> Having an awareness of the BlueGrace brand is extremely important. It's critical to our sales people and expedites our sales process greatly if buyers are aware of us. It also drives our corporate citizenship for our communities and stakeholders, not just shareholders, but stakeholders in terms of all of the good things BlueGrace is doing across communities. When you talk about purpose, that's where I would shift and talk about brand understanding. Buyers may have heard about BlueGrace, but do they understand how we help businesses be better? So, we spend a lot of time driving purpose and understanding so our clients and prospects understand how we help their business grow.

From what we understand, what consumers expect from DEIA+B value communication is to identify a genuine connection between the brand and what they stand for. The latter can be interpreted in a variety of ways, but what we insist in this chapter, and this book entirely, is that what brands stand for should stem from the core of their purpose. How does the brand purpose connect back to the DEIA+B values they claim in any communication efforts, or day-to-day operations? Why should your consumers care about such values when they engage with your brands in any way or purchase your products? What is the clear connection between your brand purpose and the values your consumers find important when they consume your products? Without having a clear understanding of this connection and an appreciation for the importance of brand purpose-driven value communication, all of the time, effort, and budgets that feed your DEIA+B initiatives are going nowhere, and may even backfire—regardless of your brand's intention.

In the following section, we introduce a great example of a brand that practices their DEIA+B initiatives with a clear brand purpose, and reflects such values across various different aspects of their brand communication, operations, and consumer experiences. By looking closely at the example, we hope to give a realistic example with hands-on guidance for how any brand should deliver DEIA+B with authentic and significant brand value through high-quality communication to consumers.

11.4 Case: CONQUERing

Among all the brands in the industry practicing their purpose-driven communication to their consumers, CONQUERing could serve as a role model for a purpose-driven value communication deeply rooted in their brand operation as well as consumer-brand interactions. We had a fortunate opportunity to interview Tammy Nelson, the CEO and founder of a jewelry brand, CONQUERing. Founded in January of 2020, CONQUERing has grown exponentially to be recognized in 2022 by Inc. 5000 as one of the 500 fastest-growing companies in the United States, which is only within two years since its very first introduction to the market (Inc. 5000, 2022). While celebrating its incredible success and accomplishments in the first few years, Nelson also pointed out that the brand has faced some challenges along the way: "I would say that if I had to name just one thing, that was the biggest challenge in our time, it has been to find a way to create sustainable, consistent growth that we have more control over."

She then emphasized the importance of the clear brand mission that CONQUERing was built upon, and how she believes in the power of brand purpose in driving sustainable and consistent growth together with the brand's consumers:

> We have a saying, I guess we call it our mantra, which is, "Our rings won't change the world, but those who wear them will." And it's really the core of what we do. Our mission is to help people feel empowered. And so we know that that comes from within our customers to feel empowered. But we want to give them the tools to feel empowered during their day. And so that is really the core of why we exist and why we created the business and how we market ourselves.

What's noteworthy about her insight here, particularly, is that at the core of the business is brand purpose and mission, which will direct every aspect of how the brand is positioned, operated, and therefore interacting with its consumers. With the mission of "Helping people feel empowered," CONQUERing strives to deliver the mission in multiple ways for its consumers to genuinely feel empowered through their brand experience. We then followed up with a question asking what believability means to her as a leader of the fast-growing brand, and how important it is to cultivate believability among its consumers. She emphasized the concept of authenticity along with believability:

> To me, believability is another way of saying authenticity. And so for us, we really believe in the idea of show versus tell. And what we mean by that is, I mentioned that I work mostly in marketing our business. But I can market all day long. And I can say, "Our products are great, our service is awesome, our shipping is fast, it's high quality, it's unique," I can say a million things. But unless the product, the experience they have with our product and the experience that they have with our service match what I'm saying, that ruins believability. And it also takes away from the authenticity of our brand and what we stand for.

Moreover, she also brought up the deep connection between marketing and brand believability by addressing how marketing plays a critical role in enhancing or ruining believability.

> I believe that marketing and customer experience go absolutely hand in hand. And you can't have a solid brand if the experience doesn't match. Because that's what breaks down that trust and the believability in who you are. If you're saying something and then you're not delivering upon it. So for me, believability has to do with having people experience what you tell them they're going to experience, for it to actually match.

Likewise, how they implement their DEIA+B initiative in their brands reflects exactly what she emphasized: "Deliver what you say to your consumers." She shared a specific example with a consumer who was looking for a bigger size ring and finally found CONQUERing's inclusive sizing options that made her stay loyal to the brand after all.

> A core part of our belief system is we're not here just to make certain people feel empowered. We are on a mission to help everyone feel empowered. So some of the ways that manifest themselves in our brand is—one example is we have the largest range of sizes of any major jewelry brand. So we go all the way from a size four all the way to a fourteen, or actually we just launched a fifteen. And it sounds like, "Oh, okay, lots of companies are size inclusive," but in jewelry it's very, very, very infrequent. Many companies only offer sizes six, seven, eight, or seven, eight, nine. Because it's expensive to offer all these sizes, to develop the sizes and then carry them. But we don't want anyone to feel excluded. So we work really, really hard and we invest a lot of money in doing that.

The brand also goes further to offer products for various different groups of people in marginalized communities in the society, including but not limited to, those who have different physical or mental abilities:

> We also are focused very much on communities that maybe have different abilities. So our jewelry, we have a whole line of jewelry within our brand of braille jewelry for people who are vision impaired. We have a piece that is focused on supporting people who are deaf or hard of hearing. We have products that are focused on people with ADHD or autism. So we're always looking to find ways to be inclusive. Our designs are very universal too, and we try not to label things as men's versus women's and/or kids versus adults. We try to focus everything in a very inclusive nature and universally, so that we can empower. Again, it's all tied back to how we can have the most people to feel empowered.

Just like that, CONQUERing delivered its own promises by reflecting DEIA+B values universally across product choices and offerings, labeling considerations, etcetera so that consumers naturally accept the idea that the brand CONQUERing authentically and genuinely cares about the DEIA+B as the core value guiding every aspect of it. That way, consumer skepticism toward the brands' DEIA+B value communication is significantly lowered, which in turn, helps boost brand believability in the long term. In addition, Nelson also mentioned that employee perception toward the brand purpose and mission becomes increasingly important as well:

> I would say all of our employees are very much empowered to do the right thing. I guess for our customers, they don't have to come to me to say, "Hey, can I make an exception on this return policy?" Or "We got this compelling story from a customer; can I send them something? A free ring or whatever?" Everyone is empowered to help people feel empowered. It would be pretty sad if our whole mission was to help people feel empowered and then we didn't empower our own employees. So I would say that's the biggest fundamental way that our employees act, is they feel that they can do what they need to do to provide a great experience to our customers.

Not only direct consumers of the brand, but the employees who will be interacting with the consumers daily should also be able to agree with the brand mission that is practiced across the company. When the brand CONQUERing helps everyone feel empowered, the definition of everyone includes those who work for the brand. This is exactly what purpose-driven value communication should look like as a solution to the potential setbacks from consumers related to brands' DEIA+B communication. It is not something that is a unique or shiny strategy that enables successful purpose-driven value communication, but it is a universal and realistic day-to-day practice that applies DEIA+B mission across all aspects of brand positioning, operation, and consumer interaction, which ultimately leads to a positive and purposeful consumer experience.

11.5 Application: Conscious Consumers and Brand Value Co-creation

According to the integrative framework of brand value co-creation suggested by Ramaswamy & Ozcan (2016), brand communication empowered by a digitized atmosphere co-creates values among consumers and brands by positioning consumers as the core and essential player in establishing and maintaining a valued brand. That is, brands and brand building should be considered as a combined and collective effort of capabilities, engagements, and experiences through the interaction of individuals within a brand to evolve, invent, or redefine something new (Ramaswamy & Ozcan, 2016). Taking a similar approach, Merz et al. (2018) add support to this idea that brand value co-creation is a multidimensional concept encompassing consumer-owned resources including brand knowledge, brand skills, creativity, and brand connectedness; and consumer motivations including brand trust, passion, and brand commitment. This work also exemplifies the growing role of consumers in actively creating brand value together with the brand itself. Therefore, the same rule applies to how brands should practice their social responsibility initiatives: through brand value co-creation with its consumers. A great example of this was also given by Tammy Nelson, the CEO and founder of CONQUERing, by highlighting the importance of communicating the brand purpose to its consumers by actually showing what they stand for and engaging the DEIA+B mission to the extent that consumers feel it through their brand interactions:

> Very important. It's very, very important for us to communicate it, but we also are very careful to work to show it and not just tell it. I know that may

sound like a broken record, but I'll give you an example. Just a couple days ago I posted a video where I was telling a story about a random stranger that I met that I gifted a ring to. And following her receiving this ring, she almost looked like she was going to burst into tears. And she just kind of stopped, and she thanked me and said that it was the first ring that she had ever been able to have in her entire adult life because no one carried her size. And she was just so appreciative. So when I think about it from a branding perspective, it's so much more impactful for me to show that we gifted this ring to someone who had never been able to have a ring. Because most companies aren't inclusive enough to carry a ring size that would fit her. That's so much more impactful than me saying, "Oh, and we have the most ring sizes of any jewelry brand. We carry sizes four to fifteen." So it's very, very important for us to share our mission and our values, but we always aim to share it in a way of showing it versus just telling it.

Indeed, the significance of brand value co-creation does not simply sit on its typology, but also leads to noticeable influence on perceived corporate social responsibility (CSR) and brand authenticity. Muniz and Guzmán (2023)'s recent empirical study found that by leveraging brand value co-creation, consumer perception of CSR authenticity was significantly enhanced, which then also positively influenced brand equity. Findings of this study demonstrate that consumers do believe that a brand is co-creative by allowing them to participate in the value creation process, which helps the participating consumers to perceive brands' CSR activities more authentically. Now that consumers are becoming more aware and conscious of what brands are doing in terms of their production, employee treatment, marketing communications, and more, it is reasonable to accept that consumers are a crucial part of creating brand value together.

Some of the younger generations, such as Generation Z consumers, who responded to our focus group questions agreed that it becomes more important for brands to communicate their core value or purpose to its consumers, and they personally prefer such brands that are socially aware, standing out from their competitors in the same market category:

> I think it's really important, especially in this day and age, and especially as a way to stand out from other brands. Right now, we're struggling to come up with them off the top of our head; it's like, what are they actually trying to… what's their goal? I think that it's very important to stay on top of the competitors as well as social causes.

Even though some of them did not necessarily remember what a brand mission statement was exactly, the perception of brands that are doing socially responsible activities consistently in relation to their brand operations or communication, seems very important for cultivating believability toward a brand:

> I can't really recall any mission statements or anything, but that part is very important, communication aspect, but also showing that through a video, visuals, makes it believable and having consistency with that.

One particular example that some of the Generation Z consumers brought up during the focus group sessions is Disney and their DEI mission statement and what has been in fact "reflected" through their storyline:

> I think again, another example of Disney. For me, I feel like they're successful at it, but I also feel like at the same exact time they're failing at it. This is why. We read off their mission statements or something for diversity or something. They kept mentally in all the different mission statements that they have had for different realms of Disney, it always says, "All people," they're doing this for all people globally. They use words like they're really being inclusive of everybody. When we think of Disney, yes we can think of they're being more inclusive in terms of Black people, Indian people, Asian people, they are, but all at the same time, they're kind of failing at it because we all know there's a lot of controversies when it comes to the stories, for instance. It's like they have this like DEI statement where it's like, "We care about all people, we care about this, we care about global, we care about this." You guys care, but only to an extent. Because it's like "You guys are fabricating the history and the values for your primary audience, which really is the white audience." It's all at the same time, it's like they're putting it out and it's like it's successful, but then it always seems to be they get some sort of backlash. They're just really good at covering it up or putting something over it for the meantime.

Therefore, applying social responsibility—DEIA+B as part of that—into day-to-day brand experiences should start from acknowledging the role of consumers in creating brand value together with your brand. Without knowing your people—your clients, consumers, employees, and stakeholders—social responsibility efforts of any kind, including DEIA+B initiatives, will be cheap, not the authentic silver and gold that your brand is trying to create. In the next section, we introduce how to measure social responsibility efforts in a credible way.

11.6 Metrics: Employee Experience (EX), Charitable Giving, and Philanthropy

Now that we talked about how important it is to direct consumer focus on brand purpose in DEIA+B initiatives, and how to practically implement it in brands' perspectives with a great example of CONQUERing, it is time to think about how to measure the success of such efforts. Are there any golden metrics that consumers and brands could employ to examine how valuable socially responsible brands' efforts are? Among several options that may be applicable in this context, we introduce three categories in this section: Employee experience (EX), charitable giving, and philanthropy.

Charitable Giving and Philanthropy

Measuring social responsibility at a brand can be as simple as quantifying the amount of dollars a brand provides to charitable causes. Money talks, and authentic philanthropic partnerships—whether it be through a foundation or one-time gifts—matter to conscious consumers.

Establishing a codified corporate philanthropy strategy—whether through consistent financial commitments or creation of a foundation—can build believability. Corporate philanthropy has been proven to be beneficial for brands worldwide, but few have implemented a formal strategy (Casajús-Burutaran et al., 2023). For brands just getting started in the charitable sector, here are some ways to build authentic and quality philanthropic efforts:

- Financial donations: contributions to nonprofit organizations or charitable causes;
- Community grants: allocated funds to local organizations;
- Annual giving: programs to support ongoing charitable initiatives;
- Corporate foundation: a separate legal entity established by a corporation to manage and oversee philanthropic activities in line with their mission, vision, and purpose;
- In-kind donations of goods or services: non-monetary resources including products, equipment, or professional services, given to nonprofit organizations.

Beyond these purely financial options, brands often establish partnerships or sponsorships for particular causes. These are avenues for brands to provide financial support for events, organizations, or initiatives in line with their mission in exchange for brand awareness through promotion of a specific cause.

Our research supports these points as "donations" are one of the keywords mentioned most frequently among our focus group participants when we asked them what would be considered as authentic brand behaviors specifically related to supporting any social mission:

> In a world like this, let's consider Toms, because I know Toms, they donate a certain amount of shoes or whatever to a certain community or something? Yeah. I feel like yes, people do like their stuff. But I think that's what makes them more successful because they actually do seem to care to be socially responsible. I feel like it adds on. I feel like most of these brands, yes, they're in it for only money, but I feel like they could be way more profitable if they did assume social responsibility.

> I kind of think a lot of times money doesn't really lie. If it's like they're donating to this cause that speaks to my values, then for me it's hard to look at that a different way.

Similarly, donations and giving back to the society for the particular cause a brand stands for have been also considered quite important in the brand's perspective as well. Tammy Nelson also added to the point that everything is aimed at the core brand purpose, including their philanthropic efforts regarding who they donate portions of their profits to: "Everything about what we do is aimed at that purpose. So, for example, our philanthropic efforts, we donate a portion of our profits. And we select organizations that share our passion for empowering others. So when we're making a donation, we're looking for a charitable organization that is committed to that same thing."

Employee Experience (EX)

Opportunities for brands to develop socially responsible employees include:

- Volunteer Time Off: Employees get paid leave to volunteer for an approved charity or community organization.

- Employee Grant Stipends: Employees get funds to donate to a charity of their choice.
- Automatic Payroll Deductions: Employees can choose to have a portion of their paycheck donated to a charity of their choice.
- Employee Volunteer Programs: Companies encourage and support employee participation in volunteer activities.
- Matching Gifts: Companies match employee donations to eligible nonprofit organizations.

All of the efforts listed above can build believability for employees as they can literally buy into any given brand's social responsibility efforts on an individual basis—in addition to any corporate efforts the brand supports more broadly. Thanks in part to the prevalence of employee narratives in owned and earned media in particular, consumers notice the quality of employee experience at brands and organizations worldwide when considering brands to believe in. Employee experience is one big way to measure how a company takes their employees seriously and reflects their core values and commitments to social responsibility. Consumers do not only evaluate based on what they put their partial profits to support which values in the society, they also pay attention to how a company treats its employees to authentically reflect DEIA+B in their workplaces:

> I guess I would say Nike probably doesn't have the greatest reputation because of how they treat their employees internationally. I know that there's a lot of factories in China that are producing this and they don't get treated that well. I don't know if that's directly like DEI, but a lot of these companies kind of do well and could take advantage of people that are, I would say, maybe underprivileged. I don't know if that's the right title to put on them, but I would say that a lot of these companies need to probably be more successful in being diverse and accepting of everyone.

The importance of an engaging and inclusive employee experience is well-noted among the CMOs we interviewed. Among other things, generosity is an effort that supports a healthy brand culture. Clare Scott, CMO of Ryan Companies, emphasizes generosity and giving back as a brand value that the company has supported for a long time, which she believes ultimately extends to the client satisfaction:

> A giving back standpoint, that's been an anchor of Ryan forever. We're known for that generosity, that the way that we give not only as an

organization but the way that we encourage and support our individual employees in giving, the way that charitable work is just woven into the culture of every office. I could cite a million different examples of that, but it's just a big part of who we are and a serious point of pride for our employees, and something that I think is impactful for our clients.

Brand Profile: Ben and Jerry's

B Corp Certification represents a certification provided by B Lab, a nonprofit organization, certifying the "businesses that meet the highest standards of verified social and environmental performance, public transparency, and legal accountability to balance profit and purpose" (B Corporation, 2023). Obtaining B Corp Certification may offer brands an opportunity to gain a third-party assessment to objectively evaluate their ongoing efforts toward any socially responsible activities by a holistic investigation into the business operations, structure, and different work processes in addition to active reviewing procedures of potential consumer complaints and possible on-site visits.

Ben & Jerry's Homemade Holdings Inc. is a B Corporation that has been socially responsible with an authentic brand story from the start. Ben & Jerry's was founded by Ben Cohen and Jerry Greenfield in 1978, and their first location was in a renovated Vermont gas station. The brand grew and was acquired by Unilever in 2000, expanding into more than thirty-three countries worldwide (Unilever, 2012).

Their purpose is manifest in their threefold mission statement as follows (Ben & Jerry's, 2025a):

- Ben & Jerry's is founded on and dedicated to a sustainable corporate concept of linked prosperity. Central to the Mission of Ben & Jerry's is the belief that all three parts of its mission must thrive equally in a manner that commands deep respect for individuals inside and outside the Company and supports the communities of which they are a part:
    - Product Mission: To make, distribute, and sell the finest-quality ice cream and euphoric concoctions with a continued commitment to incorporating wholesome, natural ingredients and promoting business practices that respect the Earth and the Environment;

- Economic Mission: To operate the Company on a sustainable financial basis of profitable growth, increasing value for our stakeholders, and expanding opportunities for development and career growth for our employees;
- Social Mission: To operate the Company in a way that actively recognizes the central role that business plays in society by initiating innovative ways to improve the quality of life locally, nationally, and internationally.

In addition to product, economic, and social mission, Ben & Jerry's upholds three "Core Values":

- Human Rights & Dignity: We are committed to honoring the rights of all people to live with liberty, security, self-esteem, and freedom of expression and protest, and to have the opportunity to provide for their own needs and contribute to society;
- Social & Economic Justice: We are committed to achieving equity, opportunity, and justice for communities across the globe that have been historically marginalized, recognizing that this is tied to fair livelihoods that enable individuals, families, and communities to thrive;
- Environmental Protection, Restoration, & Regeneration: We are committed to a positive, life-giving environmental impact that restores degraded natural environments and enables increased diversity and abundance of ecosystems.

In addition to B Corp Certification, Ben & Jerry's has committed to transparency with the publication of annual social performance reports since 1989—today, they're called Social & Environmental Assessment Reports (SEAR).

Ben and Jerry's backs up their commitments to social responsibility in their mission statement and values with partnerships and charitable giving through the Ben & Jerry's Foundation. The Ben & Jerry's Foundation origin story is that, in 1985, Ben & Jerry's went public, and Ben gave 50,000 of his shares, along with a Board of Directors decision to commit 7.5 percent of the company's annual pretax profits to launch and sustain the Foundation.

Causes Ben & Jerry's supports include racial justice, climate justice, and Fairtrade. Examples of partnerships they uphold include implementing and sourcing ingredients from Fairtrade Certified suppliers since 2005

(Ben & Jerry's, 2025b). The Ben & Jerry's Foundation was founded in 1985, and has given more than $50 million in grants to community organizations. Today, the Foundation gives funds through Community Development Financial Institutions (CDFI)—private sector financial intermediaries that have community development as their primary mission and develop a range of programs and methods to meet the needs of low-income communities (Ben & Jerry's Foundation, 2025).

Co-creating Inclusive Brand Culture

Throughout this chapter, we addressed various perspectives to understand how to communicate a brand's social responsibility initiatives appropriately and effectively to its employees, stakeholders, clients, and consumers. We first identified a noteworthy problem associated with value miscommunication and potential negative consequences. Then, we suggested a solution to redirect the focus of communication to brand purpose that is centered on the brand identity and mission reasonably connected to the brand's day-to-day operations. From there, we introduced a role model example of the brand CONQUERing case study demonstrating what a well-implemented, socially responsible brand mission might look like in real-world consumer interactions and brand design. We finished up by providing how to apply such an example to your own brand by acknowledging the role of conscious consumers in brand value co-creation, and then introducing practical ways to measure the success of socially responsible efforts and initiatives. By reviewing this chapter, we hope to have provided useful insights for the current and future strategic communication professionals who aim to incorporate social responsibility into their business operations in a mindful and strategic way.

Key Terms

Authenticity
B Corp Certification
Brand purpose
Brand reputation
Brand value co-creation
Diversity, Equity, Inclusion, Access, and Belonging
Donations
Employee experience (EX)
Miscommunication
Public transparency

Discussion Questions

1 Define social responsibility in your own words.
2 What brands have taken an authentic approach to their social responsibility efforts, and what makes their approach effective?
3 How can, and should, brands measure the effectiveness of their social responsibility initiatives?

Activity

Charitable Giving and Philanthropy Comparative Analysis: Evaluate three Fortune 500 brands' philanthropic efforts. How do they prioritize charitable giving and philanthropy?

12

Brand Resonance

What is brand resonance? Brand resonance is a combination of emotional attachment and credibility that brands develop and sustain with employees, stakeholders, clients, and consumers. Brand resonance can be measured with metrics including brand affinity. Brand indifference is a problem brands face when consumers lack preferences and have emotional detachment from brands. Artificial intelligence (AI) is one tool that helps brands to personalize their connections with consumers to gain resonance. AI can also help brands to automate and streamline processes to resonate with new audiences in innovative ways. Spotify is presented as a brand that leverages AI in elements of their marketing strategy to help their brand to gain resonance with consumers through authenticity and innovation. Brand affinity is a metric that can help brands quantify their resonance.

Chapter Outline

12.1 Introduction: What Is Brand Resonance?	292
12.2 The Problem: Brand Indifference	292
12.3 The Solution: Believable Brand Resonance	294
12.4 Application: Artificial Intelligence (AI)	297
12.5 Case: Spotify	303
12.6 Metrics: Brand Affinity	306
Key Terms	308
Discussion Questions	308
Activity	309

12.1 Introduction: What Is Brand Resonance?

Brand Resonance: A combination of emotional attachment and credibility brands develop and sustain with employees, stakeholders, clients, and consumers.

We define brand resonance as a combination of emotional attachment and credibility that brands develop and sustain with employees, stakeholders, clients, and consumers. This concluding chapter of the book further explores the two norms that every believable brand upholds and sustains with clients, customers, employees, and stakeholders: Emotional attachment and credibility. These norms are touched on in Part I of this book as the norms of believable branding. Believable brands must cultivate emotional attachment and maintain credibility with clients, consumers, employees, and stakeholders. Believable brands do this by co-creating values including authenticity, consistency, innovation, and quality with clients, consumers, stakeholders, and employees throughout all touchpoints and delivery of products, services, and experiences. When these values are co-created and norms of emotional attachment and credibility are upheld, brands resonate with audiences. When these values fail to be upheld, emotional attachment and credibility wane, and brand indifference may set in.

12.2 The Problem: Brand Indifference

Brand indifference is defined as a lack of preference and emotional detachment from brands (MBLM, 2024b). Research by leading industry firms shows that understanding brands and consumers' or clients' interactions as a relationship can be helpful as customers' and clients' relationships with brands range from brand intimacy to brand hatred. Brand indifference is a point in a customer's or client's journey where, due to inconsistent communication or user experience, ranging from cumbersome checkout processes to slow loading times to convoluted customer service to lack of personalization, a customer or client becomes apathetic (MBLM, 2024b). Oftentimes, brand indifference is indicated by metrics including decreasing engagement rates, decreasing customer lifetime value, abandoned carts or contracts, and decreasing net promoter scores. When brand indifference sets in, customers and clients often begin looking for a more believable brand experience.

Thinking of a brand as a relationship can be helpful when discussing emotional attachment in particular, as research shows that brand indifference leads a large number of consumers to break up with brands before the three-year mark (MBLM, 2024a). Our research shows that emotional attachment and credibility can be built through personalized marketing, quality products, and memorable customer experiences, and can be lost through negative customer service interactions, poor product quality, inauthentic branding or value propositions, and inconsistent branding. Providing high-quality products and services, consistent branding and touchpoints, and authentic branding early on in a customer or client's journey can increase emotional attachment and the credibility of your brand.

Acquiring a new customer can cost five times more than retaining an existing customer (Gallo, 2014). If a brand can move past indifference to believability through emotional attachment and credibility within the first three years of the relationship, consumers will be more likely to stick with the relationship (MBLM, 2024b).

Declining quality, differing values, and disappointment are all contributing factors signifying brand indifference, so it makes sense that improved quality, consistent customer engagement, and increased reliability can help to overcome brand indifference (MBLM, 2024b).

In 2023, Southwest Airlines lost hundreds of millions of dollars due to more than 16,700 canceled flights and two million stranded passengers during the month of December. They admitted to causing "a tremendous amount of anguish, inconvenience, and missed opportunities for our customers and employees" as social media erupted with angry posts showcasing varying degrees of indifference and anger (Gannon, 2023; McCorvey, 2023). Southwest managed to post a net income for that year, and through reimbursements, refunds, apologies, and sales, attempted to regain emotional attachment and credibility with their customer base.

It's possible to move past brand indifference with brand resonance: Cultivating strong emotional attachments and maintaining credibility through authentic branding, consistent communication and feedback, innovative products and services, and quality across the board on all deliverables—products, services, and customer service alike.

12.3 The Solution: Believable Brand Resonance

Brand resonance is built with elements of emotional attachment and credibility. Brand believability comprises norms of emotional attachment and credibility along with values including authenticity, consistency, innovation, and quality. Emotional attachment and credibility are defined below, and are validated by metrics including brand affinity.

Emotional Attachment

We define emotional attachment as a positive affect with clients, consumers, employees, and stakeholders. Our research has found that emotional attachment is more important to executives and consumers than ever before. This finding is backed by industry research and reports (MBLM, 2022; Piper Sandler, 2024; Prophet, 2023).

But what is emotional attachment and how does it help brands build believability? Our in-depth interviews with chief marketing officers (CMOs) at leading companies and organizations in the United States show that love and authenticity are synonyms for believability. Innovation and a willingness to fail fast, while being authentic and vulnerable about failures, are key to developing this emotional attachment. Clear communication about what went wrong and how the brand desires to fix it helps clients, consumers, employees, and stakeholders to buy into what the brand is and stands for.

According to president and CMO Mike Benson, the key values of CBS are unification, accessibility, and optimism. As the former head of marketing at Amazon Prime Video, Benson values arguments grounded in data and creativity but notes that love and trust are powerful emotional bonds to cultivate within and outside of an organization.

"Customer love is foundational to me," Benson said.

> Love is a powerful emotion, and most people seek it. When you create an emotional bond with your customers, trust follows. You need to foster love first for trust to develop. I encourage the team to be empathetic marketers who deeply understand our audience and find ways to surprise and delight them, as they build and foster a love for our content, and thereby, our brand(s). Building an authentic, emotional bond with your customers makes them feel a strong attachment to you, much like a relationship. If there's strong love and connection, you can weather any rough patches.

CMOs in general note that emotional attachment creates a deeper relationship with consumers and enables innovation and experimentation. CMOs on the business to business (B2B) side of industry recognize there are rational, functional values and benefits to sales while at the same time accounting for the emotional elements of how buyers make decisions.

Leah Larson, CMO of Madison Air, argues that developing disruptive and nontraditional brands provides opportunities to build bridges to new customers through innovation and value creation. At the same time, producing quality deliverables is key to developing credibility, fulfilling the promise that a brand will deliver on what it says it will, consistently.

Credibility

We defined credibility as whether or not a brand delivers on their promises to provide high-quality products and/or services. Credibility is a foundational norm to some of the more institutionalized industries in society, including the medical field.

"Credibility is just table stakes, especially in a clinician's office," Darren Wennen, CCO of Caerus Corp., says.

> If you're not credible, you're not going to get in the door or stay there for very long. Some people may feel that just "making stuff up as you go along" can be effective. But when you are dealing with human health, you need to make sure you understand the implications of your statements and actions. But, to really build your brand you need to figure out the clinician's current belief, or objection, and what do you want them to believe about your product? A positive belief, for example, may be that the product's mechanism of action differs from competitors making it more effective. Marketers need to consider what are the rungs of that bridge that are going to get them from current belief to future or desired belief? And it often

varies by clinician. For some clinicians, it's published clinical evidence. For others, it's practical use. They need to have experience with a particular device and have it be effective before they're going to recommend it broadly.

Similarly, in STEM fields, emotional attachment and credibility go hand in hand, but credibility comes first.

"I think that's a great way to think about it, is the sequencing. I think credibility is first, and I think I could never sell emotion with a bunch of engineers, because a lot of these folks are engineers by training, especially on the construction and design side," Clare Scott, CMO of Ryan Companies US, Inc., says.

We come in, we tell them why we think we are credible, why we think we can do the job, and then we hit them with the emotion of, "We get you. We understand what you want to do. We want to be your partner in transforming this place." They go hand in hand, but I think the credibility has to be there first for the business that we do. Even if it worked externally with clients, I could never get my folks internally to buy into that.

Word of mouth recommendations are key to establishing credibility, and are bolstered by consistency in brand marketing. Credibility is also bolstered by research and assessment of whether or not a brand delivers on their promises. For example, it's one thing to build a brand promise and it's another to deliver on that promise.

At the University of Minnesota, CMO Ann Aronson notes they regularly send out surveys to constituents asking about the effectiveness of various brand attributes that comprise and evaluate the UMN brand's believability.

"We ask constituents about all kinds of different attributes at the U. We ask about providing health care to Minnesotans, providing a high-quality education, conducting research that improves Minnesotans' quality of life, discovering cures for chronic diseases, supporting student success, all those things," Aronson says.

We ask if these things are important to people and if they think that we do a good job of it. To me, whether or not we do a good job of it is their believability in us. Do they think that we're really delivering on it? We can give them messages about it, but whether they believe we're doing well says whether they believe in us.

12.4 Application: Artificial Intelligence (AI)

Artificial intelligence (AI) became central to branding in the twenty-first century. As computing technology and the internet evolved heading into the 2000s, integrated and digital marketing eras were born. Google began to revolutionize the advertising market by using algorithms and predictive analytics to personalize advertising on web browsers. E-commerce and online retail brands like Amazon began to emerge and take up space in the market. Rideshare apps including Uber and Lyft revolutionized global transit, using algorithms and AI to personalize taxi rides and ridesharing for users worldwide. As the digital market became saturated, brands began to recognize the need for targeted and personalized marketing experiences in digital realms.

Today, more than a quarter of the way through the twenty-first century, brands are utilizing artificial intelligence in a variety of ways: To create content; analyze website traffic; predict future trends in consumer behavior using predictive analytics, and more. AI can automate expensive and complex creative tasks, including product design, but AI integration has the potential to adversely affect a brand when not done authentically or with the quality a brand seeks to uphold (Freitas & Ofek, 2024). For these reasons, this application section provides some tips and pointers about how brands can integrate AI authentically and ethically.

AI can complete tasks including creating captions for branded video content, changing a keyword bid to adapt to real-time market changes, or choosing to show your audience a specific ad or message based on key real-time inputs about the customer (Melinn & Boyd, 2024a). The benefit of AI for digital marketers is that it aims to create systems with human-like thinking skills, such as the ability to reason, discover meaning, generalize, or learn from experience (Melinn & Boyd, 2024b).

As AI continues to evolve, it can be used in four main realms: assistive, creative, analytical, and advisory (Zucker & Srinivasan, 2023). If you or your customers need help doing something, assistive AI can provide support in the form of chatbot customer service and/or programmatic advertising. If you need to create something, creative AI can create mood boards, ideate keywords for campaigns, create copy recommendations, and more. If you need to better understand something, analytical AI can provide forecasting and web analytics in addition to optimizing sales leads. If you need to decide something, advisory AI can recommend budget distributions and scheduling suggestions. In the midst of all of these opportunities to leverage AI, it's important to consider how ethics and governance play a role in AI systems. Brands and organizations must attain user permissions to gather and analyze data. Below are some tips on how to integrate AI ethically to gain resonance.

Ethics and Governance

Before activating artificial intelligence (AI) tools of any kind with customer, consumer, or client data, brands must ensure compliance with privacy laws and policies. Because the use of AI often involves the collection and analysis of large sets of customer data, even if a target market is not in a region where privacy laws are strict, marketers must adhere to privacy regulations including the California Consumer Privacy Act (CCPA), European Union's General Data Protection Regulation (GDPR), and other relevant local laws and policies. Knowing what data are allowed to be legally collected and how to protect the data once collected is crucial. There are also sector-specific regulations to be aware of, including HIPAA in the health care sector.

Helpful questions to ask when considering using user data in AI applications include: Do you have explicit consent from customers to use their purchase history and behavior data for personalization? Does your brand have consent to use subscribers' data for machine-learning purposes?

It's one thing to understand how AI works and to use it on a personal level. It's another thing to implement an effective and ethical AI system. Assuming your brand or organization has your legal team's backing to feed consumer or client data into an AI system, before your brand or organization implements AI on a broad scale, it's important to evaluate whether or not you have the personnel who can carry out AI analysis in an authentic, effective, and ethical way.

Step 1: Viability assessment: Is your brand well positioned to implement or leverage a proprietary AI system? Do you have the personnel and the funding to support and sustain this implementation? AI is a highly complex field, and there are often significant upfront costs.

Also, digital marketers often have to climb a steep learning curve to get up to speed with the latest AI technologies. If your brand is ready, you'll likely need to hire a firm to develop the software you'll need, or outsource to have an agency conduct AI analysis for you, or pay for a license to AI software. Brandwatch, Sprinklr, Hootsuite, Mailchimp, and Sprout Social are all platforms that use AI in various ways for branding. This type of software can be expensive.

Step 2: Data preparedness: Do you have access to the quality and quantity of data required for AI? Is your data clean, organized, and free from biases? Ensure that your data are CCPA and GDPR-compliant and adhere to any other applicable legal regulations. Similarly, the team needs to ensure that the data are stored securely in compliance with data regulations and policies.

Stage 3: Ethical and legal compliance: How will the implementation of AI affect data privacy and security? Are there ethical considerations like potential biases, questions about IP ownership, or unfair practices? Conduct an ethical audit, potentially involving third-party ethical consultants. Review and adhere to data protection and privacy laws that apply to your industry, jurisdiction, and customer base.

Stage 4: Technology and team readiness: Is your team ready to implement an AI system?

Stage 5: Monitoring and feedback: How will you measure the success of the AI implementation? What are the KPIs and metrics that will indicate whether the AI is performing as expected? Accountability is also important here as it should be clear who is responsible for each aspect of an AI project. There should also be a framework in place for ethical review and oversight. Build in a feedback loop that allows for ongoing adjustments and improvements.

Clearly define what success looks like, quantitatively and qualitatively, before launching the AI implementation.

As one example of what AI implementation might look like in real time, let's say you are setting up a generative AI chatbot to manage queries on an E-commerce site. It's important to follow these steps (Boyd & Williams, 2024a; Melinn & Boyd, 2024a):

1 Documentation: Identify the type of data the chatbot will collect and how it will be used.

2. Review: Recruit your internal ethics or legal board to review and approve the chatbot's programming and intentions, and ensure users are informed clearly that they are interacting with a machine and have the option to opt out at the beginning of every engagement.
3. Audit: Set up an audit trail to log all interactions the chatbot has with users and continually audit the AI algorithms for any inherent biases and correct them.
4. Monitoring: Set up the chatbot's programming with sentiment and the ability to flag conversations where users express strong emotions like frustration or anger, to be escalated and reviewed manually by a human agent.
5. Disclosure: Add a disclaimer to your brand's website, stating how the chatbot will use data.
6. Compliance: Have your ethics or legal team review the audit and monitor steps and procedures to make sure they comply with GDPR or equivalent regulations.

These considerations of ethics and governance are important to consider before adopting or implementing AI systems. Use cases and options of how a brand or organization may utilize AI are described in detail below.

Web Analytics and KPIs

Web analytics platforms are a major way AI is implemented in digital marketing and branding. Google Analytics 4, also known as GA4, enables brands to measure the return on investment (or ROI) of various content strategies.

Using GA4, you can look at your key performance indicators (or KPIs) to see how users are engaging with your content. It can tell you, for example, which content pieces are getting the most traffic and how long users are spending on different content pages. You can then use these GA4 insights to adjust your content strategy to make it more effective (Boyd & Williams, 2024b). For example: Are there web pages getting less traffic that could be optimized to gain more traffic by updating headers, subheadings, photo captions, and keywords? Are there web pages gaining lots of traffic that could be monetized or include calls to action or language leading to conversions?

Branded Content Creation and Strategy

Content marketing is a core element in an overall digital marketing strategy. Artificial intelligence (AI) tools can be particularly effective in this part of a campaign because AI can help you to create content, customize content, schedule content, and edit or evaluate content. In addition to entering prompts to help write content, Generative AI can edit content for flow and can enhance the tone of voice for various content. Tools that can help to craft and schedule content include Buffer, Hootsuite, and Sprout Social, which are all examples of social media management platforms that provide AI-driven tools to help with effective content scheduling.

When it comes to content creation, it's important to remember that Generative AI is an emerging technology and might not create excellent content on the first try, or at all. So, use AI tools for idea generation, keyword research, and content research, and be conservative with your implementation; create drafts and be prepared to edit accordingly. Text content can be created with Generative AI tools including ChatGPT, Clearscope, MarketMuse, Claude.ai, and Sudowrite.

Beyond text content, Generative AI can create multimedia content including images, video, infographics, graphics, and photographs. Generative AI can also modify and enhance existing visual content, in order to make it more engaging to better resonate with various audiences. Emerging generative AI tools introduced to the market almost daily can create AI images; convert text to video or text to speech with an AI voice; and create video avatars, photographic representations, and full-fledged music for podcasts and videos. Key AI tools for visual content include Stability AI, Lumen5, DALL-E, and Synthesia.

It's important for brands to evaluate the permissions and ethics of each generative AI platform out there before utilizing them. It's also important to ensure brands have permissions to enter any and all data and content entered into any Generative AI system.

A/B Testing

Beyond creating content, digital marketing involves a lot of testing and learning. A/B testing is simply testing two different options for content—

email subject lines, ad copy, blog posts, and similar. Based on results of the tests, brands can decide what option works best over another. AI-powered tools such as Hubspot, Mailchimp, Google Optimize, Adobe Target, Unbounce, Optimizely, and Convert all enable efficient and effective A/B tests. You can then use the results of these tests to optimize your content and dynamically adjust campaigns as necessary, based on real-time performance. HubSpot, for example, uses AI to help it efficiently deploy A/B testing.

Market Segmentation

If your brand has permission to use AI to analyze customer data, AI can help with audience segmentation. You can use machine learning algorithms to analyze customer data and divide your audience into different customer segments. This segmentation might be based on demographics, behaviors, preferences, and so on. Tools including Algolia and RecSys can even make content suggestions based on your audience segments.

Email Marketing

AI tools can be particularly helpful in email marketing campaigns. If you use AI tools to analyze customer behavior and segment your audience, you can then segment your emails so that you're delivering customized content to different customer segments. If your brand is compliant with data privacy laws such as GDPR, you can also use AI to create an email marketing campaign for inactive subscribers by identifying who hasn't interacted with content and targeting them with specific content and campaigns.

AI tools and AI-driven platforms such as Automizy, Mailchimp, Salesforce, and HubSpot all can help you create more personalized email content, including targeted subject lines. You can also use AI to determine the best times to send the emails by testing a percentage of your audience with various subject lines or send times. Personalization can enhance customer experience and increase brand reputation— for example, Marriott hotels uses Einstein AI prediction capabilities to help it deliver hyper-personalized emails to its customers (Boyd & Williams, 2024c).

Fiscal Management

AI tools can gather data in real time, even and especially in the financial sector when it comes to budget allocation. AI tools can alert you to when different parts of a campaign are draining budgets or where you might need to invest further to take advantage of sudden opportunities. In other words, you can make data-driven decisions in real time to maximize ROI.

AI tools that can help with your budget allocation include Google Ads Smart Bidding, Adobe Advertising Cloud, AdRoll, WordStream's Smart Ads, and Facebook's Campaign Budget Optimization feature.

Dynamic pricing is another area where AI can prove very beneficial for digital marketers. You can implement AI algorithms that adjust pricing strategies in real time based on market demand, stock levels, customer trends, and competitor prices. This again enables you to maximize ROI in a fast-changing environment. Uber, Airbnb, and Amazon have all implemented AI-driven dynamic pricing to enable them to optimize pricing in real time. Key AI tools used for dynamic pricing include Feedvisor, RepricerExpress, and Prisync (Boyd & Williams, 2024a).

Personalization is one of AI's superpowers in providing custom experiences for clients and customers especially in e-commerce and on streaming services. AI can be trained to analyze user behavior and preferences and can make recommendations accordingly. Spotify, the world's top music streaming service, is a case study in how AI can be leveraged to build believability and market share.

12.5 Case: Spotify

Spotify is the world's largest audio streaming platform and maintains its competitive advantage with creativity, data-driven insights, and innovation. Riding on the tails of Kazaa, Napster, and other websites designed to download, trade, and share mp3s at the turn of the century, Spotify began to revolutionize the music streaming industry when it was founded in 2008. Today, Spotify is the number one most home-screened app and is used by more than 626 million users, including 246 million subscribers in more than 180 global markets (Spotify Advertising, 2024b). Economically, Spotify's market share is 32 percent (Leu, 2024).

Spotify makes the biggest share of its revenue through its premium subscription model, as approximately 40 percent of their users are paid subscribers. Spotify maintains its market dominance with artificial intelligence and data-driven, innovative, and personalized products and services that create emotional connection with users and subscribers.

Spotify resonates with its users with data-driven insights to create highly personalized, engaging, and innovative marketing campaigns. Their "Spotify Wrapped" feature, which gives users a yearly summary of users' listening habits, has become a viral sensation. Beyond personalized news, podcasts, and music delivered straight to users' inboxes and dashboards, Spotify advertises out of home and on television with creative billboards, bus advertisements, and more.

Spotify leverages data and innovation to analyze and attempt to capture the attention of younger audiences including Generation Z and Generation Alpha. Spotify's operating costs include licensing expenses toward record labels, distributors, and artists. In recent years, Spotify has increased its spending in research and development, including analysis of proprietary and partner data to create human-grounded and culturally nuanced content and experiences that help marketers navigate the future. For example, Spotify shares their findings in reports about youth culture: "Culture Next 2024: Gen Z Trends" (Spotify Advertising, 2024c); and in reports about podcasting trends: "2024 Podcast Trends Tour" (Spotify Advertising, 2024a). One key takeaway Spotify has released as a result of their user data and research is that Generation Z desires more connection and positivity (Spotify Advertising, 2024c). Three points that come directly from Spotify's Podcast Trends Tour report (Spotify Advertising, 2024a) are:

- Podfluencers: 63 percent of Gen Z trust their favorite podcast host more than their favorite social media influencer, which means connection is key.
- Breaking Borders: Generation Alpha in particular are using podcasts as passports, as 41 percent of Gen Alpha's podcast streams came from a different country in 2023.
- Generation Z loves the arts: They streamed content related to art, drawing, film, theater, anime, and more by +31 percent YoY.

Spotify's values are to be innovative by moving fast and taking big risks; to be sincere; to be passionate; to be collaborative; and to be playful

(Haggard, 2024). Jenny Haggard is Spotify's Global Thought Leadership director, which is part of the Business Brand Marketing Team that manages many of these data-driven insights and helps to turn them into marketable products. According to Haggard, it's important to know your audience, capture young audiences, and move at speed or die (2024). One key question to ask is: What is unique about your audience? Another element of innovation is to give teams permission to be creative, to take risks, and to fail.

Spotify knows that AI streaming intelligence helps their listeners and consumers to find what they love and anticipate what they'll love. When Spotify started in 2008, they were designed as a utility platform that helped users look for something and find it. As the platform evolved, they focused more on curation in an attempt to personalize their offerings based on analyzing user data. At Spotify, they leverage AI to combine streaming intelligence and personalized experiences for listeners and users. Each of their attempts to appeal to users has evolved over time—for example, their popular Spotify Wrapped feature began as My Spotify and evolved based on testing and user data.

In addition to gathering data, it's important to structure that data. At Spotify, one way they structure their data is geographically—they focus on specific regions of the world.

At Spotify, innovation is also about surprise. One question Spotify's team asks is: How can we surprise people? Another is: What problem does my brand solve? This answer in particular should stay the same and also evolve.

"We want people to feel better; we want to leave people feeling better than we found them," Haggard said (2024). Another question relating to innovation is: If you could create anything what would it be? "As marketers we have the opportunity and privilege to dream big. Clients come to Spotify and say we want to do something innovative or amazing. Take risks," Haggard said (2024).

Spotify uses artificial intelligence to interpret data, create interactive experiences, and create targeted digital campaigns grounded in users' musical preferences. Personalized recommendations are what set Spotify apart from the competition—namely, playlists and streams that create emotional attachment with artificial intelligence (AI).

Spotify sets the standard for the music industry in some ways as it shares the popularity of artists based on its algorithmically curated playlists it promotes—ranging from most streamed artist charts to top podcasts. In addition to more than 100 million tracks and 6 million podcasts, Spotify streams 350,000 audiobooks.

One challenge Spotify faces is that "we are an audio jail. Some partners think of us as a music platform only. Now, we are trying to build out our pillars with podcasts and audiobooks in addition to music. Also, video." Spotify has found a niche as users' "essential daily companion" as Spotify has found their users "feel happier after scrolling Spotify than social media" (Haggard, 2024). At the same time, Spotify is competing with YouTube for the podcast market domination, and is attempting to build out its interface for offering users access to video podcasts. This is the next frontier, in addition to other opportunities Spotify will pursue based on incoming user data.

Tangible examples of cultivating creativity and innovation include hosting a "Hack Week," dedicated time to brainstorming creative potential new products and services if money was no object. Asking the question "What if" has led to some of Spotify's most successful innovations. Questions Spotify is tackling as a result of their 2024 Hack Week include "What if… Spotify could help parents tackle bedtime storytime? Spotify could help deaf people experience music?" (Haggard, 2024). For example, Spotify's popular Discover Weekly feature came out of a Hack Week brainstorm. Then, as individuals on teams, how do you get your creative juices flowing? Focus on what makes you creative even if it's five to ten minutes per day. As a brand, it's important for staff to find their source of creativity and carve out time for it. Creativity is a gift, and it's important to encourage it. It's brands' opportunity and privilege to encourage creativity as a brand.

Innovation is also about listening and having dialogue across backgrounds and experiences—and to collaborate and listen.

12.6 Metrics: Brand Affinity

Brand affinity is one metric that can help measure brand resonance. Brand affinity is defined as an emotional connection and relationship that captures the hearts of consumers (Marcy, 2019). Brand affinity relates directly to the emotional attachment brands co-create with consumers, and can be cultivated with authentic and innovative marketing that creates loyalty and increases brand awareness and recall. Affinity has been adopted by Google Ads, who has implemented "Affinity Audiences" to their ad campaigns. Affinity audiences are broken out based on passions, habits, and interests, and are one way to show how users' online behaviors and data show their affinity for various brands (Bonderud, 2022).

Accessibility can help enhance brand affinity on websites and social media in particular. A majority of social media videos are viewed without sound, so it's important to include captions for all multimedia published across social media platforms. Alt text, or descriptions, are also important to include for all photographs for those who are visually impaired. Videos on social media—in particular, Stories on Facebook and Instagram—are immersive, authentic, inclusive, and accessible. Seventy-three percent of people in the United States agree Stories enable them to experience new things outside their everyday lives; 65 percent say Stories help them feel closer and more up to date with friends; 57 percent say Stories make them feel part of a larger community; and 62 percent say they plan to use Stories even more in the future than they do today (Meta, 2024). For these reasons, and the fact that social media videos get more engagement than static images, it's important to publish video content to build brand affinity. In addition to posting content, it's important to respond to comments, ratings, and reviews—whether good or bad. If a negative comment, rating, or review comes in, it's important to respond instead of ignoring it. Responding to negative comments, ratings, and reviews is part of being consistent. Being consistent helps build believability, and responding to all comments, good and bad, with authenticity and consistency, builds affinity. Another way to increase brand awareness and affinity is to meet consumers and customers where they are—which means posting outside of 9-to-5 business hours. Sprout Social regularly publishes guides on top posting times across social media platforms.

Brand affinity can be built with individuals, and it can also be built in communities. Facebook groups, Reddit forums, and even hashtags can provide communal gathering places for employees, stakeholders, and consumers in digital realms. Physical meetups and events can provide opportunities to build brand affinity as well. Fandom plays a role in brand affinity, too. Some brand communities name themselves—for example, Taylor Swift's fans are "Swifties"; Nicki Minaj's fans are "Barbz"; Beyonce's fans are "the Beyhive." Fans of Fiskars, a Finnish housewares company, call themselves Fiskateers, and fans of T.J. Maxx discount designer clothing stores call themselves Maxxinistas. Within communities brands and brand ambassadors create, customers can form connections with others, which helps build brand affinity, too. To increase engagement among brand communities, brands can post followers-only content, promotions, and discounts to encourage people to experience the benefits of being part of your community. Loyalty programs on apps and websites—including perks like free shipping—can also help build brand affinity.

Encouraging engagement in communities and with the brand, across platforms and in person, helps brands to build affinity with customers. Brand affinity is similar to brand sentiment, and can be measured in a few different ways. As mentioned throughout this book, it's important for your brand to decide what KPIs are most important when it comes to measuring various elements of believability. When it comes to brand affinity, engagement rate is one such metric that clearly shows customers' affinity toward and with the brand. Engagements can be calculated as how many times a person interacts with your content, and can include likes, comments, shares, and in some cases, clicks. From there, engagement rate can be calculated as a percentage of your audience that has engaged with your content. To calculate engagement rate, divide the number of engagements (how many times a person interacted with your content; including likes, comments, shares, and in some cases, clicks) by the total reach × 100.

Key Terms

Brand affinity
Brand indifference
Brand intimacy
Brand resonance
CCPA

Credibility
Engagements
Engagement rate
Emotional attachment
GDPR

Discussion Questions

1. What is brand resonance and how can brand resonance help build a believable brand?
2. Why does brand indifference pose a threat to brand believability?
3. In your opinion, what is more important or valuable for brands to pursue and uphold—emotional attachment or credibility? Why?

Activity

Brand Affinity Exercise: Choose a brand and evaluate its brand affinity by analyzing its digital communities, fandom, influencers/brand ambassadors, loyalty/reward programs, and physical meetups/events. Based on your findings, which element of brand resonance is strongest for this brand: Emotional attachment or credibility? Why?

Appendix A: Methods

Our original research presented in this book draws insights from in-depth interviews with 20 chief marketing officers (CMOs) in the United States; 17 focus groups with 89 consumers; and ethnography at and participation in academic and industry conferences including the International Communication Association (ICA); American Academy of Advertising (AAA); Sustainable Brands; Digital Summit; International Association of Business Communicators (IABC); and AdWeek's Brandweek. Our triangulated qualitative data collection occurred from January 2023 through March 2025, and continues today. Our interview sample was cultivated in a purposive manner based upon (CMOs) employed at U.S. brands and organizations to inform the study's research questions, goals, and purposes. This purposive sampling began by contacting CMOs with contact information available through LinkedIn with connections to the University of Minnesota. We initially identified 104 total interviewees on LinkedIn employed as CMOs with connections to the University of Minnesota. We contacted 66 of them for interviews and began interviewing those who responded. Our initial interviewees suggested 17 additional contacts—some with connections to the University of Minnesota, and others without. We conducted a total of twenty total in-depth interviews through our combination of purposive and snowball sampling. Each interview was conducted via Zoom, and lasted 30 to 90 minutes with an interview guide approved by the University of Minnesota Institutional Review Board (IRB) that included questions on the topics of branding, believability, growth, strategy, and social influence. Our 17 focus groups took place in person at the Hubbard School of Journalism and Mass Communication's focus group suite on the University of Minnesota's Twin Cities campus. Our 89 focus group participants were recruited through the University of Minnesota's Hubbard School of Journalism and Mass Communication's SONA Subject Pool. Each focus group lasted 60 to 120 minutes with a focus group guide approved by the University of Minnesota Institutional Review Board (IRB) that included questions on the topics of branding, believability, growth, strategy, and social influence. Focus group participants were full-time students that identified as members of Generation Z. All focus group participants were granted extra credit for their participation. Focus group and in-depth interview transcripts were anonymized, transcribed by confidential transcription service Rev, and imported into qualitative analysis software NVivo. NVivo is a qualitative data analysis software with content analysis, annotations, and data visualization capabilities provided to the researchers via license from the University of Minnesota Libraries. Initial findings from our qualitative data analysis are presented in this book. We give our sincere thanks to our interviewees and our dozens of focus group participants for their time, wisdom, expertise, and passion for believable branding.

Appendix B: Interviewees

Name	Title (CMO = Chief Marketing Officer)	Brand
Mike Benson	President and CMO	CBS
Mark Derks	CMO	BlueGrace Logistics
Jaime Hunt	Vice President for Communications and CMO	Old Dominion University
Clare Scott	CMO	Ryan Companies US, Inc.
Katie Alvino	CMO	College of Saint Benedict and Saint John's University
Andrew Farrant	CMO	Global Jet Capital
Darren Wennen	CMO / Chief Commercial Officer (CCO)	Caerus Corp.
Leah Larson	CMO	Madison Indoor Air Quality
Lizzie Spier	CMO	Halara Cannabis
Dr. Jesse Lillejord	Founder and CMO	Chiro for Moms / Chiro for Kidz / Pelvic Floor for Moms
Glenn Bottomly	CMO	Taylor Corporation
Ann Aronson	CMO	University of Minnesota
Amy L. Halford	CMO	Thrive Pet Healthcare
James Plesser	Assistant Dean and CMO	Carlson School of Management, University of Minnesota
Chris Brandt	CMO and Chief Brand Officer (CBO)	Chipotle
Tammy R. Nelson	CMO	CONQUERing
Jon Althoff	President and CMO (Chief Marketing/Mission Officer)	Dakota County Regional Chamber of Commerce
Sherri Gilligan	CMO	Mayo Clinic
Jeehye Jung	Founder and CMO	Amuse Agency
Anonymous	Founder	Anonymous

Appendix C: Brand Believability Score Assessment Sample Survey

- This brand is a believable brand: Total /6 = %
  - Emotional Attachment /1
    - I am emotionally attached to this brand. (Yes/No)
  - Credibility /1
    - This brand is credible. (Yes/No)
  - Authenticity /1
    - This brand is authentic. (Yes/No)
  - Consistency /1
    - This brand is consistent. (Yes/No)
  - Innovation /1
    - This brand is innovative. (Yes/No)
  - Quality /1
    - This brand provides high-quality products/services. (Yes/No)

References

1% for the Planet—Patagonia. (2023). Patagonia. https://www.patagonia.com/one-percent-for-the-planet.html

Aaker, D. (2014). *Aaker on Branding: 20 Principles That Drive Success*. Morgan James Publishing.

Aaker, D. (2022). *The Future of Purpose-Driven Branding: Signature Programs That Impact & Inspire Both Business and Society*. Morgan James Publishing.

About B Lab. (2023). B Lab. https://www.bcorporation.net/en-us/movement/about-b-lab

Advertising Association. (2023). New Research Shows UK Public's Advertising Experience Integral to Trust. Little Black Book. https://lbbonline.com/news/new-research-shows-uk-publics-advertising-experience-integral-to-trust

Agricultural Marketing Service. (2023). Organic Regulations. U.S. Department of Agriculture Agricultural Marketing Service. https://www.ams.usda.gov/rules-regulations/organic

Aguis, A. (2024, April 17). Customer Journey Maps: How to Create Really Good Ones [Examples + Template]. HubSpot. https://blog.hubspot.com/service/customer-journey-map

Anderson, S. (2023, May 3). How many ads do we really see in a day? Spoiler: it's not 10,000. *The Drum*. https://www.thedrum.com/news/2023/05/03/how-many-ads-do-we-really-see-day-spoiler-it-s-not-10000

Ansoff, H. I. (1957). Strategies for diversification. *Harvard Business Review*, 35(5), 113–124.

Antioco, J. (2011, April 1). How I did it: Blockbuster's former CEO on sparring with an activist shareholder. *Harvard Business Review*. https://hbr.org/2011/04/how-i-did-it-blockbusters-former-ceo-on-sparring-with-an-activist-shareholder

Apple (2024). *iPhone Upgrade Program*. Apple. https://www.apple.com/shop/iphone/iphone-upgrade-program

Arguedas, A. R., Robertson, C., Fletcher, R., & Kleis Nielsen, R. (2022). Echo chambers, filter bubbles, and polarisation: A literature review. Reuters Institute for the Study of Journalism. Retrieved September 22, 2024, from https://reutersinstitute.politics.ox.ac.uk/echo-chambers-filter-bubbles-and-polarisation-literature-review

Aronson, D. (2023, May). Unpacking Consumer Trends. Research Insights Series: Consumer Preferences and Behaviors. Sustainable Brands Brand-Led Culture Change.

Asics. (2023). Our Circular Approach to Addressing Climate Change. Asics. http://www.asics.com/us/en-us/mk/sustainability

ASICS Corporation. (2023). Methodology of Calculation for Carbon Footprint of Product. http://www.asics.com/us/en-us/mk/sustainability/carbonfootprint

Asics Global. (2023). Sustainable Materials and Processes for a Sound Earth. Asics Global. https://corp.asics.com/en/csr/planet-product/materials-and-processes?version_name=Default

Athwal, N., Istanbulluoglu, D., & McCormack, S. E. (2018). The allure of luxury brands' social media activities: A uses and gratifications perspective. *Information Technology & People*, 32(3), 603–626. https://doi.org/10.1108/ITP-01-2018-0017

Atkins, B. (2020). Demystifying ESG: Its history & current status. *Forbes*. https://www.forbes.com/sites/betsyatkins/2020/06/08/demystifying-esgits-history–current-status/

Avery, J., & Greenwald, R. (2023, May 1). A new approach to building your personal brand. *Harvard Business Review*. https://hbr.org/2023/05/a-new-approach-to-building-your-personal-brand

B Corporation. (2023). Measuring a Company's Entire Social and Environmental Impact. https://www.bcorporation.net/en-us/certification/

Bailey, C., Tilley, C., & Lelia Sandoghdar, A. (2023, September 11). *Harvard Business Review*. https://hbr.org/2023/09/what-makes-a-great-corporate-purpose-statement

Bakare, L. (2023, May). Unlocking the Power of Responsible Marketing: How to Reach for More & Keep It Real. Sustainable Brands Brand-Led Culture Change.

Baker, K. (2022, February 3). How to Understand Market Penetration and Create a Strategy With STP Marketing. Hubspot. https://blog.hubspot.com/marketing/market-penetration

Bartlett, L. (2021, January 31). *How your cannabis company can avoid a shadowban on social media*. Forbes. https://www.forbes.com/sites/lindseybartlett/2021/01/31/how-your-cannabis-company-can-avoid-a-shadowban-on-social-media/

Barzilai, S., & Chinn, C. A. (2020). A review of educational responses to the "post-truth" condition: Four lenses on "post-truth" problems. *Educational Psychologist*, 55(3), 107–119. https://doi.org/10.1080/00461520.2020.1786388

BBC News (Director). (2022, January 23). What Is Greenwashing?. BBC, YouTube. https://www.youtube.com/watch?v=0XGAMJsm6Tg

References

BBC Radio (Director). (2015, April 15). Erving Goffman and the Performed Self [Video recording]. https://www.youtube.com/watch?v=6Z0XS-QLDWM

Beaubien, S., & Gleich, C. (2023, May). Blazing New Trails for Brand Activism. Sustainable Brands Brand-Led Culture Change.

Bedbury, S., & Fenichell, S. (2003). *A New Brand World: Eight Principles for Achieving Brand Leadership in the Twenty-First Century*. Penguin Books.

Bemporad, R. (2023, May). Unpacking Consumer Trends: Research Insights Series: Consumer Preferences and Behaviors. Sustainable Brands Brand-Led Culture Change.

Ben & Jerry's. (2025a). Activism [Ben & Jerry's Homemade, Inc.]. https://www.benjerry.com. https://www.benjerry.com/about-us/jobs/global-head-of-integrated-marketing

Ben & Jerry's. (2025b). Fairtrade [Ben & Jerry's Homemade, Inc.]. Fairtrade. https://www.benjerry.com/values/issues-we-care-about/fairtrade

Ben & Jerry's Foundation. (2025). What We Do. *Ben & Jerry's Foundation*. https://benandjerrysfoundation.org/about/what-we-do/

Bengtsson, A., Bardhi, F., & Venkatraman, M. (2010). How global brands travel with consumers: An examination of the relationship between brand consistency and meaning across national boundaries. *International Marketing Review*, 27(5), 519–540. https://doi.org/10.1108/02651331011076572

BLVR. (2023, May 14). The Business Case for Belief-Led Transformation. BLVR. https://blvr.com/article/the-business-case-for-belief-led-transformation/

Bonderud, D. (2022, January 17). How to Use Custom Affinity Audiences: From Creation to Stellar ROI. Hubspot. https://blog.hubspot.com/marketing/custom-affinity-audiences

Boyd, C., & Williams, J. (2024a). Core Read: Monitoring Social Media with AI. American Marketing Association's Digital Marketing Institute. https://my.digitalmarketinginstitute.com/courses/module_v2/tr-aifdm-1-efk1087/2345/TR-AI-1-10003-x7c3a

Boyd, C., & Williams, J. (2024b). Implementing AI-Driven Digital Marketing. American Marketing Association's Digital Marketing Institute. https://my.digitalmarketinginstitute.com/courses/module_v2/tr-aifdm-1-efk1087/2345/TR-AI-1-10003-x7c3a

Boyd, C., & Williams, J. (2024c). Using AI for Content Creation. American Marketing Association's Digital Marketing Institute. https://my.digitalmarketinginstitute.com/courses/module_v2/tr-aifdm-1-efk1087/2345/TR-AI-1-10003-x7c3a

Brandt, M. (2010, July). *Perspectives on Internal Branding*. TAITRA, TrueBrand.

Bumachar, L. (2023, May). Strategies and Tactics for Driving Behavior Change at Scale: Content Creators for Good: A Brand Guide to Collaborating with Influencers. Sustainable Brands Brand-Led Culture Change.

Cambridge Dictionary. (2024, February 28). Endemic. https://dictionary.cambridge.org/us/dictionary/english/endemic

Cambridge Dictionary. (2024). Post truth. https://dictionary.cambridge.org/us/dictionary/english/post-truth#google_vignette

Cambridge Dictionary. (2025). Mission statement. https://dictionary.cambridge.org/us/dictionary/english/mission-statement

Carroll, R. (2014, June 28). Silicon Valley's culture of failure... and "the walking dead" it leaves behind. *The Guardian*. https://www.theguardian.com/technology/2014/jun/28/silicon-valley-startup-failure-culture-success-myth

Casajús-Burutaran, A., Ambos, T. C., & Probst, G. (2023). Do you have a corporate philanthropy strategy? *MIT Sloan Management Review*. https://sloanreview.mit.edu/article/do-you-have-a-corporate-philanthropy-strategy/

Chandler, D., & Munday, R. (2011). Brand awareness. In *A Dictionary of Media and Communication*. Oxford University Press. https://www.oxfordreference.com/display/10.1093/acref/9780199568758.001.0001/acref-9780199568758-e-248

Charello, M. (2024). *Essentials of Social Media Marketing*. Edify Publishing.

Charters, S. (2009). Does a brand have to be consistent? *Journal of Product & Brand Management*, 18(4), 284–291. https://doi.org/10.1108/10610420910972800

Cherel-Bonnemaison, C., Erlandsson, G., Ibach, B., & Spiller, P. (2021, September 22). Buying into a More Sustainable Value Chain. McKinsey & Company. https://www.mckinsey.com/capabilities/operations/our-insights/buying-into-a-more-sustainable-value-chain

Chernev, A. (2020). *Strategic Brand Management* (3rd edition). Cerebellum Press.

Cheung, M. L., Pires, G. D., Rosenberger, P. J., & De Oliveira, M. J. (2020). Driving consumer–brand engagement and co-creation by brand interactivity. *Marketing Intelligence & Planning*, 38(4), 523–541. https://doi.org/10.1108/MIP-12-2018-0587

Chimata, P. (2023, March 27). The Value of Organic Certification to Consumers. University of Minnesota College of Liberal Arts. https://cla.umn.edu/heller-hurwicz/news-events/profile/value-organic-certification-consumers

Chipotle Mexican Grill. (2018, September 24). Chipotle launches new "For Real" campaign placing its real ingredients in the spotlight. PR Newswire. https://www.prnewswire.com/news-releases/chipotle-launches-new-for-real-campaign-placing-its-real-ingredients-in-the-spotlight-300717411.html

Chipotle. (2022, April 5). Fans Can Roll Burritos at Chipotle in the Metaverse to Earn Burritos In Real Life. Chipotle. https://newsroom.chipotle.com/2022-04-05-fans-can-roll-burritos-at-chipotle-in-the-metaverse-to-earn-burritos-in-real-life

Chipotle. (2024, April 24). Chipotle Announces First Quarter 2024 Results—Apr 24, 2024. Chipotle Mexican Grill. https://newsroom.chipotle.com/2024-04-24-CHIPOTLE-ANNOUNCES-FIRST-QUARTER-2024-RESULTS

Chouinard, Y. (2023). Yvon Chouinard Donates Patagonia to Fight Climate Crisis. Patagonia. https://www.patagonia.com/ownership/

Christine, M. (2024, August 15). How to Create a Social Media Influencer Playbook. Digital Summit Minneapolis.

Clifbar. (2023a). Clif Bar & Company's Sustainability Journey. Clifbar. https://www.clifbar.com/stories/our-sustainability-journey

Clifbar. (2023b). Responsible Sourcing Practices. Clifbar. https://www.clifbar.com/responsible-sourcing

Clifbar. (2023c). CLIF Kid Becomes First Kids Snack Bar Brand to Be Climate Neutral Certified. Clifbar. https://www.businesswire.com/news/home/20230420005313/en/CLIF-Kid%C2%AE-Becomes-First-Kids-Snack-Bar-Brand-to-be-Climate-Neutral-Certified

CONQUERing (2024). Our Story. CONQUERing. Retrieved March 10, 2024, from https://myconquering.com/pages/our-story

Corporate Knights. (2023). The 2024 Global 100: Overview of Corporate Knights Rating Methodology. https://www.corporateknights.com/wp-content/uploads/2023/09/2024-Global-100-Methodology.pdf

Corritore, M., Goldberg, A., & Srivastava, S. B. (2020, January 1). The new analytics of culture. *Harvard Business Review.* https://hbr.org/2020/01/the-new-analytics-of-culture

Court, D., Elzinga, D., Mulder, S., & Vetvik, O. J. (2009, June 1). The consumer decision journey. *McKinsey Quarterly.* https://www.mckinsey.com/capabilities/growth-marketing-and-sales/our-insights/the-consumer-decision-journey

Crane, A., LeBaron, G., Allain, J., & Behbahani, L. (2019). Governance gaps in eradicating forced labor: From global to domestic supply chains. *Regulation & Governance*, 13(1), 86–106. https://doi.org/10.1111/rego.12162

Creamer, M. (2012, May 2). James Dyson: "I don't believe in brand". *Ad Age.* https://adage.com/article/adages/design-icon-james-dyson-i-brand/234494

Cunningham, A. (2017). *Get to Aha!: Discover Your Positioning DNA and Dominate Your Competition.* McGraw Hill.

Dahl, L. & Young, L. (2018, October 4). How to Create Short Videos and Promote Them for Just a Dollar-a-Day [Video recording]. https://www.youtube.com/watch?v=i0Ss7RRm-mw

Davis, T., & Higgins, J. (2013). A Blockbuster Failure: How an Outdated Business Model Destroyed a Giant. Chapter 11 Bankruptcy Case Studies. https://ir.law.utk.edu/utk_studlawbankruptcy/11

Dawes, J. G. (2016). Brand growth in packaged goods markets: Ten cases with common patterns. *Journal of Consumer Behaviour,* 15(5), 475–489. https://doi.org/10.1002/cb.1595

Decker, A. (2024, July 3). The Ultimate Guide to Brand Awareness. HubSpot. https://blog.hubspot.com/marketing/brand-awareness

Digital Marketing Institute. (2023, November 21). AI in Digital Marketing—The Ultimate Guide. American Marketing Association Digital Marketing Institute. https://digitalmarketinginstitute.com/blog/ai-in-digital-marketing-the-ultimate-guide

Dolan, K. (2013, June 6). The soda with buzz. *Forbes.* https://www.forbes.com/forbes/2005/0328/126.html

Doward, J. (2020, March 1). Children as young as eight picked coffee beans on farms supplying Starbucks. *The Observer.* https://www.theguardian.com/business/2020/mar/01/children-work-for-pittance-to-pick-coffee-beans-used-by-starbucks-and-nespresso

Dressler, M., & Paunovic, I. (2021). The value of consistency: Portfolio labeling strategies and impact on winery brand equity. *Sustainability,* 13(3), Article 3. https://doi.org/10.3390/su13031400

Dunlavy, G. (2024, July 3). Gen Z and brand accountability—Why authenticity is the key to reaching our generation. *Ad Age.* https://adage.com/article/opinion/gen-z-and-brand-accountability-why-authenticity-key-reaching-our-generation/2567996

Estudio, T. (2024, February 28). What Is Spatial Design? Virtual, Augmented and Mixed Reality UX. Medium. https://uxtbe.medium.com/what-is-spatial-design-virtual-augmented-and-mixed-reality-ux-c4419a349f10

Fair, L. (2022, April 8). $5.5 Million Total FTC Settlements with Kohl's and Walmart Challenge "Bamboo" and Eco Claims, Shed Light on Penalty Offense Enforcement. Federal Trade Commission. https://www.ftc.gov/business-guidance/blog/2022/04/55-million-total-ftc-settlements-kohls-and-walmart-challenge-bamboo-and-eco-claims-shed-light

Fair Trade USA. (2023). Fair Trade Certified. Retrieved July 24, 2023, from https://www.fairtradecertified.org/

Faithfull, M. (2024, August 13). Impossible opens Chicago pop-up amid meatier brand positioning. *Forbes*. https://www.forbes.com/sites/markfaithfull/2024/08/13/impossible-opens-chicago-pop-up-amid-meatier-brand-positioning/

Federal Trade Commission. (2015, December 9). Nordstrom, Bed Bath & Beyond, Backcountry.com, and J.C. Penney to Pay Penalties Totaling $1.3 Million for Falsely Labeling Rayon Textiles as Made of "Bamboo." Federal Trade Commission. https://www.ftc.gov/news-events/news/press-releases/2015/12/nordstrom-bed-bath-beyond-backcountrycom-jc-penney-pay-penalties-totaling-13-million-falsely

Ferraro, C., Hemsley, A., & Sands, S. (2023). Embracing diversity, equity, and inclusion (DEI): Considerations and opportunities for brand managers. *Business Horizons*, 66(4), 463–479.

Ferris, T., Lawlor, J., & Ketterer, E. (2023, June 2). Guidance for "sustainable" claims after dismissal of H&M "greenwashing" class action. Reuters. https://www.reuters.com/legal/legalindustry/guidance-sustainable-claims-after-dismissal-hm-greenwashing-class-action-2023-06-02/

Forsey, C. (2023, February 20). Instagram Shadowban Is Real: How to Test for & Prevent It. HubSpot. https://blog.hubspot.com/marketing/instagram-shadowban

Freitas, J. D., & Ofek, E. (2024, September 1). How AI can power brand management. *Harvard Business Review*. https://hbr.org/2024/09/how-ai-can-power-brand-management

Gallo, A. (2014, October 29). The value of keeping the right customers. *Harvard Business Review*. https://hbr.org/2014/10/the-value-of-keeping-the-right-customers

Gallup, Inc. (2024). Americans' Trust in Media Remains at Trend Low. Gallup.Com. https://news.gallup.com/poll/651977/americans-trust-media-remains-trend-low.aspx

Gallup, Inc. (2025). How to improve employee engagement in the workplace. Gallup.Com. https://www.gallup.com/workplace/285674/improve-employee-engagement-workplace.aspx

Gannon, P. (2023, January 26). Southwest's holiday meltdown cost big money. *Axios*. https://www.axios.com/2023/01/26/southwest-meltdown-q4-earnings-loss

Gelles, D. (2022, September 14). Billionaire no more: Patagonia founder gives away the company. *New York Times*. https://www.nytimes.com/2022/09/14/climate/patagonia-climate-philanthropy-chouinard.html

Geyser, W. (2022, October 14). Diversity, Equity & Inclusion (DEI) in Influencer Marketing: Racial & Gender Inequalities Report. Influencer Marketing Hub. https://influencermarketinghub.com/dei-influencer-marketing-report/

Ghorbanzadeh, D., & Rahehagh, A. (2021). Emotional brand attachment and brand love: The emotional bridges in the process of transition from satisfaction to loyalty. *Rajagiri Management Journal*, 15(1), 16–38. https://doi.org/10.1108/RAMJ-05-2020-0024

Gibbons, S. (2017, November 5). UX Mapping Methods Compared: A Cheat Sheet. Nielsen Norman Group. https://www.nngroup.com/articles/ux-mapping-cheat-sheet/

Gibbs, B. (2024). Structuration theory. Britannica. https://www.britannica.com/topic/structuration-theory

Gifford, G. (2024, August 14). Dominate Local SEO: Your Playbook for Impactful Google Business Profiles and Customer Reviews. Digital Summit Minneapolis.

Gomez, R. (2024, October 16). Brand Awareness: What It Is and Strategies to Improve It. Sprout Social. https://sproutsocial.com/insights/brand-awareness/

Google (2024). *Sustainability Reports & Case Studies—Google Sustainability*. Sustainability. https://sustainability.google/reports/

Greene, C., & Kremen, A. (2003). U.S. Organic Farming in 2000–2001: Adoption of Certified Systems. Agricultural Information Bulletin. http://www.ers.usda.gov/publications/pub-details/?pubid=42492

Grimes, M. G., Williams, T. A., & Zhao, E. Y. (2019). Anchors aweigh: The sources, variety, and challenges of mission drift. *Academy of Management Review*, 44(4), 819–845. https://doi.org/10.5465/amr.2017.0254

Groeschel, C. (2008). *It: How Churches and Leaders Can Get It and Keep It*. Zondervan.

Guardian. (2024, May 11). Target Pride merchandise only available at select stores after rightwing backlash. *The Guardian*. https://www.theguardian.com/business/article/2024/may/11/target-pride-merchandise-backlash

Gunther, M. (2004, January 12). For Roy Disney, the company founded by his uncle Walt is much more than a business. Marc Gunther sat down with him to learn what made him so mad at CEO Michael Eisner, and why he's leading a mouse hunt. *CNN Money*. https://money.cnn.com/magazines/fortune/fortune_archive/2004/01/12/357915/index.htm

Haggard, J. (2024, August 14). The ABCCs of Marketing: Reimagine the Basics for Your Most Creative Marketing Plans Yet. Digital Summit Minneapolis.

Hale, J. (2022). Sustainable Funds Landscape—Highlights and Observations. Morningstar, Inc. https://www.morningstar.com/funds/sustainable-funds-landscape-highlights-observations

Handley, R. (2024, June 25). How to Do Keyword Research for SEO in 2024. Semrush Blog. https://www.semrush.com/blog/keyword-research/

Hargrave, M. (2024, April 2). What Is Market Saturation? Investopedia. https://www.investopedia.com/terms/m/marketsaturation.asp

Harrison, E. (2023, May). Unpacking consumer trends. Research Insights Series: Consumer Preferences and Behaviors. Sustainable Brands Brand-Led Culture Change.

Hartley, J., & Knell, L. (2022). Innovation, exnovation and intelligent failure. *Public Money & Management*, 42(1), 40–48. https://doi.org/10.1080/09540962.2021.1965307

Hatch, M. J., & Schultz, M. (2008). *Taking Brand Initiative: How Companies Can Align Strategy, Culture, and Identity Through Corporate Branding* (1st edition). Jossey-Bass.

Heath, C., & Heath, D. (2007). *Made to Stick: Why Some Ideas Survive and Others Die* (1st edition). Random House.

Heid, S. (2023, May). *Uncertain Times Require Decisive Brand Action: Blazing New Trails in Brand Activism*. Sustainable Brands Brand-Led Culture Change 2023, Minneapolis, Minnesota.

Henkel, S., Tomczak, T., Heitmann, M., & Herrmann, A. (2007). Managing brand consistent employee behaviour: Relevance and managerial control of behavioural branding. *Journal of Product & Brand Management*, 16(5), 310–320. https://doi.org/10.1108/10610420710779609

Hootsuite. (2024). Brand Sentiment Analyzer. Hootsuite, Inc. https://www.hootsuite.com

Horsley, C., & George, M. (2024, July 24). Learning from Ferrari: Emotive Brand Positioning. Kantar. https://www.kantar.com/inspiration/brands/learning-from-ferrari-emotive-brand-positioning

Horst, J. (2023, May 22). How Brands Can Build a Purpose Movement by Prioritizing People. Sustainable Brands, Minneapolis, Minnesota.

Huang, M.-H., & Dev, C. S. (2020). Growing the service brand. *International Journal of Research in Marketing*, 37(2), 281–300. https://doi.org/10.1016/j.ijresmar.2019.10.001

Hunt, J. (2023, May 1). Charting A Course Toward Transformation. Council for Advancement and Support of Education (CASE). https://www.case.org/resources/issues/may-june-2023/charting-course-toward-transformation_v

Iglesias, O., & Ind, N. (2020). Towards a theory of conscientious corporate brand co-creation: The next key challenge in brand management. *Journal of Brand Management*, 27(6), 710–720. https://doi.org/10.1057/s41262-020-00205-7

Iglesias, O., Ind, N., & Alfaro, M. (2017). The Organic View of the Brand: A Brand Value Co-creation Model. In J. M. T. Balmer, S. M. Powell, J. Kernstock, & T. O. Brexendorf (Eds.), *Advances in Corporate Branding* (pp. 148–174). Palgrave Macmillan UK. https://doi.org/10.1057/978-1-352-00008-5_9

Inc. (2022). Inc 5000 2022: Meet the companies winning in a time of spectacular growth. *Inc.* https://www.inc.com/inc5000/2022

International Labour Organization. (2024). Annual Profits from Forced Labour Amount to US$ 236 billion, ILO Report Finds. International Labour Organization. https://www.ilo.org/resource/news/annual-profits-forced-labour-amount-us-236-billion-ilo-report-finds

Jackson, S. T. (2021). Climate change. In Encyclopedia Britannica. https://www.britannica.com/science/climate-change

Jay, A. (2023, May). AI, Sustainability and Behavior Change: Opportunities And Risks for Brands. Sustainable Brands Brand-Led Culture Change.

Jenkins, H., Ford, S., & Green, J. (2013). Introduction: Why media spreads. In *Spreadable Media: Creating Value and Meaning in a Networked Culture*. New York University Press.

Jones, P. (2024, January 10). Market Penetration: What It Is & Strategies to Succeed. Semrush Blog. https://www.semrush.com/blog/market-penetration/

Kakroo, U. (2015, October 26). 5 ways to use storytelling in your social media marketing. *Social Media Examiner*. https://www.socialmediaexaminer.com/5-ways-to-use-storytelling-in-your-social-media-marketing/

Kantar (Director). (2024, May 15). *Blueprint for Brand Growth explained in 6 minutes—Kantar* [Video recording]. https://www.youtube.com/watch?v=0hDBfMn1jLk

Kingsley, S. (2023). Carbon Neutral and Net Zero—What Do They Mean? World Economic Forum. https://www.weforum.org/agenda/2022/08/carbon-neutral-net-zero-sustainability-climate-change

Koekkoek, M., Marx, A., & Wouters, J. (2017). Monitoring forced labour and slavery in global supply chains: The case of the California Act on Transparency in Supply Chains. *Global Policy*, 8(4), 522–529. https://doi.org/10.1111/1758-5899.12512

Kohler, L. (2022, February 14). The rise of the chief purpose officer. *Forbes*. https://www.forbes.com/sites/lindsaykohler/2022/02/14/the-rise-of-the-chief-purpose-officer/

Kolster, T. (2020). *The Hero Trap* (1st edition). Routledge.

Kolster, T. (2023, May 22). How Brands Can Build a Purpose Movement by Prioritizing People. Sustainable Brands.

Lampert, C. (2023, May). Strategies and Tactics for Driving Behavior Change at Scale: Content Creators for Good: A Brand Guide to Collaborating with Influencers. Sustainable Brands Brand-Led Culture Change.

Lavin, S. (2023, May). Lessons in Brand-Led Culture Change: Righting Wrongs, Scaling Impact and Recovering from Pushback. Sustainable Brands Brand-Led Culture Change.

Leu, P. (2024). Spotify—Statistics & Facts. Statista. https://www-statista-com.ezp2.lib.umn.edu/topics/2075/spotify/#statisticChapter

Li, C., & Bernoff, J. (2008). *Groundswell: Winning in a World Transformed by Social Technologies.* Harvard Business Review Press.

Limoncelli, S. A. (2017). Legal limits: Ending human trafficking in supply chains. *World Policy Journal,* 34(1), 119–123. https://doi.org/10.1215/07402775-3903628

Liu, Y., Li, K. J., Chen, H. (Allan), & Balachander, S. (2017). The effects of products' aesthetic design on demand and marketing-mix effectiveness: The role of segment prototypicality and brand consistency. *Journal of Marketing,* 81(1), 83–102. https://doi.org/10.1509/jm.15.0315

Logman, M. (2007). Logical brand management in a dynamic context of growth and innovation. *Journal of Product & Brand Management,* 16(4), 257–268. https://doi.org/10.1108/10610420710763949

Loureiro, S. M. C., Hollebeek, L., Rather, R. A., Ruivo, L., Kaljund, K., & Guerreiro, J. (2023). Engaging with (vs. avoiding) personalized advertising on social media. *Journal of Marketing Communications,* 1–22. https://doi.org/10.1080/13527266.2023.2289044

Lund, N. F., Scarles, C., & Cohen, S. A. (2020). The brand value continuum: Countering co-destruction of destination branding in social media through storytelling. *Journal of Travel Research,* 59, 1506–1521. https://doi.org/10.1177/0047287519887234

Magids, S., Zorfas, A., & Leemon, D. (2015, November 1). The new science of customer emotions. *Harvard Business Review.* https://hbr.org/2015/11/the-new-science-of-customer-emotions

Mailchimp. (2023, February 21). Visual Branding: How to Build a Visual Brand Identity. Mailchimp. https://mailchimp.com/resources/visual-branding-and-storytelling/

Mailchimp. (2024). Brand Development: Navigate Growth in Competitive Markets. Mailchimp https://mailchimp.com/resources/brand-development/

Mainwaring, S. (2023, May). Brand-Led Culture Change. Sustainable Brands.

Marcy, W. K. (2019, June 28). Using Brand Affinity to Get Clickable Banners. Hubspot. https://blog.hubspot.com/agency/using-brand-affinity-to-get-clickable-banners

MBLM. (2022). *Brand Intimacy Study 2022.* https://content.mblm.com/bis-study-2022-report

MBLM. (2024a). *Consumer Trends.* MBLM. https://mblm.com/lab/features/consumer-trends/

MBLM. (2024b). Indifference. MBLM. Retrieved October 20, 2024, from https://mblm.com/lab/features/indifference/

McCorvey, J. J. (2023, February 9). Southwest Exec Vows Fixes but Rebuffs Calls for Cash Hardship Payments to Fliers. NBC News. https://www.

nbcnews.com/politics/congress/southwest-executive-tell-congress-messed-hearing-holiday-flight-fiasco-rcna69858

Mccuan, J. (2004, November 1). It's not easy being green. *Inc.* https://www.inc.com/magazine/20041101/seventh-generation.html

McKinsey Global Institute. (2008). The Carbon Productivity Challenge: Curbing Climate Change and Sustaining Economic Growth. https://www.mckinsey.com/capabilities/sustainability/our-insights/the-carbon-productivity-challenge

Melendez, M. J. (2023, May). Responding to Cultural Tipping Points: Co-creating a Brand Culture for Good. Sustainable Brands Brand-Led Culture Change.

Melinn, C., & Boyd, C. (2024a). Ethics, Privacy, and Law When Using AI. American Marketing Association's Digital Marketing Institute. https://my.digitalmarketinginstitute.com/courses/module_v2/tr-aifdm-1-efk1087/2345/TR-AI-1-10003-x7c3a

Melinn, C., & Boyd, C. (2024b). What Is AI in Digital Marketing? American Marketing Association's Digital Marketing Institute. https://my.digitalmarketinginstitute.com/courses/module_v2/tr-aifdm-1-efk1087/2345/TR-AI-1-10003-x7c3a

Merriam-Webster. (2023). Greenwashing. https://www.merriam-webster.com/dictionary/greenwashing

Merz, M. A., He, Y., & Vargo, S. L. (2009). The evolving brand logic: A service-dominant logic perspective. *Journal of the Academy of Marketing Science*, 37(3), 328–344. https://doi.org/10.1007/s11747-009-0143-3

Merz, M. A., Zarantonello, L., & Grappi, S. (2018). How valuable are your customers in the brand value co-creation process? The development of a customer co-creation value (CCCV) scale. *Journal of Business Research*, 82, 79–89.

Meta. (2024). Stories Ads. Meta for Business. https://www.facebook.com/business/ads/stories-ad-format

Millman, D. (2011, September 27). How Starbucks transformed coffee from a commodity into a $4 splurge. *Fast Company*. https://www.fastcompany.com/1777409/how-starbucks-transformed-coffee-commodity-4-splurge

Millman, D. (2013). *Brand Thinking and Other Noble Pursuits* (1st edition). Allworth.

Mitchell, A. (2023, May). Culture Changing Communications: How Brands Can Build a Purpose Movement by Prioritizing People. Sustainable Brands Brand-Led Culture Change.

Mitchell, K. (2021, April 12). 3 ways companies can embed purpose into their organizations. *Harvard Business Review*. https://hbr.org/

sponsored/2021/04/3-ways-companies-can-embed-purpose-into-their-organizations

Montaña, J., Guzmán, F., & Moll, I. (2007). Branding and design management: A brand design management model. *Journal of Marketing Management*, 23(9–10), 829–840. https://doi.org/10.1362/026725707X250340

Mordowanec, N. (2024, January 4). Lululemon founder blasts company's push towards diversity. *Newsweek*. https://www.newsweek.com/lululemon-founder-blasts-company-diversity-chip-wilson-1857526

Morville, P. (2004, June 21). User Experience Design. Semantic Studios. https://semanticstudios.com/user_experience_design/

Mulcahy, R., Riedel, A., Beatson, A., Keating, B., & Mathews, S. (2024). I'm a believer! Believability of social media marketing. *International Journal of Information Management*, 75, 102730.

Mullen, L. (2021, March 17). The Positive Impact of Organic Foods. University of Colorado Boulder Environmental Center. https://www.colorado.edu/ecenter/2021/03/17/positive-impact-organic-foods

Muniz, F., & Guzmán, F. (2023). The impact of brand value co-creation on perceived CSR authenticity and brand equity. *Journal of Product & Brand Management*, 32(8), 1338–1354. https://doi.org/10.1108/JPBM-02-2023-4340

Napoletano, E. (2023, June). What Is ESG Investing? r. Forbes Advisor. https://www.forbes.com/advisor/investing/esg-investing/

NASA (2021). Earth Science Communications Team at NASA's Jet Propulsion Laboratory: Overview: Weather, Global Warming and Climate Change. In *Climate Change: Vital Signs of the Planet*. NASA. https://climate.nasa.gov/resources/global-warming-vs-climate-change

Natarelli, M., & Plapler, R. (2017). *Brand Intimacy: A New Paradigm in Marketing*. Hatherleigh Press.

National Geographic Society. (2019). Climate Change. In *National Geographic Society Encyclopedia*. http://www.nationalgeographic.org/encyclopedia/climate-change/

Nespresso. (2024). Preventing and Eradicating Child Labor from Nespresso's Supply Chain. Nestlé Nespresso. https://nestle-nespresso.com/views/preventing_and_eradicating_child_labor_from_nespressos_supply_chain

Neumeier, M. (2005). *The Brand Gap: How to Bridge the Distance Between Business Strategy and Design* (2nd edition). New Riders.

Nielsen. (2025). *Brand Lift Studies*. Nielsen. https://www.nielsen.com/solutions/marketing-optimization/brand-lift/

NielsenIQ, & McKinsey & Company. (2023). *Consumers care about sustainability—And back it up with their wallets*. https://nielseniq.com/

global/en/insights/report/2023/consumers-care-about-sustainability-and-back-it-up-with-their-wallets/

O'Callaghan, C. (2020). Post-Truth—An overview. In *International Encyclopedia of Human Geography* (2nd edition). ScienceDirect. https://www.sciencedirect.com/topics/social-sciences/post-truth

Oxford Languages (2016). Oxford Word of the Year 2016. https://languages.oup.com/word-of-the-year/2016/

Padula, J. (2023, May). Strategies and Tactics for Driving Behavior Change at Scale: Content Creators for good: A Brand Guide to Collaborating with Influencers. Sustainable Brands Brand-Led Culture Change.

Park, H., & Steinke, A. J. (2023). *Brand Thinking Generation Z Focus Groups* [Dataset]. University of Minnesota Hubbard School of Journalism and Mass Communication.

Peters, A. (2021, February 17). People are more likely to trust—and buy—purpose-driven brands. *Fast Company*. https://www.fastcompany.com/90605135/people-are-more-likely-to-trust-and-buy-purpose-driven-brands

Pierce, S. C. (2010). Turning a blind eye: U.S. corporate involvement in modern day slavery. *Journal of Gender, Race & Justice*, 14(2), 577–600.

Piper Sandler. (2024). Taking Stock with Teens. Piper Sandler. https://www.pipersandler.com/teens

Prophet. (2023). *Prophet's 2023 Brand Relevance Insights Report*. Prophet. https://relevantbrands-2023.prophet.com/public-outreach-campaigns-in-an-era-of-low-trust/

Qualtrics. (2024a). What Is CSAT and How Do You Measure It? Qualtrics. https://www.qualtrics.com/experience-management/customer/what-is-csat/

Qualtrics. (2024b). Market Segmentation: Definition, Types & Best Practices. Qualtrics. https://www.qualtrics.com/en-gb/experience-management/brand/market-segmentation/

Qualtrics. (2024c, January 10). Consumer Trust Languishes at 2016 Levels. Qualtrics Newsroom. https://www.qualtrics.com/news/consumer-trust-languishes-at-2016-levels/

Qualtrics. (2024d). The Complete Guide to Brand Architecture. Qualtrics. https://www.qualtrics.com/experience-management/brand/brand-architecture/

Quaratino, L., & Mazzei, A. (2018). Managerial strategies to promote employee brand consistent behavior: The new frontier for brand building strategies. *EuroMed Journal of Business*, 13(2), 185–200. https://doi.org/10.1108/EMJB-02-2017-0008

Quesenberry, K. A. (2022, June 22). Why you need to be an influencer brand and the 3 Rs of becoming one. *Entrepreneur*. https://www.entrepreneur.com/science-technology/why-you-need-to-be-an-influencer-brand-and-the-3-rs-of/428086

Raman, S. (2017). Key Concepts: Strategic Planning. Harvard Kennedy School. https://projects.iq.harvard.edu/files/hks-communications-program/files/ho_sushma_raman_2017_brief_-_strategic_planning.pdf

Ramaswamy, V., & Ozcan, K. (2016). Brand value co-creation in a digitalized world: An integrative framework and research implications. *International Journal of Research in Marketing*, 33(1), 93–106. https://doi.org/10.1016/j.ijresmar.2015.07.001

Red Bull Media House. (2024). About Us. https://www.redbullmediahouse.com/en/about-us

Reichheld, F. (2006). *The Ultimate Question: Driving Good Profits and True Growth* (1st edition). Harvard Business School Press.

Reichheld, F., Darnell, D., & Burns, M. (2021). *Winning on Purpose: The Unbeatable Strategy of Loving Customers*. Harvard Business Review Press.

Ridder, M. (2024). Red Bull—Statistics & Facts. Statista. https://www.statista.com/topics/12039/red-bull/

Riserbato, R. (2022, July 12). What Is Market Share & How Do You Calculate It? Hubspot. https://blog.hubspot.com/marketing/how-to-calculate-market-share

Romanchuk, J. (2024, September 11). 5 Dos and Don'ts When Making a SMART Goal [+ Examples]. HubSpot. https://blog.hubspot.com/marketing/smart-goal-examples

Romaniuk, J., Dawes, J., & Nenycz-Thiel, M. (2018). Modeling brand market share change in emerging markets. *International Marketing Review*, 35(5), 785–805. https://doi.org/10.1108/IMR-01-2017-0006

Ryan Companies. (2016, December 14). About Ryan Companies https://www.ryancompanies.com/about

Rynarzewska, A. I., Tanner Jr, J. F., & Edmondson, D. R. (2024). An introduction to the "The role of inclusion, diversity, equity, & access (IDEA) in today's global marketing environment" special issue. *Journal of Global Scholars of Marketing Science*, 34(1), 1–4.

S&P Global (2023). Dow Jones Sustainability World Index. S&P Dow Jones Indices. https://www.spglobal.com/spdji/en/indices/esg/dow-jones-sustainability-world-index/

Sabrina, D. (2023, August 4). How to Create a Compelling Brand Identity. Entrepreneur. https://www.entrepreneur.com/starting-a-business/how-to-create-a-compelling-brand-identity/456707

Schein, E. H., & Schein, P. A. (2021). *Humble Inquiry: The Gentle Art of Asking Instead of Telling* (Expanded edition). Berrett-Koehler Publishers.

Scott, M. (2020, January 21). The Global 100 Difference. Corporate Knights. https://www.corporateknights.com/rankings/global-100-rankings/2020-global-100-rankings/global-100-difference-2/

Segijn, C. M., & van Ooijen, I. (2020). Differences in consumer knowledge and perceptions of personalized advertising: Comparing online behavioural advertising and synced advertising. *Journal of Marketing Communications*, 28(2), 207–226. https://doi.org/10.1080/13527266.2020.1857297

Semaan, R. W., Ashill, N., & Williams, P. (2019). Sophisticated, iconic and magical: A qualitative analysis of brand charisma. *Journal of Retailing and Consumer Services*, 49, 102–113. https://doi.org/10.1016/j.jretconser.2019.03.011

Semrush. (2024). Market Explorer: Research New Markets for Growth. (2024). Semrush. Retrieved August 2, 2024, from https://www.semrush.com/market-explorer/

Seventh Generation. (2024). Our Company. https://www.seventhgeneration.com/company

Sisodia, R. (2023). Explore Conscious Capitalism's Philosophy. Raj Sisodia. https://rajsisodia.com/conscious-capitalism.html

Smith, K. (2023, October 25). 4 ways to measure and track brand awareness *Brandwatch*. https://www.brandwatch.com/blog/how-to-measure-brand-awareness/

Somers, M. (2024, June 26). *5 enduring management ideas from MIT Sloan's Edgar Schein*. MIT Management Sloan School. https://mitsloan.mit.edu/ideas-made-to-matter/5-enduring-management-ideas-mit-sloans-edgar-schein

Spotify (2023). Tips for Creating a Successful Hack Week. For the Record. https://newsroom.spotify.com/2023-03-16/tips-for-creating-a-successful-hack-week/

Spotify Advertising. (2024a). *2024 Podcast Trends Tour*. https://ads.spotify.com/en-US/trends/podcast-trends/

Spotify Advertising. (2024b). *Spotify Advertising*. https://ads.spotify.com/en-US/

Spotify Advertising. (2024c). *Culture Next 2024: Gen Z Trends*. https://ads.spotify.com/en-US/culture-next/gen-z-trends-report/

Sprout Social. (2024, April 10). Best Times to Post on Social Media in 2024. Sprout Social. https://sproutsocial.com/insights/best-times-to-post-on-social-media/

Statista. (2024a). Cannabis Product Usage by Type. Statista. https://www-statista-com.ezp3.lib.umn.edu/global-consumer-survey/tool/10/gcs_usa_202403

Statista. (2024b). Biggest Social Media Platforms by Users 2024. Statista. https://www.statista.com/statistics/272014/global-social-networks-ranked-by-number-of-users/

Statista. (October 21, 2024c). Brand Awareness by category in the U.S. as of September 2024 [Graph]. Statista. Retrieved October 31, 2024, from https://www-statista-com.ezp2.lib.umn.edu/forecasts/997052/brand-awareness-by-category-in-the-us

Steinke, A. J. (2022). *The Institutionalization of Solutions Journalism.* University of Minnesota. https://hdl.handle.net/11299/241318

Stengel, J., Lamberton, C., & Favaro, K. (2023, May 1). How brand building and performance marketing can work together. *Harvard Business Review.* https://hbr.org/2023/05/how-brand-building-and-performance-marketing-can-work-together

StrawberryFrog, & Dynata. (2024). Purpose Power Index. https://www.purposepowerindex.com

Sullivan, T. (2023). *Brand Management & Strategy: Building & Sustaining A Valuable Brand.* Stukent, Inc.

Sustainable Brands—Clif Bar & Company. (2023). Sustainable Brands. https://sustainablebrands.com/brands/clif-bar

Sutcliffe, C. (2023, September 13). Report reveals generational divide in trust around advertising. *Marketing Week.* https://www.marketingweek.com/report-generational-divide-trust-advertising/

Swaminathan, V., Sorescu, A., Steenkamp, J. B. E. M., O'Guinn, T. C. G., & Schmitt, B. (2020). Branding in a hyperconnected world: Refocusing theories and rethinking boundaries. *Journal of Marketing,* 84(2), 24–46. https://doi.org/10.1177/0022242919899905

The American Customer Satisfaction Index (ACSI)—National Cross-Industry Measure of Customer Satisfaction. (2024). The American Customer Satisfaction Index. Retrieved July 29, 2024, from https://theacsi.org/

The Ellen MacArthur Foundation. (2023). Fashion and the Circular Economy. https://ellenmacarthurfoundation.org/topics/fashion/overview

The Paris Agreement. (2023). United Nations Climate Change. https://unfccc.int/process-and-meetings/the-paris-agreement

Thomson, M., MacInnis, D. J., & Whan Park, C. (2005). The ties that bind: Measuring the strength of consumers' emotional attachments to brands. *Journal of Consumer Psychology,* 15(1), 77–91. https://doi.org/10.1207/s15327663jcp1501_10

Townsend, S. (2023, May). Harnessing the Power of Brands. Sustainable Brands Brand-Led Culture Change.

Trader Joe's. (2018, May 1). It's About Values (Episode 2). Retrieved May 1, 2018, from https://www.traderjoes.com/home/podcast.html

Trader Joe's. (2022, May 23). A Trader Joe's Journey from Portland (ME) to Portland (OR) (Episode 50). https://www.traderjoes.com/home/podcast.html

Trader Joe's. (2023, December 31). Neighborhood Shares—Every Store, Every Day. Trader Joe's. https://www.traderjoes.com/home/neighborhood-shares.html

Trader Joe's. (2024). Donations and Sponsorships. Trader Joe's. https://www.traderjoes.com/home/contact-us/donations-and-sponsorships.html

Tuchman, R. (2022, June 21). How success happened for Selina Sykes and Laura Fruitman, CEO and CMO of The Uncovery. *Entrepreneur*. https://www.entrepreneur.com/growing-a-business/how-success-happened-for-selina-sykes-and-laura-fruitman/428007

Unilever. (2012). Ben & Jerry's. Retrieved from https://www.unileverusa.com/brands/ice-cream/ben-jerrys/

United Nations. (2021). The Climate Crisis – A Race We Can Win. https://www.un.org/en/un75/climate-crisis-race-we-can-win

United Nations. (2023a). Sustainability. United Nations; United Nations. https://www.un.org/en/academic-impact/sustainability

United Nations. (2023b). The 17 Goals: Sustainable Development. United Nations Department of Economic and Social Affairs. https://sdgs.un.org/goals

U.S. Census Bureau. (2023). Community Resilience Estimates. Census. Gov. https://www.census.gov/programs-surveys/community-resilience-estimates.html

U.S. Department of State. (2023, June). *2023 Trafficking in Persons Report*. United States Department of State. https://www.state.gov/reports/2023-trafficking-in-persons-report/

U.S. EPA. (2014, November 5). Learn About Sustainability [Overviews and Factsheets]. United States Environmental Protection Agency. https://www.epa.gov/sustainability/learn-about-sustainability

U.S. Green Building Council (USGBC). (2023). LEED Rating System U.S. Green Building Council. https://www.usgbc.org/leed

U.S. Securities and Exchange Commission (2022). SEC Charges Goldman Sachs Asset Management for Failing to Follow Its Policies and Procedures Involving ESG Investments. U.S. Securities and Exchange Commission. https://www.sec.gov/news/press-release/2022-209

Vallaster, C., & Kraus, S. (2011). Entrepreneurial branding: Growth and its implications for brand management. *International Journal of Entrepreneurship and Small Business*, 14(3), 369–390. https://doi.org/10.1504/IJESB.2011.042759

Varsha, P. S., Akter, S., Kumar, A., Gochhait, S., & Patagundi, B. (2021). The impact of artificial intelligence on branding: A bibliometric analysis (1982–2019). *Journal of Global Information Management (JGIM)*, 29(4), 221–246. https://doi.org/10.4018/JGIM.20210701.oa10

Wall Street Journal. (2023, April 21). Greenwashing: When Companies Aren't as Sustainable as They Claim (video). https://www.youtube.com/watch?v=2NsBcVrPQok

Whitaker, A. (2024, February 20). Rethinking public outreach campaigns in an era of low trust. *Forbes*. https://www.forbes.com/councils/forbesagencycouncil/2024/02/20/rethinking-

Wieser, V. E., Luecke, M. K., & Hemetsberger, A. (2021). Charismatic entrainment: How brand leaders and consumers co-create charismatic authority in the marketplace. *Journal of Consumer Research*, 48(4), 731–751. https://doi.org/10.1093/jcr/ucab035

Wohl, J. (2018, October 25). Chipotle says month-old ad campaign is already paying off. *Ad Age*. https://adage.com/article/cmo-strategy/chipotle-month-ad-campaign-paying/315403

Wong, J. (2024, August 13). Council post: The importance of diversity in modern marketing. *Forbes*. https://www.forbes.com/councils/forbescommunicationscouncil/2023/04/17/the-importance-of-diversity-in-modern-marketing/

Yildirim, E. (2023, December 21). Not all failures are created equally, says Harvard expert—How to learn from your mistakes more easily. CNBC. https://www.cnbc.com/2023/12/21/harvard-professor-dont-fail-fast-fail-often-fail-intelligently.html

Zerkalenkov, Z. (2024, January 8). Brand Identity: What It Is and How to Create a Strong One. Semrush Blog. https://www.semrush.com/blog/build-brand-identity/

Zhexembayeva, N. (2023, May). Regeneration, Reinvention and Revamping Retail. Sustainable Brands Brand-Led Culture Change.

Zhukova, N. (2023, April 21). Market Segmentation: Types, Examples, and Strategies. Semrush Blog. https://www.semrush.com/blog/market-segmentation-strategy/

Zhukova, N. (2024, February 8). How to Calculate Market Share [Formula + Guide]. Semrush Blog. https://www.semrush.com/blog/how-to-calculate-market-share/

Zote, J. (2023, June 30). What Is Social Commerce? Stats, Trends and Tips Marketers Should Know for 2023. Sprout Social. https://sproutsocial.com/insights/social-commerce/

Zucker, M., & Srinivasan, S. (2023, October 4). AI in Marketing: Four Ways to Maximize Value. Prophet. https://prophet.com/2023/10/ai-in-marketing/

Index

A/B testing 301–2
accessibility
    digital 307
AIDA funnel 78, 82, 98–100, 138–40
analysis
    social media 217–19
    SWOT 193–6, 198, 230, 259
Ansoff Matrix 130–1
artificial intelligence (AI)
    branding and 297
    customer service and 10, 297
    data preparedness and 299
    ethical and legal compliance and 299
    ethics 298
    generative 301
    implementation 299–300
    monitoring and feedback 299
    personalization 298
    technology and team readiness 299
    viability assessment 298–9
analytics
    dashboards 30–1, 171, 218
    data 31
    website 217–18, 300
Asics 254–5
assessment 181, 193, 197, 286, 296
audit
    AI 300
    brand 230
    content 158
    ethical 299
    social media 158, 196, 218
    website 158, 218
authenticity 19–20, 59–61, 81–2, 203, 239, 271–2

Baby Boomers 137, 191
B Corporation 10, 17, 47, 242, 265, 286
behavioral
    characteristics 146–7
    segmentation 120–1
belonging 195, 270
Ben & Jerry's 286–8
brand
    affinity 306–8
    alignment xiii, 96, 239, 257
    ambassador 59, 98, 156, 159, 165
    architecture 222
    awareness 245
    believability 10–13
    bombardment 204–6
    channels 134–5
    co-destruction 11
    communication 12, 154–5
    community 32–3, 86–7, 162, 307–8
    defined 11–12
    drift 57
    engagement 30–1, 170, 232, 241–2, 293, 308
    experience (BX) 70, 81–2
    growth 108–11
    guidelines 231
    identity 84–5, 110
    indifference 292–3
    intimacy 30
    love 294
    loyalty 16
    messaging 170
    mission 288
    monitoring 196–7
    penetration 112–15

perception 206–7
personality 85, 89
positioning 206–8
promise 41
purpose 39–42
reputation 189, 274, 302
resonance 292
sentiment 231–3
skepticism 14
stagnancy 174–5, 231
story 50–1, 42–3
storytelling 50–1
trust 16
value 11
value co-creation 16–17
value continuum 11
values 61–2, 68–9
vision 41, 79, 91
branded house 222–3, 230
branding
  purpose-driven 23
  rebranding 189–93
  sustainable 164

California Consumer Privacy Act
  (CCPA) 119, 298–9
call to action (CTA) 32, 156, 171
carbon
  neutral 252
  offset 252–3
CBS 226–9
chief purpose officer 39–40, 260
Chipotle 45–6, 66–7, 142–4
Chiro for Moms / Chiro for Kidz 91–5
clicks 31, 156, 164, 170–1, 183
Clif Bar & Company 264–5
climate crisis 236, 241, 251–2, 254–8, 263
College of Saint Benedict and Saint
  John's University 188–93
communication
  multichannel 141, 144, 187–8
  omnichannel 141, 145, 187
community engagement 86–7, 241

competitive advantage 1–2, 19, 33, 115, 195
CONQUERing 277–80
Conscious Capitalism 242–3, 246–7
consistency 19–23, 57–8, 66, 79, 82–3, 109
consumer
  data 135, 184–8
  perception 197–8
  sentiment 183, 188, 197–8
content
  calendar 158–9
  creation 301
  organic 163–4, 263–4
  visual 165
core values 141–3, 145, 193, 204, 207, 285
Corporate Knights' Global 243–4
Corporate social
  activism (CSA) 270
  advocacy (CSA) 270
  responsibility (CSR) 270
credibility 18, 51, 56, 67, 154, 293
customer
  experience (CX) 88, 95–6, 98, 165, 206, 210–11
  relationship management (CRM) 115
  Satisfaction Score (CSAT) 103–4

Desperate Housewives 123–4
digital
  currency 10
  marketing 10, 159
  marketing trifecta 159
diversification 131
diversity 273
donations 283–5

echo chamber 153
eco-conscious 240, 250
education 18, 34, 47, 56, 164, 185
emotional attachment 59, 64–5, 292
empathy map 96, 99, 103
employee

Index

engagement 57–8, 69, 72–3
experience (EX) 56, 58, 72–4, 283–5
resource groups 61
endemic 20, 34, 69
endorsed brand architecture 224–5
engagement
    customer 293
    community xiv, 86, 164, 241
    social 245, 307
    rate 31, 308
Environmental and Social Governance (ESG) 253, 262, 270
exploitation 237–8

Fair Trade 260–3
feedback loop 199
figure storming 176
filter bubble 154–5
firmographic segmentation 120, 131, 146
fiscal management 303
followers 31–2, 158, 164, 171, 308

General Data Protection Regulation (GDPR) 298
Generation Z 137, 204, 239, 258, 272–4, 281–2
geographics 113, 120, 131, 146–7
goals
    SMART 51–3, 158
    social 243
    sustainability 259–60, 263
greenwashing 252–3
gross rating points (GRPs) 148–9
groundswell 87
growth accelerators 109–10

Halara Cannabis 86, 126–30
house of brands 223–4
hybrid brand architecture 225–6

impressions 89, 148–9, 164, 171, 185–6, 188
inclusivity 65–6, 82, 92, 195, 288, 307

inconsistency 23, 57, 252, 271, 292–3
influencer
    advertising 163
    campaign 162–3
    engagement 164
    legal contracts 163
    macro 161
    marketing 161
    mega 161
    micro- 161
    mid-tier 161
    nano 161
    representation 162
    sponsorships 216
innovation 23–8, 56–8, 65–6, 85, 175, 229
intellectual property (IP) 23
internal branding 70–2
it factor 79–80

journey map 95–102

key performance indicators (KPIs) 30, 148, 159, 164, 170–1, 300
keywords 156–7, 197–8, 231–2, 284, 297, 301

linear thinking 168–9
Liquid I.V. 241–2
logo 79, 84–5, 231

market penetration 131
market share 108, 110, 112–15, 121–2, 127, 241
market
    development 131
    penetration 131
    share 112–5
marketing
    content 10, 108, 264, 301
    email 170–1, 302
Mayo Clinic 27, 62, 65–6, 124–5
McKinsey's Consumer Decision Journey (CDJ) Model 139–40

Index

media mix 215–17
mentions 32, 158–9, 164, 170–1, 232, 246
mergers and acquisitions 61, 66, 226
Millennials 271
misalignment 226, 228
miscommunication 272–4
mission statement 40–1, 49–50, 157, 166, 282, 286

net
  profit 33, 171, 177–8
  zero 252

online reviews and ratings 10–1, 32, 51, 97, 140, 218–19
organic 260–1, 263–4
outreach
  brand 149
  community 86, 93
  consumer 135–6, 142, 144, 150
  local 69

partnership 46–7, 49–50, 160–2, 167, 240, 283–4
Patagonia 265–7
performance
  brand 20, 30, 113, 174, 230, 247
  employee 56
  environmental 286
  management 43
  marketing 109
  social 286–7
performative activism 237–9
position map 211–15, 259
post-truth 3, 12–13, 39, 208
profitability 19, 33, 88, 177, 272, 294
profit margins 49, 176–8
pulse survey 72–4

quality 27–8

reach 42, 126, 135–7, 148, 171
Red Bull 165–8

relative market share 113–14
research 182–3
  brand 164, 206
  competitor 216
  consumer 239–41, 258, 271
  content 301
  customer experience 206
  industry 72
  internal 63
  keyword 301
  market 113, 119, 201, 209, 215, 231
Responsibility Assignment Matrix (RACI) 111–12
return on investment (ROI) 162, 164, 171, 178, 300, 303
revenue 52, 61, 67, 112–14, 176–7
Roblox 34
Ryan Companies US, Inc. 43–5

saturation
  keyword 157
  market 108–9, 114, 202, 297
  media 144
segmentation
  behavioral 120
  core 118, 121–3, 129, 131
  demographic 120
  firmographic 120
  geographic 120
  market 117–25
  psychographic 120
  secondary 118, 126
Seventh Generation 47–9
shadowban 128
shareability 19, 29–32, 294
shareholders 10, 38, 49, 176, 241, 276
share of voice (SOV) 215–17, 219
social
  commerce 10, 160
  debts 246
social listening 119, 154, 181, 197–8, 219, 232
Spotify 303–6
stakeholders 10, 236, 270, 282, 287–8

statement
  mission 40–1, 49, 157, 166, 195, 265
  purpose 24, 39–42, 47, 49, 208
  vision 40–1
strategy
  brand 174
  editorial 156, 158
  marketing 162
structuration theory 16–7
Sustainable Development Goals 256
sustainability 250–1

target
  audience 144–8
  persona 144–8
Thrive Pet Healthcare 208–11
total addressable market (TAM) 114–15

Trader Joe's 68–70
transparency laws 238
trust
  brand 16, 137, 204, 208, 271, 280
  building 141–2
  consumer 66, 135–7, 148, 204, 265
  customer 57
  public 136

URL click 171
user
  data 298, 304–5
  experience (UX) 78, 95, 165, 292
  generated content (UGC) 11, 160, 197

value proposition 16, 49–50, 109, 156–7, 259, 261

About the Authors

Allison J. Steinke is an award-winning researcher and communications professional on faculty at the University of Minnesota Hubbard School of Journalism and Mass Communication, USA. She teaches undergraduate and graduate courses in branding, digital and social media, marketing, and management, and has presented her research on branding, innovation, solutions, and institutions at conferences around the world.

Haseon Park is a leading scholar in digital consumer and brand relationships on faculty at the University of Minnesota Hubbard School of Journalism and Mass Communication, USA. She teaches courses in branding and media planning. Her research focuses on branding, influencers, social networks, and advertising.